THE ABYSS ABOVE

SILKE-MARIA WEINECK

THE ABYSS ABOVE

PHILOSOPHY AND POETIC MADNESS IN PLATO, HÖLDERLIN AND NIETZSCHE

STATE UNIVERSITY OF NEW YORK PRESS

Published by
STATE UNIVERSITY OF NEW YORK PRESS
ALBANY

For information, address
State University of New York Press
90 State Street, Suite 700, Albany, NY 12207

Production and Book Design, Laurie Searl
Marketing, Patrick Durocher

Library of Congress Cataloging-in-Publication Data

Weineck, Silke-Maria, 1963–
    The abyss above: philosophy and poetic madness in Plato, Hölderlin, and Nietzsche/
Silke-Maria Weineck.
        p. cm.
    Includes bibliographical references and index.
    ISBN 0-7914-5427-4 (hc : alk. paper) – ISBN 0-7914-5428-2 (pbk. : alk. paper)
    1. Philosophy–History. 2. Poetry–History and criticism. 3. Literature and mental
illness–History. 4. Plato. 5. Hölderlin, Friedrich, 1770–1843. 6. Nietzsche, Friedrich
Wilhelm, 1844–1900. I. Title.

B66 .W45 2002
190–dc21

                                                                    2002017726

10 9 8 7 6 5 4 3 2 1

for my families

CONTENTS

ACKNOWLEDGMENTS

All traces of merit this book may be found to have lead back to Arkady Plotnitsky, prince amongst advisers. The attention he lavished on my project far exceeded all standards of generosity and care known to the academy, and I cannot thank him enough. No matter what he says.

I think of Charles Bernheimer (†) with gratitude and sadness; he was the rarest of mentors, teaching me not just what to know, but how to know it, more than I can say. Thank you much also to Jean-Michel Rabaté, for consistently and abundantly displaying the most wondrous of academic virtues, intellectual generosity.

Madness, at its core, is a condition of profound solitude. To all the friends I have kept and lost, whose companionship and whose touch have made me happy and human, my deep gratitude. Separate thanks to Susanne Gödde and Michael McShane, excellent friends who know Greek, to Imke Meyer, who always listens and always answers, and to Gwen, who now as ever continues to provide her own lovely brand of sanity in the form of passionate intelligence, silly novels, bubble bath, gossip, laughter, and long-distance consultations of various kinds. Marc Lipschutz helped in ways that are difficult to articulate.

To my mother and father, who, parents that they are, erroneously but fervently believe that I can do whatever I set my mind to.

To Paul, who kept the faith throughout the years we worked together; and to all the Sunsteins, who took me in for a while so graciously and so warmly. My children, Stella and Leon, have accepted that this is not, as far as they are concerned, "a real book," and I appreciate their tolerance.

Last, to my brother Jens (†) whose figure stood in the shadows of my mind throughout. I still cannot make out whether his gesture in this twilight is a greeting, or a warning, or both. "The wounded ones are silent, for nothing can heal them but the wound which is floating too far in the distance," he once wrote. I have not tried to make the wounded speak here; I wouldn't dare.

I thank the Program in Comparative Literature and Literary Theory at the University of Pennsylvania for its generous support, and my superb new colleagues and friends at the German Studies Department and the Program in Comparative Literature at the University of Michigan for giving me a new intellectual home.

The author and publishers would like to thank the following for permission to reproduce copyrighted material:

Cyrus Hamlin, " 'Stimmen des Geschiks': The Hermeneutics of Unreadability (Thoughts on Hölderlin's 'Griechenland')," with the kind permission of the Bouvier Verlag.

Friedrich Hölderlin, *Essays and Letters on Theory*, trans. and ed. Thomas Pfau, with the kind permission of the State University of New York Press.

Paul Celan, "Tübingen, Jänner," with the kind permission of the Fischer Verlag.

Philippe Lacoue-Labarthe, "The Caesura of the Speculative," *Glyph* 4 (1978):57–84, with the kind permission of the Johns Hopkins University Press.

Plato, *Plato's Phaedrus*, trans. with introduction and commentary by R. Hackforth, with the kind permission of Cambridge University Press.

Versions of the following parts of this book have appeared in other publications: the reading of the *Ion* in *Arethusa* (31:1998, 19–42), part of the Hölderlin chapter in *Seminar* (36:2, 2000, 161–181), an excerpt of the Nietzsche chapter in *Journal for Nietzsche Studies* (15:1998, 34–49), and the second part of the conclusion in *Orbis Litterarum* (54:4, 1999, 262–275). I thank the editors and publishers for their kind permission to include this material in this book.

ABBREVIATIONS

The following abbreviations will be used throughout:

PSW   Platon. *Sämtliche Werke in zehn Bänden*. Griechisch und Deutsch. Nach der Übers. Friedrich Schleiermachers, erg. durch Übers. von Franz Susemihl u.a. Hg. Karlheinz Hüser. Frankfurt/M.: Insel, 1991/Paris: Les Belles Lettres, 1991. All quotations from this edition appear in my translation.

RP   *The Republic of Plato*. Trans. with notes, an interpretive essay, and a new introduction by Allan Bloom. New York: Basic Books, 2/1991.

FA   Friedrich Hölderlin. *Sämtliche Werke ('Frankfurter Ausgabe')*. Historisch-kritische Ausgabe. Hg. Friedrich Sattler. Frankfurt/M: Stroemfeld/Roter Stern, 1988. I provide both the original German text and my own translations.

WBD   Friedrich Hölderlin. *Werke, Briefe, Dokumente*. Nach der Kleinen Stuttgarter Hölderlin-Ausgabe, hg. von Friedrich Beißner. Ausgewählt und mit Nachwort von Pierre Bertaux. München: Winkler, 1963. I provide both the original German text and my own translations.

KSA   Friedrich Nietzsche. *Sämtliche Werke. Kritische Studienausgabe in 15 Bänden*. Hg. Giorgio Colli und Mazzino Montinari. Deutscher Taschenbuch-Verlag: München, 1988. I provide both the original German text and my own translations.

Nietzsche's works will be abbreviated as follows:

GT   *Die Geburt der Tragödie*

WL   *Über Wahrheit und Lüge im Außermoralischen Sinne*

UB   *Unzeitgemäße Betrachtungen*

MA   *Menschliches, Allzumenschliches*

M   *Morgenröthe*

FW   *Die fröhliche Wissenschaft*

JGB   *Jenseits von Gut und Böse*

GM   *Zur Genealogie der Moral*

GD   *Götzendämmerung*

EH   *Ecce Homo*

Z   *Also sprach Zarathustra*

For the convenience of my English-speaking readers, all quotations from German scholarly works have been translated into English; I have retained the original passages in the endnotes.

FUTURE PERFECT

CASSANDRA, OR THE BELATED TRUTH OF MADNESS

Apollo desired the Trojan princess Cassandra enough to offer her anything she might wish for. After choosing knowledge of the future, she refused to honor her side of the bargain. Since Greek gods cannot take back what they give, she now had the inhuman gift of seeing and saying the truth. She saw Troy fall; she knew that the wooden horse was dangerous; and she told the Trojans that she would die in Agamemnon's house. To anyone who listened, however, she was a madwoman, for Apollo had amended his gift so that nobody would ever believe what she knew: "All heard, and none believ'd the prophecy."[1]

I have always thought of Apollo's revenge as the cruelest of punishments, and of Cassandra's story as the most profound tale of supreme madness. Supreme madness, in this study, denotes any form of madness that generates a knowledge that is not given to those who are not mad, a knowledge, moreover, that—like prophecy—can be neither verified nor refuted by the rational operations of the sane mind, which must disregard it or accept it on faith.

Reflection on supreme madness sets up a paradoxical relationship between madness and reason: the moment we assume that mad speech is true, we necessarily cease to think of it as mad, even though we may still consider the speaker to be a madman. As truth or knowledge, the revelation granted by supreme madness can be confirmed only in retrospect, *nachträglich*. The story of madness must be read in reverse, for the validity or invalidity of mad thought can never be guaranteed in advance by the methods devised to legitimate the operations of rational thought. Not all madness hides a truth, after all, and since the verification of mad truth cannot itself be mad, any philosophy of madness must necessarily be a hermeneutic of mad utterance.

This structure presents itself most hauntingly in Greek mythology and Attic tragedy. The meaning of prophecy, as Tiresias and the mad Sybil of

1

Delphi speak it, is dark until its truth has become manifest. And since by virtue of its very logic it must be obscure or ambiguous in order not to be averted, the only accurate tense for the movement of revelation is future perfect: this will have been true.

These days, attempts to listen to the speech of the mad are by and large confined to the hospital or the therapy room. To be sure, empirical psychology is fascinated by madness and "creativity" (the contemporary, somewhat insipid, term of choice in this regard). Cases in point are, to name just a few, Stephen Diamond's *Anger, Madness, and the Daimonic*, Arnold Ludwig's *The Price of Greatness*, Kay Redfield Jamison's suggestive study *Touched By Fire*, Russell Monroe's *Creative Brainstorms: The Relationship Between Madness and Genius*, Albert Rothenberg's *Creativity and Madness*, or anthologies like *Creativity and Madness: Psychological Studies of Art and Artists*.[2] Yet, the hospital and the brain-scan lab are nothing like the institution of Delphi, even though both serve to frame and accommodate madness. Psychiatrists and psychologists will call what they hear a symptom, and they will think of the symptom as a manifestation of a cause, a disorder, mental or (more and more often) physiological. Mad speech still points to a truth, but it is a truth only about the mad themselves, their minds or their bodies. This conception of the symptom is deaf to the word's etymological root, *symptomatikos*, accidental, coincidental. A symptom that merely coincides with madness can be set free—the Sybil can be mad, and her words can be a symptom of her madness, but the symptom is not confined to her madness. In the hospital, conversely, the ravings of the modern psychotic will bespeak nothing but the disorder he embodies.

Cassandra's story, in contrast, speaks of the broken contract between desire and knowledge. In order to know, she is to surrender her body and her own desire. Who can tell whether this is a fair price? Socrates might have known, but he decided against his carnal love for the boys as well as against secure knowledge, famously claiming once to know only that he knew nothing. From the *Symposium's* Alcibiades, we know much about his resistance against the flesh, but not so much about the attraction that the mad rituals of prophets and bacchantic dance, promising knowledge beyond anything the labor of philosophy can attain, might have held for him. I think, with Nietzsche, that his sanity must have been a burden to him at times. Nietzsche, following the *Phaedo's* version of Socrates' last days, sees him listen to the voice that says, "Play music!"[3] It might also have said, "Socrates, dance, drink, make love." Or even, "Socrates, go mad." He did not; instead, he died his death in a splendor of reason. His name has come to be read as shorthand for Western reason, his death as the beginning of Western philosophy, and although he used the word *logos* in a bewildering variety of senses, it is due to him that we think of *logos* as a word for reason itself.[4]

Socrates' thought, then, is simultaneously the most obvious and the least obvious place to start an inquiry into the constellation of philosophy, madness, and poetry. The least obvious, because Plato makes him look like the incarnation of *sophrosune*, that elusive Greek term that means something like serenity of mind, the moderation that comes out of knowledge, reason in balance—a term that comes closest to being the opposite of madness.[5] At the same time, it is Socrates who insists that to know anything is to know its opposite as well.[6] He who knows most about *sophrosune* would know most about madness as well, and the philosopher who would ban the imitative poets from his fictional republic would have to be an expert on poetry.

Whether this argument is convincing or not, Socrates indeed does seem to be the first to formulate a sustained philosophy of poetry that is also a reflection on madness. While he certainly did not invent the notion of poetic madness, he appears to be its first theoretician. I will argue that this theory of poetic madness is central to the birth of Platonic philosophy itself, and thus to that part of Western philosophy as a whole that starts with Plato.

It seems necessary to clarify the notion of madness that is at stake here. Since Foucault, the humanities have mostly understood the question of madness to be the question of the asylum. In *Madness and Civilization*, Foucault argues that the modern relationship between reason and madness, one of exclusion and internment, has replaced a previous interaction between them that was more ambivalent, more porous:

> In the serene world of mental illness, modern man no longer communicates with the madman. . . . As for a common language, there is no such thing; or rather, there is no such thing any longer; the constitution of madness as a mental illness, at the end of the eighteenth century, affords the evidence of a broken dialogue, posits the separation as already effected, and thrusts into oblivion all those stammered, imperfect words without fixed syntax in which the exchange between madness and reason was made.[7]

Modern thought in the age of reason, Foucault suggests, consolidates itself against madness, an act that characterizes its political and social institutions, its science, and its philosophy. Even though this assertion has not gone unchallenged,[8] it has set the tone for a number of subsequent studies. In contrast, this book will not concern itself with what Foucault called "the great internment" inside or outside the asylum. It presents an idea of madness that moves *within* the thinking of reason, its scope and its limits—in a word, within philosophy. More specifically, I seek to elucidate the role madness plays in the constellation of philosophy, madness, and poetry as it emerges from the writings of Plato, Hölderlin, and Nietzsche.

There are others who might have more to say about madness and poetry—Shakespeare, Nerval, or Freud, for example; this book focuses on Plato, Hölderlin, and Nietzsche instead because they have, perhaps more than anyone else, engaged both literary and philosophical modes of writing in an attempt to negotiate the respective epistemological claims of philosophy and art. As antithetical as their positions often are, they are linked by a unifying theme: the idea of madness holds a central place in the search for the specific, contradistinctive natures of poetry and philosophy. This is true for Plato's Socrates, still the philosopher par excellence; for Hölderlin, whom Heidegger called "the poet of poetry"; and for Nietzsche who—writing, celebrating and condemning in turn both philosophy and poetry—ultimately used the hammer of his thinking to shatter the foundations of a rationalist culture in which philosophy and poetry excluded each other. All of them have been both praised and blamed for the ambiguity of their style, oscillating and sometimes hovering between philosophy and poetry.

Hölderlin and Nietzsche, of course, are not only famous for their poetry and their philosophy: they are also two of the most distinguished madmen in history. Their later lives continue to fuel the critical imagination of Western culture, a culture that—despite its most conspicuous celebrations of reason—has always associated madness and genius. The chapters on Hölderlin and Nietzsche will largely abstain from speculation as to whether their work drove them mad or their madness drove their work, or from discussions of whether there are essential connections between the two. Stipulated connections of this sort, however, sometimes latently, sometimes overtly, inform a number of the most influential studies devoted to them. It is only in dialogue with some of these studies that the question of Hölderlin's and Nietzsche's madness will arise. The omission of biography comes about not because it is obvious that these things do not matter—ultimately, they probably matter immensely and immeasurably. However, biographical speculation appears invariably inadequate, if only due to the lack of a relevant interdisciplinary theory with any predictive or explanatory force, and while the phenomenon of the mad creator remains to intrigue scientists and humanists alike, we are still looking at a sporadic correlation for which no causal model has proven convincing.

TOTAL AND RESTRICTED MADNESS

The figure of the mad poet has been of singular impact on our understanding of poetry for a very long time. I will argue that the concept of poetic madness has served to distinguish the procedures of philosophy and poetry, as the controlled and repeatable labor of thought versus the spontaneous production of a text that is by definition unique. Socrates' postulate in the *Phaedrus* that "some of the highest goods have come to us by way of madness" (244a),[9] i.e., that a state of profound self-alienation[10] can give rise to the most highly concentrated expression of human existence, has proven so pervasive that it has by now become a cliché, informing readings of poetry as well as psychiatric practices, the marketing strategies of popular culture, and the vague musings of the feuilleton. In contrast, very little attention has been paid to the extent to which the notion of poetic madness is fundamental to the self-conception of Western *philosophy*. Foucault's seminal work in *Madness and Civilization* has spawned various studies devoted to the historical, political, sociocultural, and ideological aspects of ever-changing perceptions of madness in general, and it has informed a good number of critical case studies devoted to mad poets. Almost all of these books, however, are characterized by a curious omission. Taking the alliance of poetry and madness for granted, they rarely stop to consider or question the theoretical assumptions that underlie the concept of poetic or philosophical madness. At the end of *Maladie mentale et psychologie*, Foucault writes:

> There is a good reason why psychology could never master madness: psychology has only become possible in our world after madness already was mastered, after it had already been excluded from the drama. And if madness, a lightning, a scream, reappears in Nerval or Artaud, Nietzsche, or Roussel, then psychology grows silent in turn and stands wordlessly before this language, a language which borrows the meaning of *its* words from that tragic tear and from that freedom in the face of which the mere existence of 'psychologists' guarantees contemporary man a depressing forgetfulness.[11]

It is by no means obvious, however, why Foucault can invest the language of mad poets and philosophers with such unique power to transcend their historical time, which defines "contemporary man," and to cross the limits of the knowledge (or memory) allotted to those who stay confined within the realm of reason. First, Foucault has to bracket some questions: Did Nietzsche, for example, really write a language of madness, or did his madness coincide with the end of his writing? Was Nerval's writing not a non-mad *recollection* of madness rather than the language of madness itself? More importantly, perhaps, does Foucault himself not speak from the position of a cultural-historical psychologist, indebted more than he admits to Freud and to that Nietzsche who himself was a great psychologist? But even if Nerval, Nietzsche, Hölderlin, Artaud, or Roussel did transcend the limits of their time, and transcended them on the strength of their madness, we still do not know what it is in madness that would grant it access to a meaning to which historical reason—i.e., reason defined and delimited by its historical place—cannot penetrate.

Foucault, like his followers, writes the history of madness as a history of repression and oppression, and he is surely justified in doing so. Yet he also invests madness with significant privileges. In Foucault's writing, these two operations seem distinct from each other, the second one functioning like a gesture of repudiation of the first one. In this, however, Foucault stands more firmly in the very tradition he criticizes than he acknowledges. Oppression itself can breed privilege, however marginal or imaginary this privilege may be. Moreover, oppression and privilege tend to stem from the same theoretical or ideological preconceptions, so that the praise of folly will always be, to a certain extent, complicitous with the internment of the fool. Thus, Jacques Derrida maintains in his critique of Foucault that the "misfortune of the mad, the interminable misfortune of their silence, is that their best spokesmen are those who betray them best" (CHM, 36).

Simply put, both the oppression of the mad and the suspicion of those strange powers that the mad may wield are founded on the notion that madness, in various ways, constitutes the opposite of and thus possibly an alternative to reason. Derrida moves within this tradition when he claims that "[madness] simply says the other of each determined form of the *logos*" (CHM, 42). And in *Madness and Modernism*, Louis A. Sass remarks that

> [t]he madman is a protean figure in the Western imagination, yet there is a sameness to his many masks. . . . Nearly always insanity has been seen as what one early-nineteenth-century alienist called 'the opposite to reason and good sense, as light is to darkness, straight to crooked.'[12]

Sass and Derrida are certainly right to point out that the term *madness*, for all the historically and ideologically determined variance in its conceptualization, has a constant element. It is also correct, however, as Sass's study itself proves extensively for the period of modernism, that the Western imagination has at times privileged darkness over light, spirals over straight lines, and madness over good sense.

> "The highest goods come to us by way of madness."[13]
> "Sacred Madness is highest human manifestation."[14]
> "Almost everywhere it is madness that prepares the way for the new thought."[15]

These sentences span more than two thousand years, bridging the work of Plato, Hölderlin, and Nietzsche, conceivably three of the most authoritative writers on reason, philosophy, and poetry. To be sure, madness means something different in each case, and so does the reason it competes with. In each case, however, reason emerges as an incomplete form of being, perhaps a little pallid, as something good and useful but not quite satisfying, limited as to the task at hand. In these texts, *logos* reflects on itself and its limits; they are not mad texts, but reasonable disquisitions into reason.

It has been suggested, by Foucault as well as by Derrida, that madness cannot reflect on itself without ceasing to be madness. Foucault might have said that such a sustained reflection would amount to a work, while madness, as he defines it, is the absence of the work. For Derrida, who radicalizes Foucault's argument, any discursive language is already *logos*, and madness, as we have seen, is always *logos*'s other. Madness, then, cannot possibly speak itself: "To say madness without expelling it into objectivity is to let it say itself. But madness is what by essence cannot be said" (CHM, 43). The madman is locked into an interminable solitude where he cannot speak about himself *even to himself*.

To suggest that madness cannot say itself because madness is what cannot be said is not, in the end, a very satisfying proposition. While it appears plausible to say that the mad cannot speak about themselves *as mad* without entering the discourse of sanity, "expelling their madness into objectivity," they can certainly say things about themselves, and it is, after all, often precisely on the grounds of these things that we declare them mad. Speech need not be in a truthful, self-representative, and self-conscious relation to the speaker to qualify as *logos*. Moreover, there is nothing in madness that would prevent the madman from engaging in philosophy. Freud, for instance, was at times rather exasperated by Schreber's metaphysical aspirations, even though or perhaps because they amounted to a quite consistent theology.[16]

In paralleling 'saying' with 'saying itself,' 'saying itself' with *logos*, and *logos* with reason, Derrida, following Foucault rather closely in this respect, constructs a notion of a madness that is striking, and troubling, for its purity. Later on, Derrida argues that "[t]he madman is not always wrong about everything; he is not wrong often enough, is never mad enough" (CHM, 51) to engage philosophy. Certainly, this statement is meant to elucidate Descartes' quest for a perfect doubt, but Derrida, at times, also appears to be speaking for philosophy per se. A madness mad enough would amount to "a negativity so negative that it could not even be called such any longer" (CHM, 308, fn. 4). Madness as it is, as a negativity not sufficiently negative, is of lesser interest since it can, à la Hegel, too easily be called to the service of *Aufhebung*, as an instance of work. And work, to close the circle again, would be the absence of madness. But just as a negativity so negative could not be called negativity any longer, a madness so mad could not be called madness anymore, since it would lie outside the realm of all diagnosis, which is, after all, a form of categorization. It could not be called anything at all, and all discourse on this madness would be limited to speaking about its nothingness. If "[e]very concept that lays claim to any rigor whatsoever implies the alternative of 'all or nothing'," if it "is impossible or illegitimate to form a *philosophical concept* outside the logic of all or nothing,"[17] then nothing may too often be all that is left—or that is left *within* philosophy.

Common usage of the term *madness*—and this is neither surprising nor an argument against Derrida—suggests otherwise. The near endless variety in this regard implies that what we call madness is a continuum that starts well within the confines of what is considered reasonable behavior. It is possible to be a little mad, it is even considered quite charming. This is not to say that there is not something in those small follies that links them to the stains on the walls of an asylum close to my hometown where everything is white—the paint, the beds, the uniforms, the paper cups, the plates, the pills. A man I know, a poet and painter diagnosed with paranoid schizophrenia (and almost any other psychotic disturbance the current medical dictionary lists), recalls that he pissed at the wall to relieve this whiteness, which he could not bear. Perhaps these stains constitute a form of mad writing for our times, unreadable, and quickly washed away from walls prudently covered with latex paint. If this study is silent on this writing, then it is because I do not think that my critical vocabulary has anything to add to it, even though I would like to say, just once, that I saw it before me when I initially started to think about madness and poetry, and that I find it both mad and reasonable, and also poetic.

It is not only that there are acts that can be both mad and reasonable; it is a commonplace that many acts can be both or either, at certain times, under certain circumstances, if we take our clues from the history of a term that has always been used to cover the most banal and the most complex conditions or events. More interesting is the question whether the act of philosophy, the most privileged performance of reason, has a connection to madness that goes beyond "the reassurance given against the anguish of being mad at the point of greatest proximity to madness" (CHM, 59), that does not conceive of pure madness as pure silence. In his essay on Artaud, Derrida seems to suggest as much when he speaks of

> the other madness, as the metaphysics which lives *within* difference, within metaphor and the work, and thus within alienation; and lives within them without conceiving them *as such*, beyond metaphysics. Madness is as much alienation as inalienation. It is the work or the absence of the work.[18]

The project of self-reflection, central to philosophy since Socrates, is an act highly susceptible to that "other madness," even though the organized presentation of self-reflecting thought has come to be thought of as the very paradigm of reason. Sass quotes Nietzsche in the epigraph of his book: "The growing consciousness is a danger and a disease."[19] Nietzsche, on the whole, considers this disease in terms of decadence rather than of madness, but as a disease of consciousness, it may well be a form of madness. There is a point then, where an increase in consciousness is as dangerous as, or perhaps even more dangerous than, a decrease. This sounds, and in Sass's case is meant to sound, like a fundamentally late modern thought. Plato's erotic madness, however, the highest madness producing the highest rewards, is, in essence, already an encounter with the self (even though it is not always a disease, and only potentially a state of alienation). Oedipus's fall, as Hölderlin reads it, is brought about by his "insane quest for a consciousness."[20] Hegel, it is rumored, feared that he would go mad while writing the *Phenomenology of Spirit*, a profoundly self-reflective book.

The association between madness and auto-gnosis well precedes Nietzsche, even if it is, before him, most often glimpsed only in passing. As a question of individual self-reflection, it will play a subordinated role in this book; I am more concerned with the (only partially analogous) structure of self-reflecting philosophy through what Socrates calls the "the ancient quarrel" between philosophy and poetry. On philosophy's side, this quarrel has always been, in part, a struggle for identity, marked by an anxiety of contamination. But what exactly would constitute such contamination?

THE LIMITS OF MADNESS AND THE LIMITS
OF PHILOSOPHY

The most prominent question at the beginning of Western philosophy, or rather at the moment of its consolidation as philosophy with Socrates, is the question *ti esti,* what is . . . ?, replacing, according to Heidegger's powerful analysis, the question of being itself. In arguably its most significant form, it concerns its own nature, as philosophy. What is philosophy? Socrates provided a number of answers, and it is a matter of judgment whether any one can be privileged over the others. It is possible to say, however, that one has proven exceptionally persistent: the identity of philosophy lies in its difference from poetry. Socrates' banning the poets from the philosopher's city is thus an emblematic act in the self-constitution of philosophy.

To say that the identity of philosophy is determined by its difference from poetry, however, notoriously creates a multitude of new questions about the nature of this difference. It has often been suggested, in more or less subtle articulations, that philosophy and poetry relate to each other like truthful and fictional representation of the world. While it is remotely possible that Socrates really thought so, it is almost certain that Plato did not, for Plato's *Republic* is itself an elaborate self-conscious master-fiction, a tale containing many tales within itself, some of them explicitly fictional, some even explicitly mendacious. Socrates does not ban fiction but the poets, and the telling of lies is not a poet's prerogative. Not only is the lie a requisite tool of the philosopher-king, as in the education of the guardians, fiction is also indispensable to philosophy itself. When Glaucon asks Socrates to explain the parable of the cave, Socrates responds,

> you will no longer be able to follow, my dear Glaucon, although there wouldn't be any lack of eagerness on my part. But you would no longer be seeing an image of what we are saying, but rather the truth itself, at least as it looks to me. (533a)[21]

Unless Socrates wants to slight Glaucon individually, he appears to suggest that philosophy cannot abandon the image and remain teachable; if it were unteachable, it would, at least for the Socrates of the dialogues, cease to be philosophy.[22] While this passage demonstrates the inevitability of philosophical images and fictions, it also points to the fact that a substantial part of philosophy is dedicated to the problem of its own fictionality. The place and function of the image within philosophy's and poetry's respective enterprises, then, might lead to tentative answers about their difference, and recent literary theory has investigated these in some detail.[23] Under rigorous investigation, the lines that would separate the poetic and the philosophical use of fiction appear to blur as well, leading poststructuralist theory under the influence of Nietzsche and Heidegger to maintain, as Plotnitsky summarizes, that "[t]he opposition between literature and truth or literature and philosophy becomes undecidable."[24] At least in theory, and for the time being.

It is also true, though, that an image-free discourse was one of the central utopias of modern philosophy, especially of Enlightenment thought that discourages the free and frequent use of tropes perhaps more strongly than any previous philosophical style.[25] The Enlightenment project brings philosophy's concern about the dangers of poetic contamination into sharp focus. As it turns out, Plato's writings themselves, even while they retain their status as the source of all Western philosophy, pose one of the most complicated problems to a thought that would be pure. In a sharp attack on some of his contemporaries, Kant, speaking in the name of "true" philosophy, claims the inheritance of Plato against the neo-Platonist enthusiasts, and, by extension, against the poets who read Plato as one of them. He writes:

> At bottom all philosophy is probably prosaic; and the proposition to once again philosophize poetically might well be received as similar advice to the merchant would be: that he henceforward write his ledgers not in prose but in verse.[26]

The chief positions on Plato's work with regard to this issue are well-known. Those who would write the philosophic registers in verse focus on the poetic nature of Plato's writing itself, while the defenders of a pure and laborious philosophy stress the *Republic*'s ban on the poets to guard their Platonic inheritance. Kant maintains that philosophy, including Plato's philosophy, is fundamentally (*im Grunde*) different from poetry, so different in fact that philosophy will share its language with merchants rather than with poets. The sentiment expressed is not new; compared to the ban of the poets, Kant's formulation is not even very harsh. Poetic philosophy is merely comical, as comical as the idea of a poetic sales register; it is a joke, but a joke that may conceal a profound repression concerning the origin and the nature of philosophy.

A perhaps more interesting aspect of Kant's mild jest is the explicit reference to the business of exchange. Kant's analogy brings to the fore philosophy's often latent complicity with economics. He positions philosophy on the side of certifiable calculations, of the exchange of goods, of sound economics. Philosophy, unlike poetry, is accountable, and honest philosophy, one might assume, leaves the books balanced, with no remainder. It is the language of the restricted economy of reason, a language pitched against the languages of irrationality, poetry, pathos, and ecstasy that Bataille has seen as the realms where a theory of general economy would come into play—along with madness. For madness, as well, seems to be susceptible to an analysis of general economy "that makes apparent," as Bataille says in *Inner Experience*, "that excesses of energy are produced, and that by definition, these excesses cannot be utilized. The excessive energy can only be lost without the slightest aim, consequently without any meaning."[27]

It is hardly a coincidence that economic disappropriation is one of the historically most stable elements in the treatment of the mad. One of Solon's laws stated already that the mad could hold no property, and Socrates' interlocutors in the *Republic* can easily agree that the conventional definition of justice, the telling of truth and the payment of debt, does not apply as soon as we are dealing with the mad (cf. Chapter One, section II). The exchange of meaning and the exchange of goods go together, and the mad can be excluded from this marketplace because they do not play by the rules.

In stretching Kant's analogy, we might say that the poet, and especially the inspired or mad poet, is an uncountable and unaccountable figure in philosophy's calculations. At the far end, madness indeed can appear as an extraordinary expenditure of mental or physical energy that cannot be recuperated into the economies of communication, into social or philosophical meaning. *Poetic* madness, however, cannot be a silence of "words without language" (CHM, 50), and the mad poet must create more than "a lightning, a scream," even if the text he creates is ultimately nothing more than the place from which the mad scream rises. During most of the history of poetic madness, however, mad poetry was simultaneously more and less than that. The mad poet was not meant to produce a mad text. It is not madness one would have searched for in the madman's poems, but a form of order and insight, a knowledge that was not to be found by the reasonable mind, but that, once expressed and examined, was not alien to it either. While the poet was mad, his text was exceptionally reasonable, for the privilege of the madman was precisely that alienation from himself that would allow him to leave the limits of the eternally unreasonable worldly self behind—or rather the self restricted to merely human reason. The concept of poetic madness suggests a separation between author and text as radical as or perhaps even more radical than the poststructuralist theories that the contemporary conservative cultural elite loves to attack for just this postulate.

FROM DIVINE REASON TO MADNESS UNDER THE DEATH OF GOD

In the history of poetics, it was rather late that the mad poet was meant to provide an insight into his madness—if the poetry of the mad mattered at all, then precisely to the extent to which it gave insight about things beyond the individual (cf. Chapter One and Three). The shift in interest appears to occur simultaneously with the rethinking of artistic genius in the wake of the Classical Age, an operation in which Kant's *Critique of Judgment* was prominently involved. In the German tradition, this conceptual change can be traced in the move from *Genius* to *Genie*. Whereas *Genius* signifies a demonic force that, as Rainer Nägele has put it, "comes from the outside to the subject," the term *Genie* that would come to replace it relates to the individual artist:

> The shift from *Genius* to *Genie* in German takes place in the second half of the eighteenth century, and it indicates not only the point of a fundamental

shift in aesthetic and poetological conceptions but also the point where psychoanalysis radically differs from psychology. The shift in the eighteenth century can be described as an internalization of creativity, as a claim for creativity of the individual subject that in turn is located in the ego. One can also describe it as a grammatical difference: one can *have* a *Genius*, but one can *be* a *Genie*—at least, so it is said.[28]

The move from poetic madness as divine inspiration to poetic madness as an individual pathology mirrors that shift. As Nägele points out, psychoanalytic theories have reinvested the creative process with a quasi-demonic element:

> That which emerges as the unconscious in Freud's experience and in the psychoanalytic experience renders expressions like 'my' or 'your' or 'his' unconscious questionable. The unconscious appears as a phenomenon that seems to exist, just like the *Genius* of earlier times, only in a strange and not easily graspable 'in-between.'[29]

While it is true that the driving forces that emerge from Freud's unconscious are not individually determined—take the Oedipus complex as the most obvious example—they are nonetheless forces of the individual psyche as well as of the human psyche in general. Thus, the unconscious differs from "the 'genius' of former times" as much as it resembles it. The concept of a madness that does not originate in the individual's body or experience, gone even before Freud's time, seems irretrievable after him. In this light, Foucault is certainly right in saying that psychoanalysis has nothing to say about the madness of old that was more than a pathology. As Foucault's writing itself may demonstrate, however, psychoanalysis has not dispelled the legend of poetic madness either; it is alive as a cliché as well as in the most refined theories of thought, language, and reason, and literary as well as scientific studies continue to investigate the ancient association between creativity and mental deviance.[30]

The idea of poetic madness is ancient, and it is safe to assume that it precedes Plato's writing; Plato's dialogues, however, appear to inaugurate the philosophical contemplation of *theia mania*, most prominently in the *Ion* and the *Phaedrus*. I will argue that both texts, to a different extent, strive to establish an identity for philosophy as public speech that is decisively different from poetic speech in genesis, form, content, and aim. Moreover, philosophy cannot merely be different from or even superior to poetry, it must establish itself as poetry's master discourse, as that *logos* which reflects on poetry in a way poetry cannot reflect on itself. In other words, I suggest that the *Ion* and the *Phaedrus* can be read as the beginning of literary criticism. This operation depends on a concept of divine inspiration as a state that disallows self-reflection. Ironically, then, the superior status to which divinely inspired speech can lay claim is simultaneously the condition of its subjection to philosophy.

As I will show in the first chapter, especially in the reading of the *Phaedrus*, this very operation that allows philosophy to achieve hegemony over the poet, however, creates a central problem: the origin of philosophy's primal text. If philosophical reason, as dialogue, can talk only about speech that already exists, it cannot be self-founding. A purely dialogical philosophy, then, would lose its autonomy and appear as an epiphenomenon of mad texts once madness appears as the privileged access to truth. In the *Phaedrus*'s famous myth of the soul, Socrates creates philosophy's original moment as a moment of erotic madness. Thus, Socrates saves for philosophy the unmediated nature of mad knowledge; erotic madness, however, in contrast to poetic, Dionysian, and prophetic madness, is both interactive and self-reflective, and thus—potentially—philosophical in a way that poetic madness can never be. Thus, poetic text and philosophical text are not *primarily* distinguished by formal or stylistic criteria; neither do they relate to each other like madness and reason or lie and truth. Both poetry and philosophy must present whatever truth they contain in the form of potential lies, and both rely on a moment of madness to prompt them. It is the different nature of this madness that divides them, the different role it plays, and its duration: at the end of madness, the poet ceases to be a poet. Being mad and making poetry coincide; poetic madness is a mode of speech. In contrast, erotic madness is the silent pretext to philosophy, what Derrida would call an *exergue* of philosophy.[31]

Madness, the *Phaedrus* suggests, offers the original glimpse of a truth that is both unmediated and uncontaminated by and inaccessible to language. For Socrates, the metaphysical order of the eternal ideas[32] precedes language, and language, as a medium that always both over- and underrepresents the idea, must necessarily distort it. In this way, Socrates is as aware of the irreducibly metaphorical quality of all language as Nietzsche is (even though the deception inherent in language concerns a radically different realm in Nietzsche).[33] Only beauty exists both for the soul's and the body's eye; as the only concept that is equally powerful as idea and as image, it crosses the philosophical line between the intelligible and the perceptible that Socrates draws in the *Republic*. The sight of beauty, therefore, can lead to a flash of insight into the realm of truth that in its unmediated suddenness will drive the beholder mad. Philosophical desire springs from this wordless moment of madness, which it needs to overcome in order to become philosophy as *logos*. Perhaps, in the end, the language of philosophy relates to its truth as the ugly Socrates relates to the beautiful boy, and as human reason to divine madness.

Hölderlin, too, links the related projects of self-knowledge and metaphysics to madness—whether he was influenced in this by the *Phaedrus* is difficult to decide. In his translations of and his complex commentary on Sophocles' tragedies, he rewrites Antigone's language as a language of "sacred madness," and he perceives Oedipus's life as an "insane quest for a consciousness." I will suggest that Hölderlin's work recreates Antigone and Oedipus as figurations of ancient and modern philosophy, a project immeasurably more hazardous than Socrates presents it to be in his "anti-tragic theater."[34]

Antigone's deathbound decision to bury her brother appears as an act spurred by a metaphysical drive towards "the other world," a signless, timeless desert conceived against the proclaimed laws of the polis. Oedipus's murder of his father emerges as an attempt to redefine his existence on a universal plane, a vision of a self-created life without physical origin or constraint. In my reading, Oedipus and Antigone emerge as figurations of perversion, as a critique of the philosophical enterprise of transcending the limits of language and the body, entities that Hölderlin consistently associates metaphorically.

Since philosophy itself cannot overcome the mad element in philosophical desire, it is poetry that must provide the order to contain it. While Hölderlin's theory does not present an exact reversal of Socrates' constellation, the relationship between poetry and madness resembles the one between philosophy and madness that Socrates establishes in *Phaedrus*; for the mastery of madness is as crucial to the Hölderlinian poet as it is to the Socratic philosopher. For Hölderlin, too, this mastery involves a certain renunciation. As I will show in the second chapter, the tragic poet's attitude toward the mad tragic heroes is ambivalent, entailing a veiled intimacy he ultimately must forsake.

In this light, Hölderlin's famous image of the poet who grasps Zeus's lightning with his hands and passes it on to the people, "wrapped in song," is not the vision of poetic madness as which it has been read. Zeus's lightning is indeed a metaphor of madness, but of a madness controlled and enclosed by the poem, *handled* by technique, what German calls *Handwerk*. Poetry cannot sing madly, it can only sing *of* madness; if it establishes itself thus as a master-discipline, it also abandons its former claim to an immediacy of divine experience now reserved to "the stronger ones," the tragic heroes. For Hölderlin, the only madness that counts is still divine madness, and where the poets have to bear the absence of the gods, they have to bear the absence of madness as well.

Socrates tried to coax a transient language to reveal an intuition of that which is eternal. Hölderlin, in contrast, sees in language, especially in poetic language, that which remains—more permanent than any idea it might present or conceal: "Was aber bleibet, stiften die Dichter," "that which remains, however, the poets donate." And:

> . . . der Vater aber liebt,
> Der über allen waltet,
> Am meisten, daß gepflegt werde
> Der feste Buchstab, und Bestehendes gut
> Gedeutet.

(. . . the father, however, who reigns over all, most loves that the solid letter be tended, and that that which exists/that which withstands be interpreted well.)

It is the letter that counts, not the idea it is thought to represent, and even though the process of interpretation is the manner in which its continuous existence (*Bestehendes*) is maintained, it will nonetheless withstand (*bestehen*) changing interpretation. Poetry thus has a relation with time and history that is in strict contrast to madness as the quintessential interlude. This is not to say that the encounter with the tragedy and the madness of thought is not perilous: "man kann auch in die Höhe fallen, so wie in die Tiefe," "one can also fall up, just as well as one can fall down." The poet is in danger of succumbing to the temptation of "speaking priestly," as Oedipus did, and of getting sucked into the abyss above. This fall, however, would then no longer constitute poetry's original moment, but would mean the end of poetry altogether.

Nietzsche's writings on madness further heighten the sense of the danger that threatens those who use madness in pursuit of truth. Plato's and Hölderlin's spiritual universes are controlled by gods present or absent, and there is, to put it simply, always a reason for madness. Once God is dead, however, the old distinction between high and low madness, between inspiration and pathology, does not hold anymore, and any theory of mad truth, if it is to survive at all, must be inscribed in a vastly different framework.

Nietzsche's thoughts on madness, few but powerful as they are, always arise, implicitly or explicitly, in the context of God's death—a Nietzschean shorthand for a number of complex historical transformations. My reading concentrates on God's death as the event that breaks apart the complicity of theology, morality, and reason that, in Nietzsche's understanding, has sustained all philosophical and ideological belief systems to date. As Nietzsche argues, madness can come to be seen as a privileged mode of insight only as long as there is a higher force that controls human reason, as long as reason alone does not represent the highest value.

In Nietzsche's genealogical narratives, the currency of madness is strongest in the age of *Sittlichkeit*, a system of morality that regulates the performance of any significant physical or intellectual act in accordance with established rules of conduct. *Sittlichkeit* enforces collective compliance with its laws under the near absolute authority of tradition; a potentially static ethical edifice, it cannot be challenged individually, since its whole structure condemns individual opposition or deviance. Madness, Nietzsche insists, provided the only venue of revision, since it appears to combine original thought with the appearance of "total involuntariness." Paradoxically, madness clears a space of independence precisely because it is, to all appearances, a state of utter unfreedom. Divine madness—or rather, any madness that performs as if divinely inspired—is the only state of intellectual autonomy that escapes the collective's sanctions against individual aberrance, precisely because it appears as the ultimate negation of autonomous thought.

In *Madness and Civilization*, Foucault argues that the pre-Enlightenment world had a relationship to madness that was characterized by an essential openness to the realm of unreason. In contrast, Nietzsche, who senses a similar openness, suggests that madness found an audience exactly to the degree to which it was seen to represent reason itself, in its highest, divine form.

While Nietzsche salutes the madmen of early history as "superior men," he does not extol the system that produced their rare victories. Unlike Foucault, he indicates that madness owed the voice it had to the most ruthless repression of any voice of protest that was not mad, or not mad in the right way.

Ironically, the two figures whose thoughts would initiate the long decline of madness as a propelling force of history, i.e. Socrates and Christ, emerge, in Nietzsche's reading, as the quintessential madmen of old. In preaching an anticollective morality of individual conscience and redemption, Socrates and Christ would have to be, to the mind set of Sittlichkeit, either mad or criminal. Incidentally, both Socrates and Christ, to a different degree, staked their trials on the gamble of madness: Socrates claimed to be led by his daimonion, Christ by the father God himself. Sittlichkeit, however, listens to the mad only as long as their visions do not violate certain limits, as long as they accommodate, on a fundamental level, the system which they call into question, and both Socrates and Christ were executed as criminals.

The age of Platonic and Christian Moral knows only a faint echo of the power of madness to exculpate the thinkers of new thought—at least when compared to the much longer era of Sittlichkeit. Nonetheless, the legend of mad inspiration can survive as long as there is a higher authority that controls our fates—as long, in other words, as God lives in his many theist and atheist guises. The last section of this chapter before the epilogue is devoted to one of Nietzsche's most famous figures, the madman who, in the Gay Science, mourns the death of God in the marketplace. Since Nietzsche himself announced the death of God so frequently and so forcefully, it has proven tempting to read his work into this one figure. If, so the argument goes, the death of God, thought through to its last consequences, means the breakdown of all stable belief systems, at least temporarily, then the abyss that opens within these thoughts may be enough to drive their thinker insane.

Needless to say, connections between Nietzsche's thoughts and Nietzsche's madness have been drawn throughout the reception of his work, dating from the very beginning and stretching into the most recent studies of his writings. Nietzsche's pathological profile, however, hardly supports such superficially satisfactory conclusions,[35] and neither does Nietzsche's work. While he counts himself in the Gay Science among the insane thinkers whose lust for ever quicker reevaluations of all established truths poses the greatest danger to society, and while the intellectual tensions under which he operates are indeed extraordinarily high, his work consistently favors the slow labor of subtle argument over the quick dance of fancy. While his analysis of the history of morality is devastating and thorough, he acknowledges again and again that he himself proceeds under the moral restraints that binds all lovers of truths, the "moral phenomenon" of trust in reason.

If God were truly dead—and on Nietzsche's terms, he is not and may never be—then the mournful monologue of the maniac on the marketplace would be the last possible act of true madness within the history of reason.

The knowledge of his death would be the last message that a dying god could send; after that, there would be nothing we could call madness, because there would be no standard by which to measure sanity.

It is true that Nietzsche at times suggests a scenario where the lonely certainty of the maniac is indeed nothing but the knowledge of a future to come, where his experience exists, like Cassandra's predictions, in future perfect. This figure whose desperate search for God disconcerts all atheists into an uneasy silence, then, is indeed the final reincarnation of Cassandra, foreseeing not the end of Troy, but the end of everything that came after Troy. The victory of Greece remains the most important victory of our history; it not only inspired the first text of Western literature but perhaps *is* the very text of 'the West' itself. This victory, prefigured in the mad rants of the woman who defied the god of truth, could not have been won if anyone had listened to Cassandra. But then again, she did not die before she took her madness into the heart of Greece: it echoed through Agamemnon's palace, through Aeschylus's *Oresteia*, continued as shout and murmur through literature. Nonetheless, the book that frames these screams is called (defiantly perhaps?) a *science*, and *gay*.

EPILOGUE

This study is not a history, for, as Peter Szondi has said, "the *only* approach that does full justice to the work of art is the one that allows us to see history in the work of art, not the one that shows us the work of art in history."[36] The history that at times appears in these texts, I think, is not so much the history of madness but rather the history of the divine in general and of the relationship between reason and revelation in particular as they relate to writing. To rephrase, it is the history of madness *only* to the extent to which madness can differ from psychopathology and still be madness.

The following chapters trace a constellation of themes that seems to re-emerge and re-arrange itself at some of the most critical junctions in the enterprise of aesthetics. It is this same constellation I find again in Paul Celan's Hölderlin poem "Tübingen, Jänner," which addresses the condition of poetry in the second half of the twentieth century. This study closes in a reading of this poem, which is also an epilogue on the history of divine madness. In this reading, I have attempted to understand the near-impossible burden placed on a text that thinks about poetic madness in the wake of Nietzsche and Freud. Celan's meditation on Hölderlin's madness marks a parting; it speaks, in the name of poetic reason, against the sentimental mythology of suffering that characterizes the notion of madness in our time. Celan's poem surrounds Hölderlin's madness; making it unreadable, it shelters it. In that gesture, Celan ultimately abandons madness as mythos; he creates a place for it where it cannot be narrativized into a story of authenticity. Madness finally meets with silence as absolute negativity, a silence poetry must overcome in order to continue speaking.

CHAPTER ONE

TALKING ABOUT HOMER

Poetic Madness, Philosophy, and the Birth of Criticism

TALKING ABOUT HOMER

It is, at this point, impossible to trace the beginning of the Western idea of poetic madness that was certainly already part of Homer's world. Socrates, however, develops a *theory* of poetic madness[1] that has become deeply important not just to the way we understand poetry, but to philosophy's self-understanding. This theory both manifests and unfolds the tension between poetic and philosophical speaking. This chapter, therefore, will return to Plato's ancient quarrel between philosophy and poetry—not via the *Republic*, but via the *Ion*, a text that sets out to create an identity for philosophy in contradistinction to poetry, with which it competes in the marketplaces of speech.

In the first part of this chapter, I want to analyze Plato's concept of poetic madness as it first emerges in the short dialogue *Ion*. There, poetic madness serves to differentiate the procedures of philosophy and poetry as the controlled and repeatable labor of thought versus the spontaneous production of a text that is by definition unique; in the process, the *Ion* uses the idea of poetic madness to establish the necessity of criticism as a discipline different from poetry. While the dialogue does not outline the field of criticism as a concrete practice, it argues for the necessity of a discipline devoted to the knowledge of poetry, a discipline that would operate under the aegis of philosophy rather than of poetry.

I will suggest that in its relation to poetry, philosophy essentially defines itself as criticism, as a discourse *about* poetry that poetry itself cannot achieve. This operation depends on a theory of divine poetic madness, a notion, perhaps ironically, that the poets themselves appear to have cultivated. In Plato's dialogue, mad speech emerges as a speaking that eludes the

19

conscious control of the speaker; the mad poet, then, cannot claim authority over his poetry, no matter how great a poem he has produced.

In Plato's presentation, madness appears as a condition that cannot be deliberately controlled—a point Socrates makes more forcefully in the *Phaedrus*. If that is the case, then the making of poetry itself is uncontrollable. Every act of poeisis is unique and unrepeatable. Nonetheless, of course, poetry exists as *logos*, and can thus be inserted into philosophy. Philosophy, in turn, is not just accidentally or by convention but essentially speech about speech, as the reiterative structure of all Platonic dialogues shows. The last section of this chapter will develop this argument at length.

"Sing to me, Muse . . ."

In the very first line of what can be considered Greek founding poetry, in the first line of what was regarded to be, for the longest time, poetry incarnate, the poet asks for his share of divine inspiration. Homer sings, but his song appeals to another song: sing, Muse, so that this song can be sung. Homeric song commences as a song about the possibility of singing, and the first thing it says is that song must start somewhere else. The invocation creates an odd temporal twist, reminiscent of the logic of future perfect prophecy which the introduction developed. If song can begin only once the Muse has sung, how can you sing to the Muse? Conversely, perhaps the Muse has always already sung, and the invocation is an instance of the rhetorical—and profoundly poetic—figure *hysteron proteron*. In either case, the opening lines of the *Odyssey* reproduce the paradoxical temporality that appears to pervade all inquiries into the logic of poetic and prophetic divine intervention.

In Homer's (ritual?) invocation, poetic inspiration still appears as mythology. Socrates' *philosophy* of poetic madness takes its departure from here. One of the central issues of literary theory has always been the question of who or what is speaking when there is speech, along with the consequences this question entails for artistic production. In the nineteenth and twentieth centuries, various theoretical systems have redefined this issue, among them Marxism, Nietzsche's writing, and, perhaps most influentially, psychoanalysis. I will, however, step back from the contemporary theoretical scene in order to at least attempt to approach Plato's writing on its own terms (fully aware, I hope, of the ironies involved in this phrase). There, in one of the earliest sustained critiques of literature available to us, we already find the notion of poetry as a process that is fundamentally beyond the poet's control. To the ancient tradition, or to the extent that Socrates can be said to formulate this tradition, the notion of *creative* subjectivity appears to be deeply alien, even more alien perhaps than to psychoanalysis.[2] The notion of divine poetic madness in ancient Greece, first elaborated *theoretically* by Plato's Socrates, prefigures many of the problems that have troubled literary theory over the last decades. Although Socrates' work, especially as we have come to see it through Nietzsche's passionate critique, rather seems to indicate the inauguration of what will later become a full-blown theory of subjectivity, Plato's oeuvre also marks the place where the critique of a notion of art as subjectivey controlled representation is already philosophically formulated. It is precisely in this context that the *Ion* juxtaposes the question of poetic madness with the question of philosophy.

This is not to suggest, to be sure, that literary theory has merely come full circle since Plato. It is possible, as Foucault suggested, that the idea of a subject as a self-controlled entity that authorizes a work is relatively young and remained, at least in its purest formulations, largely contained in what has been summarily called the Age of Reason.[3] But the figure of the circle, of return, will not do, if only because repeating a state never simply means to return to it. If it is possible to point out certain convergences between Socrates' thought and poststructuralist and related matters, that does not mean that they are, therefore, identical, or even similar in structure or result.[4] The history, or, in Nietzschean terms, the genealogy of this convergence, cannot be erased. In the wake of Nietzsche, Heidegger, and Derrida, much critical thought has been given to *"Platonism,"* a homogenizing term covering widely divergent Western philosophies on the grounds that they share a small number of core assumptions. By now, however, it seems necessary to also isolate Plato from this fiction of "Platonism" as far as possible, in order to focus on those elements of Plato's writing that are uniquely his. A first step in this enterprise is to acknowledge once again a point that has been made frequently, but often much too obliquely: Plato's writing on poetry, a significant portion of his oeuvre, constitutes a scandal that has never been repeated in any influential Western work. In Book X of the *Republic*, Socrates says that he was "particularly [right] when reflecting on poetry . . . , in not admitting any part of it that is imitative" (595 a).[5] Socrates' banning the imitative poets from the ideal state might well be the most famous event in Plato's writing. Gadamer calls it "the most difficult challenge posed to the self-consciousness of the German mind in its encounter with the spirit of antiquity."[6] This is a very cautious formulation: Socrates' indictment is alien not only to the mindset of modern aesthetics (let alone merely the "German mind"), there is ample evidence that the "spirit of antiquity" found it just as strange, lethally strange in the end. Since a poet was one of Socrates' accusers at his trial, poetry as an institutuion is surely implicated in his execution. Perhaps his poetry embargo was, in itself, not enough of a scandal to warrant his death, but this death was nonetheless inflicted at least in part in the name of poetry.[7]

The banning of the poets, then, positions Socrates in a zone equally remote from "the spirit of antiquity" and the entirety of modern cultural theory and ideology. While the uniqueness of Socrates' vision of a state without poets and the importance of that vision for the whole of Plato's oeuvre can hardly be overemphasized, there is, at the same time, a danger in focusing on this passage too much. Its very prominence has obscured the diversity of Plato's writings on poetry and the poets, and there is a pervasive tendency in the criticism of Plato's work to read every statement on poetry in the light of the *Republic*'s critique of *mimêsis* and poetic *psychagôgia*.[8]

Even though at some points I will refer to the *Republic*, my topic is neither the theory of *mimêsis* nor the overtly political aspect of Plato's literary theory, and the *Republic* will therefore play a subordinate role. Even though the Socrates of the *Republic* does, to a certain extent, link madness and poetry, he does not develop a theory of the mad poet. In the *Republic*, the madness of the tyrant is presented as the breakdown of the proper hierarchy of reason, spirit, and desire (*logistikon, thumos, epithumia*); any type of poetry that caters to desire instead of to virtue—that is to say, according to Socrates, almost the entirety of poetry—potentially aids in that breakdown. Poetry in the *Republic*, then, can be a contributing factor to moral madness, but it is neither mad itself nor madly conceived. Contrary to the *Ion* (and the *Phaedrus*), the *Republic* treats poetry as a skill (*technê*), comparable with, even though inferior to, the skills and crafts that are useful to the state.

The following reading of the *Ion* will predominantly proceed along issues of philosophical strategy: Why is the figure of the mad poet of interest to philosophy? What does it contribute to Plato's theory of meaning? How does it help to accomplish the consolidation of philosophy's independence from and ultimately its hegemony over other privileged genres of discourse?

In the *Ion*, Socrates converses with a popular rhapsode of that name about the nature of his trade. Ion struggles to preserve an understanding of rhapsody as a skill or craft (*technê*) that necessarily presupposes knowledge (*epistêmê*) of the poetic product he delivers. Socrates contends that the accomplishments of rhapsody rest on divine inspiration, and that the rhapsode performs in a state devoid of knowledge, sovereign skill, and reason (*epistêmê, technê, nous*). He develops that theory in the famous monologue about the magnetic chain of divine inspiration linking poet, rhapsode, and audience. This speech contains the *Ion*'s most quoted lines: "For the poet is a light thing, winged and sacred, unable to make poetry before he is enthused and out of his mind and intelligence is no longer in him".[9]

Socrates' argument is based on two major contentions: First, if rhapsody were a skill consisting of a substantiated knowledge of poetry as such, Ion would have to be as good at performing Hesiod and other poets as he is at performing Homer, which, as he admits, he is not. Second, if rhapsody necessarily involved proper judgment of a text, Ion would have to command all the skills pertaining to the subject matter in Homer's poems, such as mixing drugs, charioteering, fishing, or commanding an army. While Ion readily admits that a physician or a charioteer is superior at judging whether or not Homer "speaks true" on such matters as medicine or the races, he is less ready to yield the rank of general—he insists with considerable tenacity that rhapsodes are experts on the skills of leading a battle. When Ion, despite Socrates' intervention, insists on the equivalence of rhapsody and warfare, Socrates somewhat impatiently faces him with a choice: "Choose, then, whether you want to be held by us to be an unjust man or a divine one . . . ." Ion, coerced rather than convinced, answers that "to be held to be divine is far finer" (542a–b). This reply is ambiguous; Ion concedes nothing but his continuing loyalty to the register of appearance and performance. These lines, in fact, might be read to reveal considerable rhetorical skill on Ion's part, indicating that he might not be quite the simpleton he seems to be.

While Socrates' famous speech on divine inspiration and the magnetic chain of poetic power (533c–535a) reverberates throughout much of Plato's oeuvre, the *Ion*, I will argue, is primarily not a text on poetry but on rhapsody, and the importance of the theme of poetic madness in this dialogue emerges only once the issue of rhapsody is explored alongside. The significance of rhapsody, in turn, becomes clear only if we acknowledge it as a precursor of criticism. To substitute 'criticism' for 'rhapsody', is, of course, a thoroughly anachronistic move. Rhapsody can only be called a criticism *ante rem*, for there is no clearly defined field of practice in Plato's Greece that we could call by that term without some simplification. This changes, however, if we are willing to define criticism, very generally, as the mediating presentation of a literary text to an audience that seeks from this procedure an elucidation of the text's meaning beyond the information the text would provide without hermeneutic intervention. There is enough in the dialogue to suggest that this is the task that Ion performs.

While the definition provided above is not enough to delineate criticism as a methodical practice, it is precisely the condition of possibility of such a concerted discipline that the *Ion* starts to investigate.[10] In other words, the dialogue presents us with nothing less than the preconception of criticism under the aegis of philosophy. In Socrates' scheme, I will argue, poetic madness actually engenders the necessity of criticism. As such, the notion of enthusiasm is the key concept in a strategy that supplants the autonomy of poetry and subjects it, ultimately, to Socratic philosophy.

Like the *Phaedrus*, the *Ion* was long regarded one of the "minor" dialogues, possibly a hoax. Even though the authenticity of the *Ion* is established by now, the dialogue has never met with the kind of rehabilitation that the *Phaedrus* has enjoyed.[11] One can speculatively generate several possible reasons for this: the practice of rhapsody is located in a gray zone between poetry and theater, alien to the modern division of cultural labor and thus perhaps of subordinate interest to latter-day readers of Plato; the dialogue's predominant mood is comical rather than ironic and might thus appear un-Socratic; Ion, unlike Phaedrus, has appeared to many as a weak mind or even a fool— Allan Bloom calls him an "empty reciter of Homer," "the most conventional agent of what is most conventional"; Goethe labels him "extremely limited," "an oaf"[12]—unworthy of his interlocutor Socrates, not even a complying pupil but one who has to be badgered into acquiescence; one might say that Plato has treated central themes of the dialogue more persuasively and with more sophistication elsewhere. I suspect, however, that a significant reason for the rather unappreciative treatment the *Ion* has received is due to the fact that the dialogue has been read as a treatise on *poetry*.[13] Read in this light, however, the *Ion* appears inconsistent or even confused, no matter how influential it has been for various theories of *furor poeticus*. Socrates' speech on poetry, habitually read as the dialogue's centerpiece and its only passage of genuine interest, is difficult to evaluate.[14] For even though it is possible to read the speech at face value, it seems at least as likely that it is a casual reiteration, or even, as Goethe suspected, a "persiflage,"[15] of an already established cliche of poetic enthusiasm.[16]

There are at least two aspects of Socrates' speech on enthusiasm that cast suspicion on his sincerity. For one, Socrates claims that he is merely repeating what the poets themselves say about their art (534a–b), a framing device that serves to effectively obscure Socrates' own position; secondly, Socrates' choice of words seems uncharacteristically "enthused" itself, pointing to the potentially parodic nature of his account.[17] More importantly, the progression of the dialogue as a whole casts ambiguity on the casual assertion of an inspirational "divine." Ion reacts to *Socrates' logoi* in exactly the same way he is portrayed as reacting to divine poetic inspiration: "Yes, by Zeus, . . . somehow you lay hold of my soul with these speeches, Socrates" (535a).[18] Socrates, then, has performatively, and with little effort, inserted himself into the "magnetic" process. Hence, the chain of inspiration, and his chain of argument that rests on that metaphor, do not appear to be very tightly linked. Unless we are meant to believe that Socrates himself is passing on a divine inspiration of his own, the origin of possession has moved to the secular in the blink of an eye. Certainly, Ion may simply be a readily impressionable soul, open to skillful *psychagôgia* not necessarily only of the divine kind. In that case, it is not the theory of magnetic links that is called into question (even though Socrates' performance of inspirational speech appears to ironize it considerably), but the validity of any specific act of divine inspiration.

In this regard, the passage points to a crucial problem that any theory of divine madness poses: how can the presence of divine influence be verified? Not every poet is visited by the gods; inspiration might stem from the Muse or from any clever philosopher (or sophist) roaming the marketplace. Divine inspiration, despite rituals of evocation, may be sudden and unpredictable: one cannot expect to go mad, not every madness is divine, not every poet is mad, and not even the mad poets are mad all the time. The poets, moreover, are the least reliable witnesses in this matter, mad or not. If they are mad, they cannot account for their madness, and if they are not, they might simulate madness, considering that "to be held to be divine is far finer" than to be thought just another common laborer.

Socrates will investigate this question of diagnosis at some length in the *Phaedrus*. In the *Ion*, he is concerned not with madness in general, but with rhapsodic inspiration, or, more precisely, the relationship between a text, its reader-custodian, and the audience of the reading. As it turns out,

Ion's enthusiasm is dubious, for during his performance, divine powers do not seem to render Ion senseless at all. Certainly, at first he seems to comply with Socrates' argument: "When I speak of something pitiful, my eyes fill with tears, and when of something frightening or terrible, my hair stands on end from fear and my heart leaps" (535c). Socrates suggests that this is rather unreasonable behavior in light of the fact that Ion sits safe and adorned in the middle of a favorable audience, and that the only explanation for such irrational affectation must be divine poetic inspiration. Ion agrees.[19] This passage is misleading, however, if naively taken at face value. In the next breath, Ion imparts that while supposedly magnetized by Homeric passion, he keeps close watch of his audience's emotional response:

> For I look down on them each time from the platform above as they are crying, casting terrible looks and following with astonishment the thing said. I must pay the very closest attention to them, since, if I set them to crying, I shall laugh myself because I am making money, but if they laugh, then I shall cry because of the money I am losing. (535e)

Ion, then, is hardly entirely in the grip of divine powers, as the radical formulations of Socrates' earlier speech had suggested. Instead, he is quite conscious of manipulating his audience, and his own passions are diametrically opposed to those of his listeners instead of being "magnetically" related to them. This incongruence unchains the links Socrates had joined. The relationship between poetic text, rhapsodic text, and the passion of the audience emerges as far more complicated than initially asserted.

Any reading of the *Ion* that subscribes to Socrates' initial claim that poets and rhapsodes operate in identical or at least very similar fashion runs the risk of falling into the same trap Socrates sets out for Ion. Valid interpretations of the *Ion* which read Socrates' objections to rhapsody as veiled objections to poetry would have to operate on the assumption that poetry and its interpretation proceed in a comparable manner.[20] If the conditions of making poetry were the main concern of the dialogue, however, then Socrates' interaction with Ion after the delivery of his speech would be curiously redundant. We would be left with a rather conventional theory of inspiration, for although the dialogue contains the seeds to challenge an uncritically received view of poetic enthusiasm, it leaves this concept more or less untouched. As a celebration of poetic *mania*, a text like the *Phaedrus* is far more subtle and profound, and as a denunciation of poetry, the *Republic* gives more sustained and more engaging arguments. Certainly, these two standard approaches are not impossible; the presence of Homer does indeed permeate the dialogue, and the status of poetry undoubtedly is at stake, if only indirectly. To read the *Ion* as a sketchy anticipation of the later dialogues' arguments, however, buries the very theme that, peculiar to the *Ion*, makes this short text so fascinating. This theme, to be sure, is not poetry. Not only does the dialogue carry the name of a rhapsode, its main concern throughout the dialogical part is the investigation of interpretation or the nature of critical knowledge. Far more space is devoted to the discussion of Ion's trade than to poetry, and, as demonstrated above, Ion himself does not fit the criteria Socrates develops for the poets. We must distinguish carefully between what Socrates says about poetry and what he says about rhapsody, for the magnetic chain may be brittle.

The Ion who, ever mindful of profit, monitors his audience's affective response, is not mad, certainly not mad enough to fit the stringent criteria Socrates has established in his speech to describe poetic madness—to be devoid of *nous*, *epistêmê*, and *technê*. The implication, I will suggest, is that there is no such thing as a mad critic, or even that criticism *must* not be mad, since it must differ from poetry to perform its task. Before Socrates, it seems that the poets had provided their own critique, a critique that did not have to take a discursive, nonpoetic form, but had consisted in a constant allusive rewriting of poetic material or in the poetic self-reflection of the lyrics of authors like Homer, Hesiod, and Pindar. Thus, the reworking of the Homeric *muthos* in the tragedies of Aeschylus, Sophocles, or Euripides constituted the main venue of its interpretation and reinterpretation. In Socrates' time, however, the poets were already sharing the task of interpretation with a growing number of nonpoets. "Talking about Homer" was in the process of becoming a veritable business for those who themselves didn't engage in the making of poetry. The Sophists, Socrates' privileged competitors in the marketplace of knowledge and *psychagôgia*, are known to have grounded their claims to wisdom to a large extent in a knowledge of the poets. The early dialogue *Protagoras*, for instance, shows Socrates in interpretive contest with the Sophist Protagoras, who stresses that "it is an important part of education for a man to be strong in poems. This, however, consists in being able to understand what the poets say, what is composed well and what not, also to explain it when asked and to give an account" (339a). In this dialogue, the practice of criticism takes on the character of a philosophical *agon* when Socrates challenges Protagoras's reading of a poem by Simonides with a close reading of his own. Socrates' counterarguments are skillful and persuasive, even though he later dismisses the enterprise of competitive interpretation as silly.

In contrast, the *Ion* does not engage in the practice of hermeneutics but begins to develop a *theory* of criticism designed to establish the fundamental difference between the *logoi* of poetry and the *logoi* of philosophy.[21]

To be sure, Plato's dividing line between poetry and philosophy has been redrawn again and again. Aristotle already struggled to integrate Platonic dialogues into his generic paradigms,[22] and to modern readers especially, Platonic writing has appeared uncommonly 'poetic.'[23] It is also true that Socrates does at times investigate formal aspects of philosophical speech and/or different poetic genres in considerable detail. It is all the more important to appreciate that Plato's understanding of 'poetry,' in contrast to later accounts, does not include the differentiation between figurative and literal language or fictional and nonfictional narratives. The *logos/muthos* distinction as fiction/nonfiction, to give a prominent example, appears post-Platonic, and in Plato's writing the two terms cannot always be cleanly distinguished.[24] Even in the *Republic*, where questions of poetic genre are of paramount importance, Socrates never advises a ban on *all* poets. Fundamentally, poets are nothing more or less than "the makers of tales" (*Republic*, 377b) and the making of tales (as *muthoi*) is as indispensable to the ideal state (cf. *Republic*, Book II and III) as the use of images to communicate philosophical ideas. Even though poets are accused of making "false" tales, the education of the guardians proceeds by tales equally false.

Needless to say, Socrates freely avails himself of what seem to us "poetic" modes of speech. It is worthwhile to note, however, that Plato's Socrates, unless in quotation, *never* speaks in verse, even though he contemplates composing music in the *Phaedo*. In fact, the verse/prose distinction might be the sole "formal" criterion to distinguish his discourse from that of the poets.[25] Aristotle notes right at the beginning of the *Poetics* that the "public classifies all those who write in meter as poets and completely misses the point that the capacity to produce an imitation is the essential characteristic of the poet."[26] For Socrates, however, whose conception of *mimêsis* is at times far more comprehensive than that of the *Poetics*, the "capacity to produce an imitation" is inherent to all speech, not only poetic speech. Language *is* imitation, but in contrast to the imitation in painting or sculpture, "language can also be true" (*Cratylus*, 431d).[27] In theory, then, Socrates cannot rule out that "true" language occurs in poetry.

If the criteria neither of form nor of hypothetical truth-value can be established to distinguish philosophy and poetry with satisfactory rigor, then another criterion needs to be found. It is here that the significance of a concept of poetic madness gains its full force, for it provides the terms on which different modes of speech can be classified according to the different nature of their production or conception. The truth of poetry, the *Ion* suggests, differs from the truth of philosophy at the point of its source. There is no great poetry as long as the poet holds on to *nous* as to a *possession* (*ktêma*, *Ion* 534b).[28] Thus, the theory of poetic madness dispossesses the poet, first of his *nous*, and then, in consequence, of his poetry. In the *Republic*, we learn that "'just as poets are fond of their poems and fathers of their children, so money-makers too are serious about money—as their own product" (*Republic*, 330c). In the *Republic*, the poets are in charge of their works, and hence accountable for them. Within the theory of poetic madness as it emerges in the *Ion*, however, poems cease to be the product of their poets.

In an important sense, every form of madness entails dispossession. It is the postulate of madness that subverts the first definition of justice the *Republic* offers:

> [I]f a man takes weapons from a friend when the latter is of sound mind, and the friend demands them back when he is mad, one shouldn't give back

such things, and the man who gave them back would not be just, and moreover, one should not be willing to tell someone in this state the whole truth.

What you say is right, he said.

Then this isn't the definition of justice, speaking the truth and giving back what it takes.

It most certainly is, Socrates, interrupted Polemarchus, at least if Simonides should be believed at all. (*RP*, 331c–d)

In this passage, truth appears to be analogous to possessions to which one has a right only as long as one is sane—in other words, it qualifies *as* a property only to the sane. Madness cancels the right to this property just as it annuls the legal right to property according to one of Solon's laws. While the notion of intellectual property is not a legal one in Greece, it plays a major role in the laws of philosophy.[29]

In the *Ion*, these implications remain unspoken. The problem of property surfaces instead in the question of criticism. To repeat, the term *criticism* is an anachronism, but rhapsody was not simply recital as some readings of the *Ion* assume or imply.[30] For while the rhapsodes might have derived their glory from the glory of the texts they treated (and the Greeks, not to forget, venerated Homer beyond any veneration for a literary text imaginable to us today),[31] they were, in their comments, certainly not bound by any pieties to the "sanctity of the text" at their disposal. The rhapsodes were free to paraphrase, embellish, interpret and comment on them at their discretion. Ion himself stresses this point when he claims that there is no one in his trade who can produce "so many beautiful meanings" (530d) out of Homer as he.

Meaning, here, is *dianoia*—one of the key terms of the text. It can mean thought and intention as well as meaning, to name just a few possible translations. At the outset of the discussion, Socrates had expressed envy of the rhapsodes for their ability to "discern [the poets'] meaning (*dianoia*)" and their task of "mediating the meaning of the poet for the audience" (530b–c). That this task implies considerable critical intervention on the part of the rhapsode is obvious: "It is surely worth hearing, Socrates, how well I have adorned Homer" (530d). Here, Ion, presumably unaware of the analogy, uses the same word Socrates had used to describe Ion's ornamental stage apparel. Ion adorns the texts he recites in the same way he decorates his own body; Socrates tells him that "it befits your art for the body to be always adorned and for you to appear as beautiful as possible" (530b), and he repeats this point later in the dialogue (535d). Ion, then, presents the body of the Homeric writings on stage, gaudily decked out for the spectacle of the text which becomes, or coincides with, the spectacle of the rhapsode. The text disappears into the performance of the critic, and the epic becomes theater. The critical act cannot be distinguished from its object. Socrates, however, will insist on this distinction.

It is worthwhile noting, by the way, that Ion concedes that the rhapsodes, to legitimize their trade, need to have a knowledge apart from any *dianoia* intrinsic to the text or its performance, even though he has no quarrel with the concept of divine poetic madness per se. It is the rhapsode, after all, not the poet who, he insists, would make a good general. Why is Ion so disinclined to give up the image of the rhapsode as a quasimilitary power? What is it in interpretation that may make it comparable to warfare?[32]

Ion makes different claims as to the object of the rhapsode's *epistêmê*. Although he has to give up these claims in the face of Socrates' superior argumentative skills, they are worth noting, not the least for a certain compatibility with latter-day notions of criticism. Ion is ready to concede that he is incompetent to judge specific subject matter; but in response to Socrates' question after the rhapsode's proper field of knowledge, he designates the whole of the poem: "Everything (*hapanta*), I claim, Socrates" (539e). Thus, he hints at the concept of a textual whole different from the sum of a text's parts, and different from the accumulated subject matter it pertains to. Ion does not, as we would wish, elaborate on this embryonic idea of poetic structure. His next attempt to carve out for himself an epistemic niche concerns a knowledge of style, of different registers of diction, "[t]he things that are appropriate, I for one suppose, for a man to say, and the sort for a woman, and the sort for a slave and the sort for a free man, and the sort for one who is ruled and the sort for one who is ruling" (540b). When Socrates refers Ion back to subject matter—"the rhapsode will know, but not the cowherd, what things it is appropriate for a cowherd who is a slave to say to calm angry cattle?" (540c)—Ion at first gives in. When Socrates extends the analogies to the general, however, he encounters resistance:

S: Well then, will he [the rhapsode] know such things as are appropriate for a man who is a general to say when exhorting his troops?

I: Yes, the rhapsode will know such things.

S: What? Is the art of rhapsody generalship?

I: I would certainly know such things as are appropriate for a general to say. [. . .]

S: Since you know military matters, do you know them through the art by which you are an expert at generalship or the one by which you are a good rhapsode?

I: For me, at least, there doesn't seem to be any difference.

S: What? You say there is no difference? Do you say that the art of rhapsody and the art of generalship are one or two?

I: To me, at least, it seems to be one. (540d–541a)

Some of Plato's readers have been inclined to read this passage as a comical interlude or as a psychographic device meant to expose Ion's self-misconception.[33] The image of the general, though, is hardly innocent: Socrates will devote much of his discussion of the perfect state to the education of the military "guardians," and he will involve the poets in this education. More important, though, is the role of the general within the poetry Ion presents. Socrates suggests that Homer, "as all other poets, too" deals preeminently with war (531c). By this time, we already know that being an expert poet (as opposed to being divinely inspired) would mean being an expert on poetry's subject matter—waging war and writing war would be the same thing. Ion-the-general, then, inserts himself into poetry as its mastermind. In assuming the rank of general, he also seizes command of the *Iliad*, taking the place of the (divine and human) commanders who direct the action of the war epic. Certainly, the epic with its central narrator lends itself to this operation more than lyric or dramatic poetry—but it is in this image of strategic usurpation that the truth of Socratic criticism surfaces. If the mad do not have a right to property, as we have seen, then poetic speech—and this is true for *all* mad speech—is up for grabs. Mad speech is relinquished by its speaker at the moment of its utterance—it is never his to begin with.

In this light, the *Ion* does not so much raise the question of the legitimacy of poetry (although, naturally, this question is implicated in the question of criticism) as it does the question of the legitimation of a poem's self-appointed guardians. Socrates early on had posed the question of a text's *dianoia* as the guiding question of the dialogue. Although Socrates will deny the poets both *nous* and *epistêmê*, he will never deny that there is *dianoia* in poetry. It is not the presence of *dianoia* that is at stake but the nature of its production. The postulate of enthusiasm, the "god within" poetic speech, entails that *dianoia* here cannot be read as the poet's intentional thought but as meaning (somehow) present in the text but not controlled by its author. If criticism, as even Ion readily concedes, should consist in the ascertainment of this *dianoia*, the critic's operation has to be fundamentally different from poetic production. It is thus that the hypothesis of poetic madness establishes the necessity of criticism.

Ion, however, is neither a competent reader of poetry *to olon*, nor is he truly inspired. Thus, being simultaneously too close and not close enough to the poet, he can neither provide nor understand poetic *dianoia*. Unlike the physician or the horseback rider, he has no expertise to contribute to Homer's subject matter, and, being *atechnos*[34] (532c) in the presence of poets other than Homer, he commands no knowledge about poetry in general (532c). Clearly, the latter charge appears more grave, opening the question of the very possibility of a discipline, or *technê*, of criticism.

To repeat, the theory of divine poetic madness establishes the necessity of a criticism of *dianoia*. Socrates sets out to prove that the rhapsode is not as much a hermeneut of meaning as he is a mediator of affect.[35] While Ion cannot account for his virtuosity there is, however, also no reliable indication that he is a bad interpreter. In fact, Ion seems ready to perform several times, and it is Socrates who holds him back with always yet another question. Socrates is either not able or not willing to distinguish between good and bad criticism before he has constructed a *theory* of criticism that would be different from a theory of poetry. And it is predominantly this theory of criticism that is at stake in the *Ion*, not the theory of *mimêsis* that is habitually associated with Plato's poetological dialogues.

Socrates readily grants the status of *technê* to the experts in painting, music, sculpture, flute playing, and singing to the lyre (532e–533c).[36] His analogies lead up to the art of rhapsody itself:

> S: . . . nor in regard to aulos playing, cithara playing, singing to the cithara, or rhapsody, you never saw a man who is clever at explaining Olympus, or Thamyras, or Orpheus, or Phemius the Ithacan rhapsode but is at a loss about Ion and has nothing to contribute about what in rhapsody he does well and what not? (533b–c)

Here, Socrates makes the explicit move towards a metacriticism where not the text, but the critic becomes the object of expertise. (In fact, all the rhapsodes mentioned besides Ion are mythical figures, poetic constructions themselves.) The issue now is not Homer, but "talking about Homer," or even talking about the rhapsodes talking about Homer. The question of poetic enthusiasm is less relevant in this dialogue than the question of critical inspiration, and poetic representation less relevant than critical representation. The *adequatio rei atque cogitationis* of the primary text, the major theme of the poetry discussion in the *Republic*, never directly gets into focus.

In Socrates' argument, the necessity of criticism implies an irreducible difference between criticism and poetry. Again, if divine madness is the sole guarantor of poetry's greatness, then this madness must be *verified*. If there is to be a critic, then first and foremost he has to be a knower of madness. To know a thing, as Socrates has pointed out, is to know its opposite as well. To know great poetry is to know bad poetry. To know madness, then, would be to know sanity (*sôphrosunê*).

Criticism, then, divides into at least two different types of *epistêmê*. First, it must be a science of the soul. Second, and more importantly, any *epistêmê* of poetry must account for the enigma of meaning. In the absence of poetic *technê*, the presence of poetic meaning cannot be accounted for by the process of poetic production in the same way that the presence of a sturdy table can be accounted for by the process of carpentry (not that the latter case is a simple one, by any means). The name of divine madness marks this unaccountability. While the *Ion* merely establishes the need to pursue the two projects I have outlined, Socrates will devote himself to the science of the soul in other dialogues, most prominently in the *Republic* and in the *Phaedrus*. The latter, moreover, will provide a tentative answer to the origin of meaning with regard to poetry, to the *technê* of speaking as truth-making, to the nature of the soul, and, again, to madness. This time, however, the philosopher, too, will go (a little) mad.

In Platonic theology, we will see, poetic meaning is always divine—or, more precisely, the divine is nothing but the ultimately unaccountable presence of meaning, a meaning philosophy can only point to, but not beget: the glory of sanity is in diagnosis, not in creation.

PHAEDRUS: MADLY MADE MEANING

In the *Ion*, drawing upon a widely accepted general notion of enthusiasm, Socrates speaks of divine madness without providing any comprehensive explanation of his terms; *Ion* investigates not so much the nature of poetic *dianoia* as the theory and practice of its critical reconstruction. The question of how, in the absence of *technê*, *epistêmê*, and *nous*, meaning is to be generated in the first place, remains open. It is only in the *Phaedrus*, Plato's great dialogue about divine madness, that Socrates returns to the question of madly made meaning. This time, Socrates, led by the promise of a fine *logos* like a donkey by a carrot, abandons his usual territory, the marketplace of the city, for the countryside. With Phaedrus, he settles down in a divinely animated place, the domain of nymphs, myths, and the wild God Pan. The talk will be of lovers, love, and speeches.

The *Phaedrus* is a notoriously difficult text, so intricately structured that it was long taken to be the badly composed product of a mind either immature or clouded by old age.[37] One of the difficulties the text poses is its self-reflexively polygeneric quality, comprising a written speech read aloud, two spoken speeches, three myths, dialogue in various atmospheric modes from flirtatious to technical, and, lastly, a prayer. This complex weave of styles corresponds to a multitude of topics broached, among them the nature of the soul, of knowledge, and of philosophy as well as the relative values of mythology, love, madness, and writing. While it is certainly legitimate, or even necessary for any reading to single out and privilege one or several themes over others, the dialogue does not, to my mind, provide a thematic integrative focus comparable to the way the *Republic* integrates its various themes into the project of discursively constructing the ideal state.

Owing to the complexity of the dialogue, the *Phaedrus* is traditionally divided in two parts, one consisting of speeches, the other analyzing and critiquing them.[38] The first part includes the speech of Lysias, read by Phaedrus, Socrates' impromptu rejoinder to this speech, and his recantation of his first speech. The first two *logoi*, a speech by Lysias and Socrates' rejoinder, advocate the cause of the nonlover over that of the lover, advising young boys to yield to the former rather than to the latter because of the dangers and unpleasantness associated with the state of erotic madness. Socrates prepares to leave when his *daimonion* interferes, commanding him to recant the insult done to the god Eros in the first two speeches. Part I would then close with

Socrates' second speech, where he extols the virtue of "certain kinds" of madness, above all erotic madness. This recantation, or palinode, to Eros expands into a theory of *anamnêsis* or recollection: the lover experiences erotic madness at the sight of a beautiful boy, which in turn triggers the recollection of the idea of beauty which his soul glimpsed on its voyage with the gods in the place "beyond heaven."

The second part of the dialogue, reflecting back on the three speeches about love, is devoted to a discussion of rhetoric, speech writing, and writing in general. It contains the famous "myth of Theuth" that criticizes writing as harmful to memory. Constituting a pseudoknowledge inferior to any knowledge that would be "inscribed in the soul," writing, severed from its author—its "father"—does not know how to address different readers differently and is thus useless to philosophical *psychagôgia*, Socrates says. Writing is helpless against (mis-)appropriations by readers. Thus, true lovers of wisdom, who might playfully divert themselves with writing, will not commit their serious knowledge to such an unstable vehicle.

The writing of poetry, however, at first seems to constitute an exception to this rule. The *Phaedrus* lends vehement support to a notion of poetry that is decidedly not authorized by the poet, a poetry that is above all authenticated as poetry only by the notion that during its production the poet's self-possession is reduced to nothing. In the *Ion,* Socrates had told the story of Tynnichos of Chalkis:

> [H]e never composed a single poem worth recalling, save the song of praise which everyone sings, well-nigh the finest of all lyrical poems, and absolutely what he called it, an 'Invention of the Muses.' By this example above all, it seems to me, the god would show us, lest we doubt, that these beautiful poems are not human or from man, but are divine and from the gods, and that the poets are nothing but the gods' speakers, each one possessed by the divinity who possesses him. And to prove this, the deity on purpose sang the loveliest of all lyrics through the most miserable poet. (534d–e)

This passage illustrates well the radical nature of the assumptions on which Socrates operated in the *Ion*. Tynnichos of Chalkis is not just a mediocre poet, he is the worst of them all, and his song of praise is not just a felicitous piece of work, it is the loveliest of all lyrics. If the least poet can write the most beautiful of poems, then poetic madness operates indeed wholly independently from the human body it avails itself of. The poet is nothing but a random conduit, and it seems that he would not even have to be a poet at all, since whatever *technê* he has at his disposal is nil. Possessing nothing, he is nothing but possessed (*katechomenoi*), an object pure and simple.

At the same time, the case of Tynnichos of Chalkis emphasizes the *uniqueness* of the divinely inspired poem, presenting it as a *single* text, an utterance of fundamentally unrepeatable quality. The central significance of the question of repetition links the *Ion* to the larger issues at stake in the *Phaedrus*. On the whole, the *Phaedrus* puts forth the notion of divinely inspired poetry within a framework quite different from that of the *Ion*. Here, only the most finely tuned soul—"the tender, virgin soul" (245a)—can become a poet, and poetry is defined both by skill and inspiration:

> ... if any man come to the gates of poetry without the madness of the Muses, persuaded that *skill alone* [emphasis added] will make him a good poet, then shall he and his works of sanity with him be brought to nought by the poetry of madness, and behold, their place is nowhere to be found. (245a)

It is here, moreover, that poetry is explicitly linked to philosophy; for certain poets, Socrates says, might be deserving of the name philosopher. At first glance it seems that this particular poetry, privileged over the mere employment of *technê*, furnishes the first conception of a poetic genre that will later be called philosophical poetry (culminating in Hölderlin). However, Socrates never says that poetry might be philosophical, only that poets who can critique their own work in retrospect might be philosophers:

> tell ... Homer and all others who have written poetry whether to be read or sung ... that if any of them has done his work with a knowledge of the truth, can defend his statements when challenged, and can demonstrate the inferiority of his writings out of his own mouth, he ought not to be designated by a name drawn from those writings, but by one that indicates his serious pursuit. (278c)

This name, needless to say, is the name of the philosopher (278d). Again, as in the *Ion*, the highest merits are not in poetry but in the reflection on poetry; poetry, as the product of divine inspiration (but not divine inspiration alone, in this dialogue), unquestionably remains subjected to philosophy, even though poet and philosopher can now inhabit the same body (but not at the same time). Thus, the relationship between poetry and philosophy remains profoundly asymmetrical (as we will see, in this it resembles the structure of desire in the relationship between the beloved and the lover). Poetry, however, is more than just one of many objects of philosophy; it rather provides philosophy's privileged object of usurpation.

The following pages will concentrate on the structural principle of recantation, which I read as one of the most important clues, possibly even the single most important one to the architecture of the dialogue. At several points, recantation serves as the rhetorical gesture that propels the dialogue forward. Socrates' first speech renounces the speech of Lysias, which constructs a situation in which a non-lover attempts to persuade a boy to yield to his desire rather than to that of his erotically inflamed rival. Socrates recasts Lysias's argument, but he also changes the parameters of the narrative hypothesis: now it is a lover *posing as* a non-lover who is speaking. The argument about the superiority of a sane sexuality over erotic madness is thus implicitly subverted, appearing as a clever deceptive device hiding precisely what it denounces: Eros. In admiration of Socrates' performance, Phaedrus recants his original endorsement of Lysias. In his second speech, the "palinode," Socrates recants the arguments of his first speech, replacing the (deceptive) attack on desire with a celebration of Eros and erotic love. In the following disquisition about rhetoric, Socrates disavows his second speech as well, calling it a "play" or a "jest." In the final scene, Socrates appears to abandon the principle of rational dialectical discourse he has just espoused when he enters into prayer to one of the maddest gods, Pan.

This repeated recurrence of complete reversal is a striking feature of the dialogue; it certainly constitutes more than the mere refutation of inferior arguments, and it is quite different from, say, Hegelian dialectic. The dialogue does not proceed by refinement, moderation, or progressive reconsideration of the original arguments but, more often than not, by complete inversion—an inversion that is less teleological than it may appear. The *Phaedrus*, I will argue, suggests nothing less than that recantation is the privileged mode of philosophical procedure itself; in this sense, Benardete can indeed single out the *Phaedrus* as the dialogue that "comes closest of any dialogue to having a structure that is a passkey for every other dialogue."[39]

Interestingly, Socrates draws upon an anecdote from poetry in order to explain the need for his palinode to Eros:

> There is for those who sin against the gods in poetry an old purification about which Homer knew nothing, but Stesichoros did. For when the latter was robbed of his sight because of his slander of Helen, he did not remain ignorant of the cause, but as one familiar with the muses he recognized it and wrote immediately his 'This Story is not true, for never did you enter the gracious ships, nor did you ever come to the fortress of Troy,' and after having composed the whole so-called palinode, he regained his sight immediately. (243a–b)

This anecdote links the theme of blindness and insight, privileged in philosophical discourse over all other themes, to the rhetorical gesture of recantation; analogously, Socrates uncovers his face, hidden under his cloak during his first speech, when he starts his palinode to Eros (the same Eros who was playfully hidden, or hiding, in Socrates' first speech). He can literally see—and be seen—again now. On his own terms that are to follow in the palinode, Socrates thus declares himself a potential lover. Vision, as well as visibility, is essential on the path to a philosophy animated by Eros.

This is hardly the end of the story, though, for vision, albeit important, is ultimately not to remain the highest form of perception. Socrates' palinode itself demonstrates that sight can in turn lead to both insight and its loss: while the onset of erotic madness depends on visual impact, the transformation of its philosophical potential into knowledge depends on the lover's soul's power to prevail over the senses. Thus, the recantation that restores vision in turn leads to the recantation of vision, just as Socrates must recant first the insult to Eros and then the hymnic palinode to Eros itself. This structural principle is mirrored in turn in the fact that Plato writes a dialogue and then, in writing, has writing denounced by Socrates.

The necessity of recantation is grounded, trivially, in the ultimate untruth of anything that can be said. The unattainability of *complete* truth is a topos familiar to all readers of Plato, crystallized in the Apology's famous "I know that I know nothing."[40] It appears, furthermore, that Socrates' truth, while unattainable, is at least approachable, that there is a line connecting the limited knowledge we can have to the absolute knowledge we cannot have, and that the philosophical mind can travel on this line until the distance to truth is almost imperceptible. This model underlies much of Western philosophy. Discussing Hegel and Rousseau, Plotnitsky notes that "Derrida correctly sees the metaphysics of proximity as the metaphysics of presence," and that "the metaphysics of presence is always a profoundly infinitist metaphysics, which has among its major sources Socrates and Plato." Furthermore, these metaphysics would entail that "the best philosophical minds . . . may come extremely close, even into immediate proximity to the absolute continuum of Absolute Knowledge. The *line* would still be their best model . . . ."[41] The line, understood as a pattern of infinity and continuity, is certainly the structural principle of Socrates' most important arguments, fables, and stories, among them, for example, the parable of the cave with its movement of knowledge from the apprehension of shadows to the vision of the sun. While the idea of the line thus links Plato to Enlightenment philosophers and most thinkers beyond, it might be more fruitful to focus on the difference between these lines. While Hegel, for example, privileges the spiral that will never lead back to its beginning, Socrates' linearity, more often than not, involves circular movements (sometimes spatial, as in the parable of the cave, sometimes epistemological, as in the theory of *anamnêsis*). Even the philosopher who sees the sun will go back to the cave. There is a decisive difference, however, between the circle of the *Republic* and the analogous figure of the *Phaedrus*. The parable of the cave contains an extreme moment where the mind gazes into the sun. In the *Phaedrus*, the voyage of the philosopher's soul, read together with the teaching of *anamnêsis*, resembles a loop. The moment of hypothetical absolute knowledge, comparable to the vision of the sun, never occurs: even the most skillful of riders "just barely glimpse the beings" and "all depart after much trouble not having partaken in the contemplation of the beings" (247d–248b). No matter how often the voyage is repeated, the soul will get only so far. The line never touches the point of full intuition; while truth can be approximated, the proximity is never infinitesimal.

I will leave the graphic metaphors, for they fail to account for the tricky temporality that Socrates introduces in the myth of the soul. Progress toward knowledge is possible within the philosopher's bodily life, his mortal existence; the eternal life of the immortal soul, however, consists in a never-ending pattern of rise and fall with neither beginning nor end. If knowledge is always the recuperation of knowledge, as the theory of recollection implies, then there can be no becoming of knowledge as in the Hegelian model, only a reconstitution. Knowledge is always already there, and "there" is always already past, since recollection is always inferior to the moment that is recollected. It is important to bear in mind that this superior form of knowledge, the state recollected, is not part of discursive life, or philosophy—since the soul acquires a body only on the descent, it is a state without body, and consequently without articulated speech.

Socrates' palinode contains at its center a variation on the theory of ideas. These entities exist "without color or shape" in a place "beyond heaven." They are eternal and immutable. The truth of being is present independent of any knowledge of this truth. In fact, direct access to the ideas is denied to all human souls in bodies. The Socratic soul, however, is eternal as well, even though not immutable, and in its disembodied state it gains proximity to the ideas. When the soul acquires a body and returns to Earth, it forgets what it has seen. Only the possibility that some souls retain a faint memory of their voyage accounts for the possibility of knowledge, inscribing it into the inescapable temporality of ascent and descent. The myth of the soul contains no hypothetically atemporal moment (as far as the soul is concerned), and thus no moment of fulfilled knowledge. While it might seem at first glance that the narrative of the soul is cleanly framed by the two moments of knowledge and remembrance—where one would be the recuperation of the other—at closer inspection, neither original knowledge nor its remembrance is ever achieved.

Hypothetically, there is no way to tell whether the soul is on the ascent or on the descent, whether it is moving towards or away from Truth. Griswold paraphrases the implications for dialogical philosophy as follows:

> The 'dialogue' . . . would seem to be an endless enterprise. . . . It might well seem that if the goal of wisdom or episteme . . . is not achievable, then it ought to be forgotten. For perpetual dissatisfaction scarcely seems desirable . . . . Given the endlessness of philosophical conversation, it would seem impossible to distinguish between progress and regress . . . .[42]

Subsequently, however, Griswold launches into his own recantation when he abandons this train of thought in favor of an excursion into the ethical dimension of the imperative of self-knowledge. The notion of self, however, is so deeply implicated in the infinite narrativity of the discourse on the soul, Griswold's palinode fails to exorcise the demons he has summoned: the problems affecting knowledge in general affect self-knowledge just as well, and the points cited above may be better taken than he had meant them to be. The transitory, self-canceling quality of philosophical speech does indeed threaten to lock it into immanence, for the dialogical process does not provide any moment at which a hypothetical transition to a higher order of meaning could occur. Speech contains no caesura of metaphysical conversion, and if transcendence is to occur, it will occur elsewhere.

In order for philosophical dialogue to become metaphysically meaningful speech, then, the potential of transcendent meaning has to be intrinsic to the very first utterance philosophy uses as its point of departure. As Socrates says in the *Theaetetus*, he can never be more than the midwife of meaning; insemination must take place outside of philosophy as dialectic; philosophy, then, is infertile. Philosophical Eros is indeed nonreproductive, since, as the *Phaedrus* suggests, it gives birth only to the self engaged in it; yet, it is not masturbatory, or at least not a solitary pleasure. 'Platonic' love, the *Phaedrus* implies, is directed at the self, not the other, yet the other is necessary. The lover is attracted to the beloved because the image of the beloved, resembling the personal god of the lover, offers understanding of the lover's own past, a pathway to remembrance. The lover seeks in the process a knowledge of himself that, even though it may be located in the other, is not a knowledge of him. Conversely, the beloved reciprocates only because he sees his beauty reflected in his lover's gaze, not because of the sight the lover would offer to an unreflected glance:

> . . . the 'flood of passion' pours in upon the lover. And part of it is absorbed within him, but when he can contain no more the rest flows away outside him, and as a breath of wind or an echo, rebounding from a smooth hard surface, goes back to its place of origin, even so the stream of beauty turns back and reenters the eyes of the fair beloved. (255c)

The homoeroticism of the passage, then, is not entirely accidental or merely culturally prescribed, even though the myth of the soul hypothetically accounts for heteroerotic engagements as well. While the man-boy encounter is not symmetrical, it does imply the possibility that the beloved can, in turn, become a lover and proliferate the process of replacements. Otherwise, the analogy between Eros and philosophy would not work. At the same time, the homosexual nature of the encounter skirts the issue of reproduction that would invariably enter the description of a heterosexual relationship. Philosophical Eros, however, must be non-reproductive since truth understood as eternal truth cannot be created. While speech can be the "offspring" of the speaker, truth, within the circular history of the soul, always either precedes or succeeds its contemplator.

Truth, then, is the ultimate object of desire if desire is defined so as to preclude, or fall forever short of, consumption. Socrates' narrative of divine eroticism clearly spells out that the flight for truth is checked as soon as physical desire is consummated. Socrates, however, does by no means advance a theory of sublimation where the object of corporeal desire would be substituted with an object of philosophical desire. On the contrary, while lust, after all, can be gratified, the passion for truth appears unfulfillable. In the transposition of corporeal to philosophical desire, the object, if anything, recedes further out of reach. "Platonism," as Derrida reads it, might consist in the assumption of *onta*—in the *Phaedrus* beings "without color or shape"—that can be talked about; it postulates at least as insistently its absence in any discourse seeking to represent it, and the incompleteness of its perception even in undiscursive intuition. Platonic infinitism does not follow an Enlightenment or Hegelian infinitism defined by the possibility of progress. Comprehensive contemplation of the ideas is not part of the soul's mythical teleology. Even at the ultimate point of the soul's voyage, contemplation will be obstructed and incomplete:

> [The gods], in this circulation, gaze on justice itself, *sôphrosunê*, and knowledge . . . . This is the gods' way of life. Of the other souls, however, some, which followed the god the best and imitated him best, could stretch out the charioteer's head to the outmost space and just barely glimpse the beings; others raised themselves up sporadically and dropped below again so that, in the violent tumult of the horses, they saw some things but not others. The rest . . . are drifting powerlessly amid the lower space . . . but *all depart after much trouble not having partaken in the contemplation of the beings* [emphasis added], and thus retreated, they stick to apparent food. (247d–248b)

There never is, and never will be, then, full contemplation of the *on*: "No non-divine soul sees all the beings."[43] At the point of its utmost fulfillment, the teleology of knowledge provides at its endpoint partial contemplation soon to be forgotten. Thus, the theory of *anamnêsis*—as put forth in the *Phaedrus*[44]—does not provide a complete original object of remembrance. Unobstructed contemplation of being is given only to the gods. Seth Benardete writes:

> Human Eros consists of two incompatible elements—the desire to be with the beloved and the desire to behold the beloved (*Phaedo* 68a3–7). Apartness precludes pairing, pairing apartness. For the divine mind, however, Socrates seems to see no such difficulty. He says that their mind feasts on the beings they behold (*Phaedrus* . . . 247e2–3). For the human soul, on the other hand, Socrates notes a difference between contemplation and consumption.[45]

It is the constitutive fact of the philosophical life that this difference can never be obliterated if Socrates indeed "wants to show that to love (*eran*) is to see (*horan*) and to ask questions (*erotan*)."[46] The palinode illustrates that this distance is the condition of self-knowledge, of philosophical subjectivity. Griswold has painstakingly demonstrated how the theme of self-knowledge dominates the *Phaedrus,* and Jacques Derrida identifies Socrates' "knowledge of truth" with "truth in the knowledge of the self."[47] As Benardete's reading implies, eroticism can lead to autognosis only when the distance to the object of desire is maintained. It is in fact more than a question of mere distance. What the lover-as-philosopher sees (and loves) in the beloved is always only the promise of self-knowledge. Self-knowledge, in turn, is the remembrance of the lover's incorporeal future and/or past, a reflection of the already-seen and yet-to-be-seen. The particularity of the beloved beyond the promise of self-knowledge he holds is of little or no relevance. The same is true for *logoi,* written or spoken. Socrates establishes the structural interchangeability of beloved and discourse very early on in the dialogue when he lets himself be seduced into the wilderness not by Phaedrus but by Lysias's lecture (or vice versa, if we follow the more ironical reading that Socrates' first speech suggests).

To see, to love, to ask questions, in other words: philosophy requires an intermediate object to mobilize it that is not the *onta.* For the lover of boys, the sight of corporeal beauty constitutes this trigger; for the lover of speeches, I suggest, it is the speech of the mad, including poetry. Lysias is Plato's prime example for a speech writer who proceeds by *technê* alone, and Lysias's speech is consequently "brought to nought" (245a) by the subsequent "mad" speeches of Socrates.

If philosophical speech by nature always refers back to speech that precedes it, it cannot by itself provide the first *logos,* its original object, just as the midwife is not involved in the conception of the child. Philosophy, like midwifery, is a *technê,* at least to the extent to which it is rhetoric and dialectical. Mad speech, in contrast, is by essence the absence of *technê.* Here a problem arises: while technical knowledge cannot be satisfactorily simulated, a state of madness can quite easily be imitated. Socrates takes advantage of this several times: "This spot seems to be divine indeed so that you should not be surprised if I will be possessed by the nymphs in the process of the speech. For already I am not that far from dithyrambs anymore" (238c–d). Later on, he again plays with the possibility of divine possession when he pretends not to recall his second speech: "Tell me this, too, for I cannot recall it on account of the enthusiasm, whether I explained love at the beginning of the speech?" (263d) It is tempting to conclude from these passages that Socrates suggests a certain rapprochement between madness and philosophy. In the first case, however, Socrates continues in prose, and in the second case, it turns out that he remembers quite well everything he said. Clearly, Socrates does not go mad, neither here nor elsewhere. (Who is to say whether he might have liked to? As Lacan says wisely, "not everyone who would go mad could.")

That does not mean, however, that there is no connection between madness and philosophy. Socrates' theory of speaking madly implies a hard distinction between the nature of speaking and the nature of the spoken. The fact that the speaker, while being mad, delivers reasonable speech is the backbone of the concept of divine madness. If the sanity of the text does not depend on the sanity of the speaker, then, conversely, the madness of a text might not depend on the madness of the speaker either. That is precisely what Socrates demonstrates in his palinode to Eros.

Any reading of the palinode must acknowledge a fundamental duality. On the one hand, the speech is a complete *logos* unto itself, and it must be regarded as such. On the other hand, it occurs in a discursive surrounding which severely modifies any claims it makes. The palinode offers so many central tenets of Socratic philosophy—*anamnêsis, adrasteia*, the body-soul divide, the enigma of beauty, the eternity of the soul, the unchangeable nature of the ideas—that it reads almost like Platonism *in nuce*. Such a reading would be naive, however, since Socrates explicitly disconnects himself from the speech before he even begins it: "[The speech] I will now speak is by Stesichoros from Himera, son of Euphemos" (244a). The following, then, will be a simulacrum, a simulacrum of mad poetry as well as of a simplistically understood Platonism. I will demonstrate, in fact, that the palinode declares the conventional understanding of Plato's teaching about the philosophy of ideas to be mad; by "conventional understanding" I mean any reading that takes for granted that, within Socratism, controlled progress toward the contemplation of the ideas is possible. On the following pages, I will demonstrate why Socrates, within a critique of both mad speech and poetry, must speak madly, and why the poets can be exiled from the state but not from philosophical discourse.

Certainly, poetic madness is merely one of the four divine types of madness Socrates postulates, and most of the dialogue's theory of madness concerns either divine madness in general or erotic madness. Like the *Ion*, the *Phaedrus* does not talk much about poets, except by implication or analogy. Still, Socrates, in his closing words, explicitly refers to the poets and claims that they, like the lovers, might be or become philosophers—by dint of a specific combination of madness and palinodic sanity.

Erotic and poetic madness can share their philosophical potential because this potential is grounded in the structure of knowledge and temporality; the theory of madness, erotic or otherwise, is implied in the theory of *anamnêsis*, the remembrance of true being, that ties in together madness, poetry, and philosophy. For the madness of the poet or the lover would be of no consequence to philosophy if philosophy were not erotic and if eroticism were not mad. This specific constellation of eros, poeisis, and philosophy—which appears in this form only in the *Phaedrus*—is centered upon the suddenness of the original moment which is a constitutive element of all three modes of knowledge, poetic, erotic, philosophical. The suddenness of divine madness, which distinguishes it from nosological insanity, correlates to the instant of devastation that the vision of beauty forces upon the lover. What the *Phaedrus* suggests, moreover, is that philosophy's original moment is just as impossible to anticipate and calculate as the instant of love and madness. It might be true that Platonism, as Derrida among others reads it, really presumes the "possibility of a discourse about what is, the *deciding and decidable* [emphasis added] *logos* of or about the *on* (being-present)."[48] Platonism, however, is not the same as Plato, much less Plato's characters. Whether Socrates is quite as optimistic is perhaps more difficult to decide than Nietzsche, Heidegger, and poststructuralist thinkers have suggested. It is certain, at least, that this "possibility," even if it exists for Socrates and Plato, constitutes one of the greatest mysteries within the larger enigma of thought and speech. Arkady Plotnitsky, discussing "Platonism," sums up one of the central tenets of poststructuralism when he writes that, due to the writings of Nietzsche, Freud, Bataille, and Heidegger, "the opposition between literature and truth or literature and philosophy becomes *undecidable*."[49] These oppositions, however—literature/truth and literature/philosophy—are not always congruent in Plato's writing. While poetry is indeed always opposed to philosophy, their respective relations to truth are already in Plato supplementary rather than incompatible.[50] In the *Phaedrus*, as the following reading will show, the event of "truth," or truth-as-event, is always accidental, and thus strongly linked to the accident of madness and the uniqueness of the poetic text. To be sure, the laborious progress of philosophy *toward* truth, albeit dependent on accident as well, strives for the very calculable method that poetry by (Socrates') definition lacks. The conversion of accidental truth to approximated truth, however, cannot be accomplished without loss. Since madness precludes communication, the mad moment needs to be narrativized into *muthos* in order to transform the instantaneous recollection of knowledge into *logos*. You cannot teach but in stories.

Accordingly, the *Phaedrus* is a dialogue about madness, but also a dialogue about story-telling, about *logos* and *muthos*,[51] about *psychagôgia* as persuasion and deception. The connection between madness and narrativity is complex. Socrates distinguishes between two general kinds of mania: that of pathological, human origin (*hypo nosêmatôn anthrôpinôn*), and divine madness, *theia mania* (265a–c). As crucial as it is that Socrates rules out pathological madness from the beginning, for the purpose of this investigation, it is even more significant that poetic and pathological madness share the name of *mania*, that they share at least one register. This is important, since poetic madness, then, is *not* a metaphor in the narrow sense, but exists as a subcategory parallel to but distinct from madness as illness, the madness of the body. Thus diagnosis, the identification of *theia mania*, is an urgent project from the start. Socrates subjects divine madness to further analysis, and he comes up with four subcategories: prophetic, ritual, erotic and poetic *mania*, sent, respectively, by Apollo, Dionysus, Eros, and the Muses.

Banal as it may seem, it is worthwhile noting that *mania* always comes *from somewhere else*, that madness is not immanent to or generated by the human mind precariously suspended between *phusis* and *theos*. The choice of words in this passage underlines this aspect: divine madness is generated *hypo theias exallagês tôn eiôthotôn nomimôn,* "by a divine complete change in established customs." *Exallagês* signifies a complete alteration of human establishment; the reversal of the familiar is stressed in the redundant *eiôthotôn nomimôn,* something like customary usages. Divine madness, then, is fundamentally alien to the *cultural* human, to the man of *ethos, nomos,* and the *polis* (remember that this dialogue is set outside of Athens, beyond the limits of *polis* and the *Politeia,* in the wilderness, an environment Socrates usually could not care less about). This phrase does not simply signify the absence or the confusion of order as some translations suggest.[52] Instead of establishing a dichotomy of reason and its absence, the complete alterity suggested by *exallagês* sets up a tripartite structure which creates a place for madness that is neither controlled by the laws of culture nor, since it is of the god, produced purely at random. *Mania,* then, is not simply the other of reason in the way that desire and spirit (*epithymia* and *thumos*) are distinct from the *logistikon* in the *Republic.*[53] The construction of reason and madness as a dichotomy might, in fact, be the most profound and most frequent simplification in many critical treatments of madness and mad speech.

In Plato's text, divine madness, without exception, is part of a fable; there is always a story to contain *mania.* Prophetic *mania* has "achieved so much for which both states and individuals in Greece are thankful" (244c); ritual madness "has secured relief" "when grievous maladies and afflictions have beset certain families by reason of some ancient sin" (244e); poetic madness serves the "glorifying [of] the countless mighty deeds of ancient times for the instruction of posterity" (245a); erotic madness, finally, is inscribed in the metahistory of the human soul, the longest and most intricate narrative of the dialogue.

All of the stories Socrates tells or alludes to—and this is where one would expect them to differ most radically from modern/postmodern stories of madness—have an end to them, an end in the double sense of a conclusion and an objective, a *telos.* In an inversion of Foucault's famous definition of madness as the absence of the work,[54] Platonic *mania* is defined by its product. Indeed it appears as if Plato's madness reverses precisely the steadiest assumptions of madness held in our century. As ritual it is a remedy instead of an ailment, as prophecy it imparts the most instead of the least reliable intelligence, as erotic madness it leads to perfect attachment instead of to perfect solitude. Madness is neither excluded from history nor an episode or a footnote to it. In fact, *mania* seems to hold a central place within what we might call the different orders of history—the history of the individual, of the great families, of the state, of the nation, of the human soul. In the *Phaedrus,* all of them, in various ways, *depend* on the interlude of madness—just as they depend on madness to be nothing but an interlude. At the same time, *mania* interrupts the usual progression of things and terminates the course of causality: in the *Oresteia,* clearly the backdrop of Socrates' example of Dionysian *mania,* only madness can stop the self-perpetuation of ancient sin.

Unlike madness as *nosis*, divine madness is necessarily intermittent.[55] The place of madness within Plato's stories is one of interim action and interim (un)consciousness. Not only does madness come from somewhere, it also inevitably *leads* somewhere. But what is it? An event? An action? A state of mind or mindlessness? It seems indeed as if we can define it only in terms of a story: *Divine Madness is when* . . . If that is true, then we necessarily have to read these stories in reverse—the only way to validate madness as *divine* is to look at that state from the point of its product, the work. Madness itself is a sudden event, beyond control and calculation, and it remains an unreadable event unless it is narrativized, recuperated by a teleological story told about it. Incidentally, this is precisely the logic of divinely inspired prophecy as it is presented most rigorously in Greek tragedy: we can read it only when it has come true. And since tragedy suggests that it is indeed the law of prophecy that it *must* be ambiguous in order not to be averted, the only accurate tense for this temporal movement at the point of its origin, in the moment of mad prophetic speech, is future perfect: This prediction will have been true. The tense of Cassandra.

If the story of divine madness can be told only in a mode of *Nachträglichkeit*, then in Socrates' system madness and oeuvre authenticate each other, but only under the gaze of a narrator who is neither mad nor a poet, but knows about both madness and poetry. This narrator is, of course, as the reading of the *Ion* has shown, the philosopher.

The *Phaedrus* gives the impression that the homogeneity of the types of *mania* is deliberately enforced. The productive ends of prophetic and poetic madness may have been familiar topoi, and the revision of erotic madness as a productive force is extensively legitimized. The integration of Dionysian *mania* into the teleology of madness, however, is perplexing. R. Hackforth stresses in his commentary on the *Phaedrus* that in "the passage before us [Dionysian *mania*] is *restricted* to the special case of curing the 'maladies and afflictions' which arise from an *inherited* curse, such as that in the families of the Pelopidae or Labdacidae [emphasis added]," whereas before this particular type of frenzy had been "conceived as at once the climax of the malady and the source of healing."[56] It seems as if Plato wants to get away from the notion of *crisis*, the critical point of suspension which Hölderlin will much later rethink under the name of *caesura*. Dionysian madness is thus detached from its connection to physical affliction, assimilated to the other types of madness, inscribed into (historical) genealogy as an interruption. By deemphasizing the sense of climax that would be immanent to the course of any dynamic condition, Socrates stresses once again the agency of an *outside* force interrupting the human story.[57]

In this sense, Dionysian madness loses its rituality, since it is not *repeatable* as any ritual would have to be. This is the double bind into which Socrates will tie poetry, too, and the stratagem by which he will once again establish the hegemony of the philosophical project over the event of mad speech. On the one hand, divine madness allows for an immediacy of speech unadulterated by misrepresentation, which appears to be the fate of all intentional *mimêsis*. Speech under the reign of *mania* cannot be a distortion of the divine since it is itself divine. If madness is defined as the absence of *technê*, then divinely mad speech is essentially unrhetorical. As such, however, it is also essentially unrepeatable. We have seen in the *Ion* how the unaccountable nature of madly engendered meaning generates the necessity of a critical paraphrase that must not be mad itself, and how the very privilege of mad speech disinherits the mad speaker of his product. The speaker can never claim mad speech as his own *while he is mad*. Since the state of *mania* is one of self-alienation, the madman cannot engage in dialogue as himself—and his exclusion from dialogue means, in effect, his exclusion from (Socratic) philosophy. Only if he acts as his own critic—that is, if he ceases to be mad—can he lay claim to the name of wisdom-lover. As a critic of his text, however, he must all but obliterate what he has produced. In order for poetry to become philosophy, it must recant itself. Here is the complete version of the passage elliptically quoted above:

> Do you now go and tell Lysias that we two went down to the stream where is the holy place of the nymphs, and there listened to words which charged us to deliver a message, first to Lysias and all other composers of discourses, secondly to Homer and all others who have written poetry whether to be read or sung, and thirdly to Solon and all such as are authors of political compositions under the name of laws—to wit, that if any of them has done his work with a knowledge of the truth, *can defend his statements when challenged, and can demonstrate the inferiority of his writings out of his own mouth*, he ought not to be designated by a name drawn from those writings, but by one that indicates his serious pursuit [emphasis added]. . . . A name that would fit him better, and have more seemliness, would be 'lover of wisdom,' or something similar. (278c–d)

This definition is ingenious. It excludes from the realm of philosophy the much praised speeches of *mania*; it does this on precisely the grounds that distinguish them as incontestable. Philosophical knowledge may be limited to being nothing more than ever-aspiring, but it is the only knowledge that is authorized by a method, by *epistêmê*, constituting philosophical authority.

PHILOSOPHY'S MAD DEMON

Philosophical authority, however, is principally nothing else but authority over previous speech. As the *Ion* already foreshadowed, control of any given text can be acquired only in an act of rephrasing, of de-divinization, of criticism. As in the *Ion*, the act of speaking about speech emerges as an act of violence, as the annihilation of what was said before in an infinite deferral of meaning as truth. The dialogical form of Plato's writing embodies this principle; it provides the philosopher—Socrates—with samples of speech that precede the philosophical speech that cancels them out in turn. Philosophy, in its dialogical form, needs speech as its object. In the process, it turns itself into new speech, serving as its next object to be subsequently obliterated as well. This infinite deferral inherent in the pursuit of truth is, of course, a well-known constituent of Platonic philosophy. Its implications, followed through, are nevertheless potentially perplexing.

As seen above, the dialogical process cannot transcend itself unless the potential of transcendence is already given in the dialogue's original utterance or in the utterance it takes as its point of departure. Analogously, the knowledge of truth cannot be produced by philosophical labor, but can only be remembered, reconstituted: we can get to know only what we have already known at some point. The knowledge to be remembered, however, has never been true knowledge but only a blurred, partial, and unreliable vision of truth, present not as a memory but as a myth (which can, of course, be understood as a form of memory—but, again, a memory outside of philosophy as it defines itself here).

Socrates' account of the being of the beings, then, is deeply paradoxical. If the original contemplation of the ideas is flawed already, then the recollection of this contemplation must necessarily be even more flawed. If even the most perfect soul in its disembodied state has never been able to see all the ideas, then there can be no full recollection of the hyperuranian beings. If there can thus be neither complete contemplation nor reliable recollection of the "place beyond heaven," then Socrates' tale is an impossible one to tell. The story of soul and being, as it appears in the *Phaedrus*, renders itself impossible at the moment its narrator assumes a position that he ascribes to the gods exclusively. As Benardete has shown, only the gods escape the double bind of eroticism that keeps the mortal philosopher at a distance from the knowledge he desires; only the gods can both see and consummate being. To cross the line between what can be seen and what can be known—the famous dividing line of the *Republic*—is to be a god, or to be— divinely—mad.

The 'divine', or 'divine madness', is the name for a hypothetical complete knowledge—a knowledge that would not be constrained by the double bind of desire. Divine madness, in other words, is the name for an impossible knowledge. Griswold points out that "[t]here is a gap between what the myth says and the telling of the myth, between its *logos* and its *ergon*,"[58] since this account of *anamnêsis* could not be given if it were true. But Socrates never pretends to tell a true story. On the contrary, he claims in retrospect that, while his speeches contained useful examples of dialectics, "everything else indeed was only spoken in jest" (265c). Spoken in jest, as play, *paidia*, the way a wisdom-lover might sometimes play at writing a law, a speech, or a poem. Socrates was diverting himself. He played, and the game was called madness:

S: [My two speeches] were contrary to each other. For one asserted that one must yield to the lover, the other, to the non-lover.

P: And both quite valiant.

S: I thought you would say, truthfully, quite mad. What they sought, however, was precisely that. (265a)

Unlike Socrates' earlier flirtations with madness, this statement must be taken seriously. It does not imply that Socrates himself was mad, only that his speeches were. And the palinode, at least, is a mad speech; mad precisely because it talked about absolute truth. It was mad because it presented the very knowledge that would have made it possible as an unattainable knowledge. Thus, it could have been spoken only from the perspective of the divine. As such, it is not philosophical—philosophy remains subjected to "the necessity of speaking in a way that is human rather than divine."[59]

Without the mad speech, however, there could have been no dialectic critique of it: Part II of the *Phaedrus* is built on Part I. Thus providing its own object, the *Phaedrus* is an anomaly within Plato's oeuvre. Usually, Socrates wards off any display of rhetoric, as in the *Ion*. The texts he refers to, apart from a few disconnected quoted lines, remain outside the dialogue; similarly, the *Republic* evokes Homer's poetry only in a few quotations. Only the *Phaedrus* presents the complete original *logoi and* accounts for their presence as well as their later recantation.

The divide between part I and part II, however, although decisive and undeniable, is not complete. Certainly, there is mad speech and philosophical speech, and the hierarchy between them seems obvious. Like instantaneous love for the beautiful boy, mad speech can serve as a gateway to philosophy, but remains excluded from it. The philosopher-midwife and his dialectical forceps will deliver the madman of his truth and leave him behind. The operations of madman and philosopher appear distinct. This distance, however, is never as absolute as it is presented. Ultimately, the progress of philosophy depends on a mad moment itself, because only mad speech can contain the seed of transcendent truth. Philosophical eros enters the scene as suddenly as corporeal eros, and, like love and poetry, philosophy is grounded in an act it cannot control. In the *Phaedrus*, the most significant turning point of the dialogue might be not the shift from display of rhetoric to dialogue about rhetoric, but the event of the *daimonion*. In retrospect, Socrates grounds the dialogue in the interference of his sign. Here is the passage again:

Do you now go and tell Lysias that we two went down to the stream where is the holy place of the nymphs, and there listened to *words which charged us to deliver a message* [emphasis added] . . . that if any of them has done his work with a knowledge of the truth, can defend his statements when challenged, and can demonstrate the inferiority of his writings out of his own mouth, he ought not to be designated by a name drawn from those writings, but by one that indicates his serious pursuit.

The nymphs are still there, but the gods are gone. All that is left is "words," powerful words drifting through the realm of Pan, the mad erotic flute-playing god to whom the last sentences of the dialogue are spoken in prayer. As pointed out before, the *Phaedrus* is justly famous for its diversity of style and genre, for the complexity of its structure. Reading the *Phaedrus* resembles looking at an intricate visual pattern that changes under one's eyes according to which strand one picks to follow. Certainly, this *changeant* quality does not betray an organizational deficiency of the text; on the contrary, its continuous transmutation under the reader's gaze serves to make the *Phaedrus* as unlike the static kind of writing Socrates condemns at the end as it could possibly be. This is a text that can "help itself" fairly well against any attempt of exhaustive interpretation, a text that conceals itself from the critical grasp. That is to say, however, that it conceals itself from philosophy itself. If philosophy, essentially, is an act of recantation, then the *Phaedrus*, in its repeated gesture of recantation, establishes itself as the very structure of philosophy that in itself cannot be recanted. While every specific recantation is subject to another recantation, only recantation itself, as a principle, does not become obsolete (similarly, Cartesian doubt is the only principle to escape Descartes' all-encompassing doubt at the beginning of the *Meditations*).

Thus, mad speech, sane speech, written and spoken speech, monologue and dialogue, dialectical speech, mythical speech, divine speech, and prayer go into the most intricate dialogical structure Plato has left behind, and not one of them escapes its revocation. Certainly, Socrates establishes a hierarchy toward the end. This hierarchy privileges spoken over written speech, dialogue over monologue, dialectic over rhetoric, deliberation over inspiration, "philosophy" over "poetry." This neat multiple dichotomy, however, leaves the status of the *daimonion* open. It is a quirk, upsetting the highly complex but apparently clearly restricted economy of speeches the dialogue seems to instantiate otherwise. Neither written nor spoken, the *daimonion* constitutes a genre all of itself. It occurs at the pivot of the dialogue. Socrates, or so he said, was ready to leave—without the *daimonion*, then, there would have been no celebration of madness, eros, and philosophy. It is the *daimonion* that delivers the strangely disembodied "words that charged us to convey a message." It is the *daimonion*, finally, that prompts Socrates' recantation of pure reason (if we can call it that): "This story is not true." In this dialogue, then, truth, or more precisely the recantation of nontruth, depends in its origin on the event of words without a speaker, an event as unforeseeable and incalculable as the event of divine madness. Thus, the *daimonion* is built into the dialogue in the same way as *mania* is written into the theory of *anamnêsis*. It might not alter the story, but without it, the story would not be told.

CHAPTER TWO

THE ABYSS ABOVE

Hölderlin: Madness, Philosophy, and Tragedy
in the Absence of the Gods

> Fatigue he felt none, he only thought it unpleasant at times that he could
> not walk on his head.
>
> —Georg Büchner

> He who walks on his head, Gentlemen, has heaven below him as an abyss.
>
> —Paul Celan

INTRODUCTION: MADNESS AND THE LABOR OF POETRY

One day in spring, the student Johann Georg Fischer called on a poet, as he
had often done before. He recounts:

> Since I was leaving Tübingen in May, I asked him for a few lines as a
> souvenir. 'As your holiness requests,' he said, 'should I do stanzas on Greece,
> on spring, on Zeitgeist?' I asked for 'Zeitgeist.'

Fischer got his lines; they are preserved. The poem is dated "24. Mai 1748"
and signed "Scardanelli."[1] It was April 1843, and the poet was Friedrich
Hölderlin. He died a few months later.

Why this strange story?

At once infinitely pitiful and morbidly comical, Fischer's anecdote plays
on the major themes of poetic madness: temporal displacement, loss of identity, and, nevertheless, *poetry*, *Dichtung*. It is an anecdote about Hölderlin, for
many *the* 'poète philosophe' and *the* 'poète fou'. It is safe to say that no writer

embodies the Romantic and post-Romantic idea of poetic madness like Friedrich Hölderlin. The Hölderlin legend started to emerge during his lifetime, and its construction, to which figures as diverse as Bettina von Arnim and Martin Heidegger have contributed decisively, is still under way. Recently, the German critic Wolfgang Lange has argued that madness was not simply the aftermath of Hölderlin's intense poetic project, as Heidegger suggests, but was indeed the project itself, a "calculated madness" representative of the modern poetic endeavor itself.[2] The thesis is elegant, and Lange uses the rather sparse evidence from Hölderlin's poetry, essays, and letters effectively. Even though Lange largely confines himself to an analysis of Hölderlin's written oeuvre, I suspect that his Hölderlin chapter draws much of its persuasiveness from the biographical facts—that is, it could not have been written in this form if Hölderlin had not gone mad. Lange insists that "if there is a hidden complex from which Hölderlin's madness springs forth, or a double-bind construction through which the 'schizophrenic' contour of his hymns becomes intelligible, then they are rather to be found on the aesthetic-poetological plane than on a biographic one."[3] While Lange thus repudiates, at least implicitly, psychoanalytical or other biographical models of explanation, he nonetheless constructs an etiology of Hölderlin's insanity, rationalizing it into a structure of causality. In this operation, he is less far removed from the biographical readers than he thinks. His attempt to distinguish between Hölderlin's personal ego and the "lyrical I," while important, does not go far enough, and the two concepts quickly collapse into each other in the equation of "Hölderlin's madness" and the "schizophrenic contour of his hymns."

Wolfgang Lange's thesis nevertheless opens up a fundamental question: Does Hölderlin himself initiate and legitimize the theories of poetic madness in terms of which his life has been read? Did he *have* a theory of poetic madness? Is he complicitous in creating the site of diagnostic criticism that his biography has become? Did he *want* to go mad, if only figuratively speaking? Lange's term of "calculated madness," coined to describe modernity's conscious struggle for the state of productive alienation that goes by the name of creative madness, denotes a potentially hazardous strategy.[4] If Hölderlin, as Lange suggests, pursued madness, his "calculation" succeeded all too well, or, depending on the perspective, failed him miserably. But did he?

As I will argue in this chapter, most of Hölderlin's theoretical writings, whether influenced by his personal condition or not, are highly suspicious of any elevation of madness, poetic or otherwise. I must admit that my evidence is perhaps as sparse as that which Lange presents, for Hölderlin does not speak much of madness.[5] This, however, is telling in itself, seeing that Hölderlin speaks about poetry very frequently. The very absence of the idea of madness from most of his oeuvre should be enough to give pause to any attempt to construct an elaborate theory of poetic madness from his writings. Hölderlin's allusions to inspiration or poetic enthusiasm, in *Hyperion* or the

Empedocles project, remain rather conventional, as Maurice Blanchot points out.[6] In my estimation, there is only one group of texts to which the issue of madness is truly central: Hölderlin's translation of Sophocles' tragedies *Antigone* and *Oedipus the King* and his annotations to the tragedies. In Hölderlin's oeuvre, then, madness is predominantly linked to the phenomenon of the tragic hero, and his theory of madness can be traced only in conjunction with an analysis of his philosophy of tragedy. To complicate matters further, Hölderlin's thought on tragedy, as much of the theory of tragedy at his time, is inextricably interwoven with his philosophy of history. This constellation—history, tragedy, madness, and philosophy itself—is the subject of the following reading. It will argue that the concept of madness the Sophocles texts put forth is not poetic in nature, that it is, in fact, fundamentally *antipoetic*; Sophocles' mad tragic heroes emerge as figurations of philosophy, or rather philosophies, that must be contained by the counterforce of poetry.

Such a reading goes against the grain of a major trend in critical history that dates back to the first half of the nineteenth century. Fischer's reminiscences quoted at the beginning of this chapter provide a perfect example of this history, an attitude that often comes close to viewing the poet as a kind of exotic local landmark. During his lifetime, Hölderlin's fame as a madman may well have surpassed his reputation as a poet—he had countless visitors, and the tone of their recollections suggests that Hölderlin's condition was a veritable sight to see in Tübingen, a place from which one would take a souvenir, perhaps a few lines on *Zeitgeist*, and a lasting memory: "As long as I live, I shall not forget how his face lit up in this moment,"[7] Fischer recalls.

Fischer's image of the lit-up face is a well-worn trope for inspiration, for the poetic spirit asserting itself as a force from the outside *during* the moment of production, reducing the poet to its vessel. "Only the Muse is still able to speak to him . . . ," as Bettina von Arnim put it.[8] In a similar vein, Roman Jakobson and Grete Lübbe-Grothues speak of Hölderlin's "strangely intact and enthusiastic wish and capacity for effortless, spontaneous, and purposeful impromptu poetry."[9] Both comments, representative of many others, postulate a continuity of poetic production as independent from the continuity of a self-conscious life. To talk of an "*intact* capacity," however, is to make a dubious choice of words, since Hölderlin's former poetry had been anything but effortless, spontaneous, or impromptu. The Muse must have had very different things to say to him.

I do not want to enter into the evaluation controversy over Hölderlin's "latest poems," as the most frequent euphemism labels them, the poems written in the tower after 1806. They have been dismissed as well as highly praised. The well-researched article by Roman Jakobson and Grete Lübbe-Grothues—who admire the late poems for their "magic grace"—aptly summarizes the major statements of early and contemporary critics; it also provides a splendidly concise synopsis of the curiosity the mad Hölderlin provoked among the intellectuals of his time.[10] No matter what position is taken, however, to my knowledge not a single one of the commentators denies a definite formal and conceptual chasm between the poetry of the period preceding and that following the breakdown.

All accounts of a totally deranged Hölderlin composing poems in blissful ease—collected in volume nine of the Frankfurt Edition—are so striking precisely because Hölderlin had been the most technical of the great poets, had worked out the most rigorous, the most mathematical systems of composition and had gone into near-agony over the tiniest detail, ever revising, discarding draft after draft. Between Hölderlin's oeuvre and the criticism devoted to it, two concepts of poetry emerge back to back: laborious technique on the one hand, the total absence of labor and effort on the other.

It is easy to recognize in the two concepts Plato's distinction between *technê* and *mania* that shaped the first sustained theory of poeisis we know. For Plato, to summarize part of the argument of the first chapter, the only poetry worth serious consideration does not come about by the methodical application of poetic technique or the self-conscious representation of ontological knowledge in a poetic text; the "highest goods" of poetry are the product of a divinely inspired state that suspends the poet's subjectivity and imbues him with a divine knowledge (*dianoia*) he does not have during a self-conscious state of mind. Unlike philosophy, which requires mastery of the tools of dialectical technique, poetry cannot be taught since the poet cannot coherently account for the process of its composition. Certainly, Plato's concept of philosophy is far from exhausted in the idea of dialectics, and as I have argued in Chapter One, philosophy, too, originates in a mad moment that it ultimately cannot account for. The process of philosophy, however, consists precisely in the sustained attempt to overcome the madness that precipitates it, and the strategies to do so can be taught, practiced, repeated, and learned. In contrast, the "good" poetic text, as opposed to poetry produced "by *technê* alone," is unique, its creation is accidental, and the process by which it emerges cannot be repeated deliberately.

The mad Hölderlin of Bettina von Arnim's description, like the Hölderlin of so many descriptions to follow, is the embodiment of this Platonic prototype. The Hölderlin passages in *Die Günderode* paraphrase in indirect speech Hölderlin's Sophocles annotations and other theoretical works of his. Jakobson and Lübbe-Grothues approvingly quote the following passage, allegedly formulated by Hölderlin and passed on through Isaak von Sinclair:

> Language forms all thought, for it is greater than the human mind, which is only a slave to language, and the human intellect will be less than complete as long as language alone doesn't evoke it. But the laws of the intellect are metric—one feels that in language, which throws a net over the intellect; while caught within it, the mind must express the divine.[11]

Certainly, Plato's gods have been replaced by a vague entity called "language," but the structure remains that of Platonic enthusiasm. It is revealing that Jakobson and Lübbe-Grothues call this remark "appropriate to the late poetic form of Scardanelli." Perhaps so, but then it tells us little about Hölderlin. Jakobson and Lübbe-Grothues see no need to question the authenticity of the passage, which, stemming from a novel, after all, is more representative of Bettina von Arnim's aesthetics than of Hölderlin's.[12] Perhaps the passage's "appropriateness" is rather due to a critical interestedness that, more than two thousand years old, reasserts itself during German romanticism, a period that often declares itself in love with Plato, but also, and perhaps as vigorously, in the twentieth century, an age largely characterized by a deep and growing suspicion of all Platonisms.

As we will see, however, Hölderlin's own account of poetic production contradicts Plato's theory as forcefully as possible. This is true not only for his early theoretical writings but also for the later Sophocles annotations that appear to be written, at least in part, after his first mental breakdown in France in 1802.[13] Certainly, the picture conveyed by the likes of Fischer and Hölderlin's own descriptions of the poetic process are not necessarily incompatible. One might argue that Hölderlin recovered from the Bordeaux interlude and went "properly" mad only in 1806,[14] the year he was confined in carpenter Zimmer's tower. There were no theoretical writings from then on, or at least none have been discovered. One might further argue, as Lange suggests, that Hölderlin's madness was a kind of solution to the aesthetic problems that so troubled him during his lucid period, that the dialectical tension in his work and thought—a tension between *mania* and *technê*—became too much to bear. Heidegger seems to suggest such a train of thought when he writes that Hölderlin was "taken away into the protection of the night of madness,"[15] but Heidegger's intentions in passages like that are difficult to intuit, and he certainly would not be arguing Plato's case. Nonetheless, perhaps the highest poetry—and surely Hölderlin's work is of the highest order—demands that the poet succumb to madness. So possibly, in the last analysis Hölderlin's life does prove Plato right, and the poet, or at least some poets, really must choose between madness and philosophy.

I do not have answers to the questions raised above. Surely they are legitimate, even crucial issues, touching upon the very essence of poetic existence. Stanley Corngold, I think, articulated the stakes and possibilities most concisely and most persuasively in the following paragraphs:

> From our own standpoint, it is hard to descry a German poetry arising in the first decade of the nineteenth century that needed Hölderlin enough to warrant a belief that his madness was a sacrifice to it. Had he known this, Hölderlin would have died mourning.
>
> On the other hand, if one thinks of Hölderlin as the modern poet who more completely than any other lived the contradictions of his culture—amid outbursts of violence and melancholy creating works from the omnipresent conflict of feeling and skill—so that in him these contradictions became objective with a definiteness of outline heightened by his abrupt

end, his madness does become the philosophical sacrifice he contemplated. And then he would not have to mourn.[16]

Like most readers who consider Hölderlin's fate, I feel that there *should* be a connection between his work and his madness, and any plausible theory to that effect holds seductive appeal. If there is no such link, then his madness is utterly arbitrary, coincidental, meaningless, a waste. This is possible, after all. It is possible that madness is precisely that: arbitrary, coincidental, meaningless. In fact, is this not the very essence of madness: the utter breakdown of causal reason? Why does it seem so hard to accept Hölderlin's madness as a fundamental collapse? Certainly, he remained, even in his madness, a poet; the poetry after 1806, however, is not the poetry that maintains his rank as one of the greatest of poets.[17] His status as the quintessential grand mad poet is based on the great hymns, not on the traditional four-line stanzas he composed at Zimmer's. The language of "Zeitgeist" has little in common with the language of "Patmos" or "Andenken."

Heidegger is one of the few readers who pay attention to the work of the second Homburg stay of 1804–1806,[18] but even Heidegger's writings, like almost all other influential commentary on Hölderlin, generally treat the poetry written in the years before 1804 and never venture into the poems after 1806—with one exception, "In lieblicher Bläue".[19] This text seems to disturb the clear distinction between works before and after 1806 for which I have argued: "*In lieblicher Bläue*" is a fragment that appears in prose form in Waiblinger's novel *Phaeton*, published in 1826. Waiblinger's hero is modeled on Hölderlin, and Waiblinger, a friend of Hölderlin, claims that the mad Hölderlin wrote the poem "in verses after Pindar's manner." This alleged manuscript is lost. Heilingrath has attempted to restore Waiblinger's prose version to its hypothetical original form. The result is impressive and highly suggestive of Hölderlin's other work; its authenticity rarely becomes an issue. It is an enigmatic text, however, in that its style does not even remotely resemble any of the poems after 1806 that are preserved in the original but is much closer to the late hymnic sketches, both in language and in quality. If Hölderlin wrote it, when did he write it? If Waiblinger is correct, must we assume that the more conventional verses from the tower are not fully representative of Hölderlin's latest work? Why are no other manuscripts of this sort preserved? Is "In lieblicher Bläue" an exception? Did Hölderlin destroy some of his latest work? Did Zimmer throw it away? Did Waiblinger get hold of an earlier sketch and mistake it for a recent composition? Can we really rule out that Waiblinger wrote it himself? Personally, I am sometimes inclined towards the last suggestion, if only because the poem seems too perfectly "mad" to be true. On the other hand, there are lines in this fragment that are so resplendent that one hesitates to credit them to Waiblinger: "King Oedipus has one eye too many, perhaps," to quote the most famous one. If Hölderlin wrote it, and if he wrote it after 1806, then he truly was a mad poet, and not a man driven mad by poetry, or a madman who happened to have been a poet—but as long as "In lieblicher Bläue" still awaits its literary detective, it seems impossible to draw any conclusions from it.

To superimpose images of Hölderin's mad life onto his earlier work is a strategy that caters to the general concerns all theorists of poetic madness share, from Plato to Freud and beyond. The notion of poetic madness serves to define poetry as more than a project or product of self-conscious labor (alone), creating a space for poetry different from all other intellectual pursuits. It also seeks to conceive of madness as more than a model of ultimate arbitrariness or the complete loss of reason. Any concept of poetic madness invariably invests insanity with meaning, with a cause and a goal, *arche* and *telos*, reinscribing the absence of reason into a reasonable teleological pattern.[20] Socrates, who appears to deny any connection between a mad poet's individuality and the process of madly made meaning, rigorously isolates poetry from the poet. Hölderlin's critics, while their basic assumptions are not incompatible with Socrates' model, are, in a way, much less radical. When Hölderlin's late poetry is brought into connection with his (later) madness, his writings are implicitly said to surpass and subvert the notion of work or labor defined as essentially both a sane and a self-conscious process. At the same time, these readings maintain a continuum between the Hölderlin who still speaks and the Hölderlin who only stammers, between *logos* and *pallaksch*.[21] This notion of poetic madness thus appears as a strategy that defends the subject through the critique of subjectivity. Hölderlin's theory of tragic madness, as will become clear, achieves a similar effect—but the place of the poet is elsewhere.

In his dissertation on Romantic criticism, belatedly seminal in Romantic studies, Walter Benjamin has argued against the pervasive misunderstanding of Romantic aesthetics underlying studies that quickly link Hölderlin's madness to his work. Benjamin, emphasizing the element of reflection in Romantic *Kunstkritik*, turns against Goethe's protractedly influential verdict that the Romantics overprivileged passion and sentiment to the near-exclusion of reflection. In this context, Benjamin sees Romantic theory as an overturning of Platonic aesthetics: "As a practice of thinking and deliberating, reflection is the opposite of ecstasy, of Plato's *mania*."[22] Hölderlin's poetological essays serve as a case in point. Benjamin's points are well taken, and his critique, along with Adorno's well-known essay on Hölderlin that explicitly argues against Heidegger,[23] serves as a welcome counterpoint to Heidegger's usurpation of Hölderlin's poetry as proto-Heideggerian thought.

In his focus on Romantic reflection, however, Benjamin runs the risk of going to the opposite extreme from those he criticizes.[24] While Hölderlin certainly was no neo-Platonist *Schwärmer*, neither did he rely on reflection alone. It is precisely the dialectic between Hesperian sobriety and Greek ecstasy that is continuously at stake in Hölderlin's work, a relation that, foreshadowing Nietzsche's work on the Dionysian-Apollinian structure of Greek culture,

Hölderlin sees already at play in ancient Greece. If Hölderlin's work can be said to overturn the Platonic construction of the relation between poetry and criticism, then it does so neither by introducing reflection into it nor by erasing *mania*, but by attempting to fuse the two practices Plato had so painstakingly distinguished. This is not to say that Plato's madmen and Plato's philosophers merge into one figure, for the tension between the two elements, even though fundamentally changed by Hölderlin's reconfiguration, remains unbroken. In this process, poetry becomes something else entirely, but so does philosophy. For Hölderlin, as I will show, it is philosophy that becomes the—potentially—mad enterprise, whereas poetry takes over the labor of order and preservation that Socrates had assigned to the philosophers.

As Lacoue-Labarthe stresses in "The Caesura of the Speculative," "the theory put forward by Hölderlin is speculative through and through".[25] Adorno, against Heidegger, had already insisted on the unerasable influence Hegel had on Hölderlin's work. This connection, along with Hölderlin's personal fate and the extensive commentary dedicated to it, more often than not obscures the fact that while his theory might be "speculative through and through," his poetics are material through and through. It is instructive simply to look at the titles that have been established for some of Hölderlin's essays and essay fragments: "On the Different Ways of Composing Poetry" ("Über die verschiedenen Arten, zu dichten"), "Succession of Tones" ("Wechsel der Töne"), "On the Method of the Poetic Spirit" ("Über die Verfahrensweise des poetischen Geistes"), "On the Difference of Poetic Modes" ("Über den Unterschied der Dichtarten"), "On the Parts of the Poem" ("Über die Partien des Gedichts"), "The Blending of the Types of Composing Poetry" ("Mischung der Dichtarten"). Only some of these titles are Hölderlin's own,[26] but they convey the often technical character of Hölderlin's various poetological projects accurately.

According to the Frankfurt edition, most of these essays date from the years 1799 and 1800, predating and preparing what is generally seen as Hölderlin's highest poetic achievements, the *Nachtgesänge*, the *Vaterländische Gesänge*, and the drafts and fragments of the late hymns. They also fall into the period when Hölderlin intensified his lifelong encounter with Greek tragedy that would culminate in his Sophocles translations. (It seems that both *Ödipus der Tyrann* and *Antigonä*, published in 1804, were finished by September 1803 at the latest.[27]) If there is a quotation representative of the spirit of these essays, it is the following remark in "Reflection":

> Where sobriety leaves you, there are the boundaries of your enthusiasm. The great poet never abandons himself, he may elevate himself as far above himself as he wishes. One can *fall* into height just as well as downward.[28]

Hölderlin's stunning image of falling upward names the danger of poetic madness unconfined by the counterforces of labor and sobriety: to lose footing in elevation, to get lost in the metaphysical realm, the abyss above. Hölderlin does not deny the poet's need for the spirits, but clearly the stress lies on sobriety and the indispensability of poetic *techne*, of craftsmanship and poeto-logical calculation.[29] To rely on the spirits alone would be to court the profound alienation of self-abandonment. While the poet can "elevate" himself above himself, he may not lose sight of what he left down below, namely, the self. Lange correctly points out that the forces of enthusiasm and sobriety must coexist:

> Being sacredly sober . . . in Hölderlin's case, must not be understood as the rationalist poetics of the 18th century understood it, i.e. as the poet's capacity to rein in his enthusiasm in retrospect . . . to correct his inspirations through critical judgment in order to render their phantasms compatible with reason. Nothing comes of that but a crooked, namely sobered poetry.[30]

The loss of sobriety marks the end of *Begeisterung* as well; poetic control cannot be retrospectively activated. The spirits need the host of the self, and it is precisely the taut tension between self and that other that the poet must bear in the act of creation. Hölderlin recasts this tension under many names: Greece and Germany, antiquity and modernity, the own and the foreign.

Sobriety, *Nüchternheit*, a term I read as Hölderlin's appropriation of the Platonic *sophrosune*,[31] is a central concept in Hölderlin's theory of history, a theory cast often, but not always, exclusively in terms of Greece and Germany.[32] In the famous letter to Böhlendorff, Hölderlin writes:

> . . . in the progress of education [*Bildung*] the properly national will always be of lesser advantage. Hence, the Greeks master the sacred pathos to a lesser degree, because to them it was inborn, whereas they excel in their talent for representation (*Darstellungsgabe*) from Homer on, because this exceptional man was sufficiently soulful [*seelenvoll*] to conquer the occidental Junonian sobriety for his Apollinian realm and thus to veritably appropriate [*aneignen*] what is foreign.
>
> With us it is the reverse. Hence it is also so dangerous to abstract artistic rules only and exclusively from Greek excellence. I have labored long over this and know now that we must not be *alike* to the Greeks in anything save that which must be the highest for the Greeks and for us, namely the vital relation and destiny/technique [*Geschick*, an importantly ambiguous term].
>
> Yet what is one's own must be learned as well as what is alien. This is why the Greeks are indispensable to us. It is only that we will not come near them especially in our own, national [character], since, as I said, the *free* use of what is one's *own* is the most difficult.[33]

The poets, in other words, have to struggle for a national-historical aesthetic as well as for an aesthetic that transcends nationality and historical time. Modernity is characterized by an inborn sobriety, but it is precisely because they are sober that the moderns will have the hardest time giving artistic expression to sobriety. The mad language of sacred pathos, however, is deeply alien to modernity, but precisely because it is alien, it is within the grasp of modern art. It is a matter of understanding what is alien to the self through what is proper to the alien. This is not to say, however, that either part will be easy to achieve. Homer's assimilation of mimetic technique (*Darstellungsgabe*) is an event of "extraordinary" magnitude; Greece's greatness is founded on this event.[34] And even the Greeks, at the pinnacle of their culture, ultimately failed[35] to create an art that would conjoin pathos and sobriety, or, in Platonic terms, enthusiasm and *techne*, *mania* and *sophrosune*.[36] The task has passed on to Hesperia, although, as Hölderlin suggests, modern art will formally excel in the conveyance of pathos rather than in clear mimetic representation.[37] It is important to keep in mind that Hölderlin here argues for a sharp distinction between the cultural foundation of poetry and that which it represents on its surface. This distinction is especially significant in Hölderlin's readings of Sophocles' tragedies where tragic language conceals the very layer it springs from.

Perhaps unwittingly, Hölderlin has written a verdict not only on modern art in general but on his own work, for as much as we might admire the intensity of pathos in his poetry, it is hard to deny its cryptic quality, or, in Lange's words, its "schizophrenic contour," balancing on the borderline of representation. In naming the danger of the abyss above, Hölderlin lays out a program for a modern aesthetic that is also a warning, and most of all a warning to himself.[38] If the more promising project for modern art is the mastery of pathos, it is also the most dangerous one, for pathos has to be counterbalanced by sobriety, and the aesthetic use of sobriety is, for modernity, "the most difficult" task. The pronouncedly technical, "sober," character of Hölderlin's aesthetic essays does not contradict his verdict on this difficulty, for it is not in theory that the difficulty arises but in poetry, and not in thought, but in its representation as far as this distinction can be made. More precisely, Hölderlin's work is characterized by the conflict between a theory of sobriety and a poetry of metaphysical pathos; the latter is as far removed from Homer's epic language as one could imagine—as Hölderlin had predicted it would be.

TRANSLATING GREECE

It has often been stressed that Hölderlin is as surely an eccentric apparition of his time as he was part of it. As Ernst Cassirer emphasized as early as 1924, "from early youth on, from the first conscious beginnings of his mental development, he sees himself placed right in the middle of the great intellectual movement that takes its clues from Kant." At the same time, Hölderlin "never unreservedly and unconditionally gave himself up to this movement, however powerfully it captured and defined him."[39] Of the numerous scholars who have devoted themselves to the constellations of idealism, Dieter Henrich has probably contributed most to an understanding of the interaction between Hölderlin and the German idealists, a relation that was simultaneously an assimilation of and a defense against the philosophy of his contemporaries.[40] Even though the focus in recent years has been on the affinities and divergences of Hölderlin and Hegel, Hölderlin's relation to Fichte,[41] fluctuating between great admiration and incisive criticism, might be more exemplary of his ambivalent perspective on "the new philosophy." On January 1, 1799, Hölderlin writes to his brother Karl:

> [The Germans] could not experience a more beneficial influence than that of the new philosophy which insists to the extreme on the universality of interest and which uncovers the infinite striving in the breast of man; and even if it keeps too one-sidedly to the great autonomy of human nature, it still is, as the philosophy *of the time*, the only possible one. Kant is the Moses of our nation . . . .[42]

Years earlier, in a letter to Hegel about Fichte, Hölderlin had spoken less charitably about the post-Kantian preoccupation with "the great autonomy of human nature." After a short *reductio ad absurdum* of Fichte's argument, he concludes that "the absolute I is (for myself) nothing." Fichte, then, appears to personify an alarming "extreme" of the post-Kantian "new philosophy" that would negate its very achievements in reintroducing a different kind of transcendence;[43] at the same time, he serves as a counterfigure to the complementary problem of ancient and pre-modern philosophy:

> [Fichte] would like to move in *theory* beyond the fact of consciousness . . . and that is just as certain and even more strikingly transcendent than if the metaphysicians so far would move beyond the existence of the world.[44]

"Wishing to move beyond" (*über hinaus möchten*) is an ambiguous phrase; the departure it names can be understood as the achievement of transcendence as well as a mere leaving-behind, an oblivion. As Hölderlin continues, it becomes clear that he is concerned with the latter possibility:

> [Fichte's] absolute I (=Spinoza's Substance) contains all reality; it is everything, and outside of it there is nothing; hence, there is no object for this absolute I, for otherwise not all reality would be in it; however, a consciousness without object cannot be thought, and if I myself am this object, then I am as such necessarily restricted, even if it were only within time, hence not absolute; therefore, within the absolute I, no consciousness is conceivable; as absolute I, I have no consciousness, and insofar as I have no consciousness I am (for myself) nothing, hence is the absolute I (for me) nothing.[45]

Fichte's philosophy of self, in this reading, potentially obliterates the self altogether. If old and new thought complement each other, as Hölderlin suggests, then the old philosophy threatened to lose the world, whereas the new philosophy runs the risk of losing the self. Hölderlin's critique of both old and new philosophy is summed up in the name of "transcendence." The critical use of the term surprises in the case of a poet whose writings may appear to be rather excessively transcendent themselves. A short and largely neglected fragment may help to clarify Hölderlin's perspective; the text was presumably written in 1799:

> The wise ones, however, who differentiate [unterscheiden] only with the mind, [and] only generally, hasten quickly back into pure Being and fall into an all the greater indifference because they believe to have differentiated, and because they take the non-opposition [Nicht-Entgegensetzung] to which they have returned for an eternal one. They have deceived their nature with the lowest degree of reality, with the shadow of reality, the ideal opposition and differentiation, and nature takes revenge by . . . [46]

The differentiation Hölderlin speaks of, I think, is the eternal metaphysical differentiation between True and Apparent World. The "wise ones" proceed too hastily in their metaphysical desire to transcend reality [Wirklichkeit]— thus, however, they do not find the True World but merely a "shadow of reality," a treacherous idealization of existence that constitutes not its highest, but its "lowest degree."

Transcendent philosophy, then, whether of the old or the new kind, is at risk to spiral into what we might call a downward transcendence. At the end of this process lurks an unspecified "revenge"—Hölderlin's ominous ellipsis opens itself to speculation. I will argue that the revenge he leaves unnamed is madness, a madness that can take the form of either a loss of self or a loss of the world,[47] depending on the kind of philosophy the wise ones practice.[48] I will further suggest that this fragment, written at a time when Hölderlin studied the Greeks with renewed intensity, constitutes an important link between Hölderlin's critique of philosophy and his thought on Greek tragedy. Hölderlin recognized the two figurations of transcendent longing in the protagonists of the two Sophoclean plays he translated, Antigone and Oedipus the King. In his reading, the tragic form itself critiques and contains the perilous desire for the 'beyond' of world and self. To be able to perform this task, the poet must be firmly rooted in both regards. As noted above, Hölderlin insists that "the great poet must never abandon his self." Analogously, he may not abandon the world either: "Die Dichter müssen auch/die geistigen weltlich sein," as Hölderlin asserts in the last two lines of his poem "Der Einzige" ("The Only One"). These lines are strikingly asyntactical; freely translated, they say that "the spiritual poets must be worldly, too," but a more adequate rendering might read, "poets must be spiritual, worldly, as well." The disconnected syntax perhaps indicates the extreme difficulty of the task; at the same time, Hölderlin's phrasing allows the terms geistig and weltlich to be in direct proximity. The hard joint, a characteristic stylistic pattern in Hölderlin's writings that omits conjunctions where they might be expected, creates a parallelism that is also a confrontation, so that identity and difference emerge in startling simultaneity.

Hölderlin's annotations to the Sophoclean plays, too, insist on the solid anchoring of poetry in the world, here in the credo of craftsmanship that characterizes bourgeois life at his time. "It would be good," Hölderlin remarks at the very beginning of his annotations to *Oedipus*, "in order to secure for today's poets a bourgeois existence—taking into account the difference of times and institutions—if we elevate poetry today to the mechanä of the ancients."[49]

No remark could be farther removed from the romantic image of the poet as the inspired outsider which is all too often projected onto Hölderlin's work and life. Certainly, he is not proposing to professionalize poetry into a middle-class career, even though the prospect of a decent income from poetry without doubt held some appeal to someone who struggled along from one humiliating tutoring position to the next; neither is he always free of romantic anti-bourgeois sentiment. It is not the life of the bourgeois that Hölderlin covets, but the status of the citizen, of someone who composes *Vaterländische Gesänge*, the songs of the fatherland, for the fatherland—the status of a poet who is not, like Rousseau, "a stranger" (cf. footnote six). At a time when the rise of the Protestant bourgeois value system as the de facto ruling ideology must necessarily define citizenship, reliability and solid craftsmanship define the work ethic to which the poet-citizen will have to subscribe:

> Among mankind, above all one has to make sure with every thing that it is Something, i.e., that it is recognizable in the medium (*moyen*) of its appearance, that the way in which it is delimited can be determined and taught.[50]

Here, Hölderlin embraces the very qualities that Plato and countless others after him had denied as significant factors in the composition of poetry—i.e., accountability, teachability, repeatability. It is no coincidence that this passage can be read like an instruction for poets and critics alike, for Hölderlin's project is, in a deep sense, the repatriation of the poets whom Socrates exiled on the grounds that they could not be trusted to be responsible critics of their own work (cf. Chapter One, section two). Hölderlin's implicit reference to Plato's *Republic* is strong enough to suggest that Hölderlin is about to reopen the case against the Greek tragic poets that had been one of the main targets of Socrates' attack.

Even though Hölderlin's thought can be read as one sustained repudiation of Plato's theory of poetry, Hölderlin is also much indebted to Plato, as has often been pointed out; thus, he does accept Plato's verdict that the poets are responsible for the transfer of the past into the present. In the age of world history, however, this task takes on an unprecedented magnitude. The whole project of cultural self-knowledge is now predicated upon historical self-knowledge, for a culture can understand itself only when it apprehends its place within world history—that is, when it understands its historical other. Thus, the responsibility for cultural self-knowledge, i.e., the very possibility of a nation's coming into its own, comes to rest on the poets as the arbiters of history, a history that, for Hölderlin, goes by the name of Greece. It is not Winckelmann's Greece anymore—Greece as a model for Germany—nor Schiller's Greece, the essence of universal harmony, nor Schlegel's Greece, the name of artistic perfection, but Greece as Germany's historical and cultural other which Germany has to understand in order to become itself.

To understand Greece does not mean to emulate Greece—on the contrary. As the letter to Böhlendorff stresses, "we must not be *alike*" to them. The note of apparent resignation in this letter—"we will not come near them especially in our own, national character"—does not indicate that Hölderlin gave up the struggle for the fusion of own and other, sobriety and pathos, mimesis and affect, speculation and spiritualization. While his poetry, in all its magnificence, perhaps failed to achieve this synthesis,[51] his translation of Sophocles' tragedies constitutes the last major project along these lines. It is Sophocles, who, according to Hölderlin's distich, understood that hymnic content can be expressed not in hymnic but only in tragic language.[52] This dialectic correlates not only to the relation between pathos and sobriety that Hölderlin sees at work in Homer, but also to the productive historical tension between Greece and Germany.

This tension itself, if it is to be made fruitful, needs an aesthetic form to represent it. Hölderlin found this form in translation. In the translations' dedication to Princess Auguste von Homburg, Hölderlin says that "I chose this business because it is bound by firm and historical, albeit strange laws. Otherwise, if there is time, I will sing the parents of our sovereigns and their seats and the angels of the sacred fatherland."[53] Translating Greece, it seems, is more urgent than singing the fatherland; translation might even be the condition of that song. Hölderlin's unprecedented translatory technique in fact emerges as the privileged operation of assimilating both the own and the foreign, for it is in his translations that Greek is both most fully preserved and most fully erased. While this is true for any act of translation, to a certain degree, it is the governing effect in Hölderlin's work. The translations, while creating a German so alien that Goethe, Schiller, and Voß thought it fit for parody,[54] oscillate between a radical literality that strains and sometimes breaks through the syntactic and semantic limits of German and a deliberate indifference to the Greek original. Compare the first lines of the interlinear translation of the Juntina version of *Antigone*, almost certainly one of the original texts Hölderlin used, to his translation:

Juntina:
O gemeinsames gleichgeschwisterliches Ismenes Haupt
weißt-du eines, das Zeus der von Ödipus-her der-Übel
ein-solches-das nicht uns-beiden noch Lebenden er-vollbringt?

(O common samesisterly Ismene's head
do-you-know one which Zeus of from-Oedipus-on of-the-evils
such-a-one not to-us-two still-living he-administers?)

Hölderlin:
Gemeinsamschwesterliches! O Ismenes Haupt!
Weißt du etwas, das nicht der Erde Vater
Erfuhr, mit uns, die wir bis hieher leben,
Ein Nennbares, seit Oedipus gehascht ward?
(Samesisterly! O Ismene's head!
Do you know something which the father of the earth did not
learn of, with us, who we are living up to here,
a nameable, since Oedipus was caught?)

Radical literality ("gleichgeschwisterlich," "Ismenes Haupt") and strik-ing deviance ("der Erde Vater" instead of "Zeus," "erfuhr" instead of "voll-bringt"), syntactic parallelism and the substitution of four German lines for only three Greek ones speak of conflicting coexisting strategies of transla-tion.[55] The result is a wild language that nowhere resembles the measured and harmonious flow that had been the ideal of former translations of Greek tragedies: "The gates of language lock the translator into silence," as Ben-jamin says in *The Task of the Translator*.[56] Hölderlin's intermittent aspirations to preserve, as much as possible, the original Greek metaphors and syntax create what resembles a linguistic battlefield: barely intelligible images—"you seem to change a red word's color"[57]—phrases broken up into their smallest components, disconnected by a profusion of punctuation, hard caesuras in al-most every verse, dislocated appositions and dependencies, conjunctions that do not conjoin but separate.

Hölderlin's method creates an effect of startling starkness and obscurity; his translations excavate, against the philological tradition of his time, a layer of violence in the Greek tragic language that conventional translations, up until today, smoothly cover.[58] His translations are intended not only to correct fellow translators, of course, but also to modify a pervasive perception of Greece, "Schiller's idealization of the harmonic universality of Greek art and . . . F. W. Schlegel's insistence on the never-to-be-rivaled perfection of the classical."[59] In his refusal to assimilate his translation to the conventions of German, Hölderlin successfully brings to the fore the otherness of Greek. Whether the effect is the same as the one ancient Greeks would have per-ceived is of no concern. In fact, his greatest achievement lies precisely in *not* recreating a hypothetical Greek experience but in revealing in the text ele-ments the Greeks themselves might have been unaware of: the layer of mad-ness and pathos that, according to Hölderlin's theory, lacks its full expression in Greek art. Thus, Hölderlin does not only allow the Greek to shimmer through the German, he also, retroactively, inserts into the Greek text the very foundation it hides. As George Steiner paraphrases, "[i]t is the 'translator's' sacred, if paradoxical and even antinomian, task to call into life . . . indwelling but hitherto unfulfilled latencies, to 'surpass' the original text in the exact spirit of the text."[60] The sacred pathos, however, that thus reveals itself is the pathos of sacred madness, a term that Hölderlin uses only in the annotations to *Antigone*. Voß, most eminent translator of his time, is unwittingly right on the mark when, in reference to Antigone's lament, he disdainfully remarks that "[o]ne thinks to hear a madwoman".[61]

Hölderlin did indeed hear the voice of madness in Greek tragedy; that he heard it is testament to the great independence of his poetic sensibility at a time when *Greece*, despite Lessing's incisive comments on the language of pathos in Sophocles' *Philoctet*, still largely stands as shorthand for reason and harmony. It is not surprising that his Antigone, "divinely mad," certainly, but mad nonetheless, was received as an affront to an intellectual community that was much more inclined to read her as the representative figure of domestic-familial virtue.

The madness of Hölderlin's Antigone does not stand alone; it corresponds to and contrasts with the madness of Hölderlin's Oedipus. While Antigone epitomizes *heiliger Wahnsinn* as "highest human manifestation," Hölderlin reads Oedipus's quest for identity as "geisteskrankes Suchen nach einem Bewußtsein," a "search for consciousness" that is "sick of mind." The respective choice of words that can be translated both as madness or mad, *Wahnsinn* and *geisteskrank*, is of great significance. Incorporating *Sinn* (sense) and *Geist* (mind, spirit), they refer to the two human faculties that tradition pitches against each other, sensation and reason, the realms conventionally divided and distributed to either poet or philosopher. As failures of sense and reason, the madness of Antigone and the madness of Oedipus complement each other; they correlate to the tension between world-perception and self-recognition that emerged from Kant's writings and defined so many of the problems German idealism set out to solve.[62] Since for Hölderlin, as I have argued above, this conflict also has a distinct historical dimension, in the last analysis Antigone and Oedipus also stand against each other like ancient and modern philosophy.[63] This ancient-modern dialectic of philosophy and madness unfolds in the difference between *Wahnsinn* and *geisteskrank*. The third section of this chapter will first suggest a summary interpretation of Hölderlin's theory of tragedy as it emerges from those passages of the annotations that refer to tragedy in general, followed by an analysis of the different stakes in *Antigone* and *Oedipus* respectively.

ANTIGONE AND OEDIPUS: MADNESS AND SIGN

In Plato's *Phaedrus* and *Ion*, madness and sanity, like human and divine order, seem to coexist without conflict. Divine interference creates an interim consciousness; the composition of poetry takes place in a caesura in which the customary order of things is temporarily altered, but neither poet nor order is changed once the interval is over. Thus, the Platonic concept of *theia mania* appears devoid of pathos, and the acquisition of mad knowledge is without tragic ramification. Nietzsche was without doubt correct to define Socrates' philosophy as anti-tragedy. Greek tragedy, as even a cursory reading of the *Oresteia*, Sophocles' Theban plays, *Medea* and the *Bacchi* demonstrates, revolves more often than not around the tragic potential of madness, or the madness implicit in tragic blindness and vision. The taming of madness, then, was a crucial factor in Socrates' anti-tragic project, and his classification of the types of *mania* in *Phaedrus* serves precisely this purpose, as far as systematization can be said to be the very antithesis of madness.

Hölderlin, even if he never explicitly says so, is, almost a century before Nietzsche, engaged in resurrecting tragic vision against the Platonic heritage.[64] In the annotations to his Sophocles translations, he seems to be the first to radically and systematically reformulate the Platonic interim action as an *interaction* of divine and human. Plato's notion of divine interference implied the utter passivity of the enthused. Such a pattern "where the revelator does everything and he who receives the revelation may not even move when he receives it, for otherwise he would have added something of himself already,"[65] is, for Hölderlin, "ein Unding" (an impossibility, literally "an un-thing"). In Hölderlin's reading, divine madness does not consist in passive reception but in a catastrophic active transgression against the gods triggered by the very madness they sent; this is the "divine betrayal" ("göttliche Untreue") that keeps the memory of the gods alive, for, Hölderlin adds in a mode of shrewd metaphysical psychology, "divine betrayal is easiest to remember."[66]

Hölderlin calls Antigone's "divine madness" ("heiliger Wahnsinn") "highest human manifestation" ("höchste menschliche Erscheinung")—i.e., not a manifestation of the divine. "The boldest moment in the course of a day or a work of art is the moment when the spirit of time and nature, the divine which seizes man, stands most wildly against the object [*Gegenstand*] he is interested in."[67] The divinely inspired Antigone turns into an "anti-theos where one, in God's sense, acts as if *against* God and recognizes the spirit of the Highest lawlessly." When divine madness passes through the human being, then, it does not leave him unchanged as a mere conduit but only constitutes him *in his own right as human*; if the anti-theos is the highest human manifestation, then it is in the sharpest difference to the gods that man comes into his own. Antigone's lawlessness in the face of God-the-law creates another kind of caesura, not an alteration of order as in Plato but the suspension of hierarchy altogether. This breakdown of order creates a realm of the unspeakable; Antigone's sacred madness is "more soul than speech," "hier mehr Seele als Sprache."

As Heidegger pronounces in his *Erläuterungen zu Hölderlin*, "[o]nly where there is language, there is world . . . . Only where world rules, there is history."[68] The languageless moment of sacred madness where theos and anti-theos stand against each other in equal measure of strength is something like an un-moment, an impossibility that interrupts world and history. This mad un-moment is the proper subject of tragedy which contains it. Tragedy is the language that surrounds the breakdown of language which draws world and history into the collapse. Sophocles' "proper language," in contrast to the tragedies of Aeschylus and Euripides, "knows to objectivize the reason of man as it wanders amongst the unthinkable."[69] That implies that tragedy can never be on the side of the tragic hero, for tragedy is language pitched against the vastness of unreason into which the tragic hero transgresses. The tragic heroes, the ones whose language and reason break down, sacrifice themselves to the reconstitution of law, language, and history that emerge anew from the collapse, "so that there be no gap in the course of the world" ("damit der Weltlauf keine Lücke hat" [624]).

For Hölderlin, Sophocles' tragedy of reason is poetry in the name of the fatherland, and thus poetry in the name of the law; its subject, conversely, is the very moment of lawlessness where the power of the father is challenged as at no other time. It is crucial not to confuse the two positions: the lawlessness of world-historical mythos, and the laws of representation, the madness of history and the sobriety of poetry. Tragedy is "calculable law," calculable not only for aesthetic but also "for higher reasons," ("aus höheren Gründen"), reasons critical to the relationship between "living meaning" ("lebendiger Sinn") and "specific content" on the one hand and "general calculation" ("allgemeiner Kalkul" [618]) on the other hand. While the fact of such a relation is "infinite," the specific, determined form it takes is not:

> Next, one has to see how the content is distinct from the lawful calculation, through what mode of operation and how, in the infinite yet continuously determined relation, the specific content relates to the general calculation; how the course and that which is to be determined, the living meaning which cannot be calculated, are put in relation with the calculable law.[70]

The poet's task is to determine the relation between general law and particular meaning in every specific case. Hölderlin here claims for poetry the responsibility that is generally allocated to philosophy as one of its privileged operations: the mediation between the general and the particular. Philosophy cannot achieve this mediation, since

> philosophy always only treats one faculty of the soul, so that the representation of this One faculty makes a whole, and the mere linkage of the members of this One faculty is called logic, whereas poetry treats the different faculties of man, so that the representation of these different faculties makes a whole, and the association of the more independent parts of the different faculties can be called the rhythm, in the higher sense, or the calculable law.[71]

The different faculties—"Vorstellung und Empfindung und Räsonnement"—seem to refer to Kant's judgment, understanding, and reason

(*Urteilskraft, Verstand, Vernunft*), but Hölderlin's departure from the Kantian terms is curious. Possibly another, older distinction is at play as well, i.e., Plato's differentiation between *logistikon, thumos,* and *epithumia.* If so, then Hölderlin turns Plato's aesthetic theory against itself: Platonic philosophy, at least in its *Republic* formulation,[72] cannot represent the law of human life precisely because it focuses on reason at the cost of affect and desire. Remember that the Socrates of the *Republic* criticizes tragedy because it treats, and thus caters to, the affects and desires rather than sovereign reason. In privileging the *logistikon,* philosophy misses the historical moment where *logos* breaks down and the other faculties of the soul gain force. Philosophical logic needs the correction of "poetic logic" which is a logic "of successions."[73]

The logic of successions is not Heraclitean flow, but neither is it static: it creates a balance centered around a caesura. As one might not be aware of the rhythm of a drumbeat until it syncopates or falters, order can be understood only through its suspension. The rhythm of the laws of succession can be perceived only from the moment of the caesura that interrupts it, when silence becomes audible.[74] Hölderlin and his contemporaries knew very well that order is always threatened by its dissolution.[75] At the same time, dissolution is the very foundation of order, as long as order is in need of periodic rejuvenation—as it always is. As a "calculable law," tragedy will always be on the side of order—but not necessarily on the side of the old order. Its heroes are the exemplary sacrifices to history as the becoming of order in its decline, the *Werden im Vergehen.*

Antigone's act is situated in the very moment of suspension, the historical turning point characterized by the absence of law. In Plato, divine madness seemed to be imbedded in and confined by history or rather narrative in general; for Hölderlin, the moment of sacred madness is the moment of *historicity* which, making the course of history possible, must first interrupt it—not as a moment in time, but a moment of timelessness. In the "equal measure" tragedy creates, hierarchic order is suspended, *à la pointe acérée,* which is, to repeat, not a moment in history but its standstill (if any such thing can be thought) from which historical time arises—timelessness awaiting its unfolding. The center of sequential order is empty, as the center of reason is madness.

Analogously, tragedy's first main function is the suspension of representation, "for tragic transport is essentially empty" (618). The poetic *mechanä* resembles the skill of an architect who balances an arch with the invisible but essential force of gravity, which pulls at every stone he uses.[76]

Hölderlin's theory of sacred madness marks a middle ground between possession and self-possession. Hölderlin locates Antigone's "highest feature" ("der höchste Zug") neither in her action nor in the way she justifies it, but in her final lament, which he reads as mockery:

> Nigh well Antigone's highest feature. The sublime mockery, to the extent
> that sacred madness is the highest human manifestation and here more soul

than language, surpasses all her other statements . . . . It is a great resource of the secretly working soul that at the point of highest consciousness it eludes consciousness and that, before the present god actually seizes it, the soul encounters him with bold, frequently even blasphemous word and thus maintains the sacred living possibility of spirit [Geist].[77]

Sacred madness, then, marks the turning point where "highest consciousness" coincides with the end of consciousness. In the moment where possession begins—"before the present God grasps" the soul—the soul reaches the pinnacle of its power in an act of self-sacrifice, a sacrifice to the supra-individual instance of Geist. This act of sacrifice is a conscious one, but consciousness cannot understand it: it is the end of self-reflection, and therefore without language. This is why the sublimity of Hölderlin's Antigone is not in her words but in her soul (hier mehr Seele als Sprache) and why her madness presents itself in the form of mockery, that is to say in a discursive mode of self-possession. In Hölderlin's reading, madness and its discourse are severed more radically than ever before—in its mockery of the law in the name of the law, the speech of sacred madness is fundamentally ironic. This act of mad irony preserves the "sacred living possibility" of Geist on the turning point of history. The continuation of Geist, then, depends on a theatrical performance that is still intimately connected to its roots in sacrifice; now, it is a theater of a self-sacrifice that is both conscious and unconscious.

Hölderlin's essay Das Werden im Vergehen ("Becoming in Perishing") identifies this turning point as a state between Being and Non-Being: "During the state between Being and Non-Being, however, the possible everywhere becomes real, and the real becomes ideal, and in free artistic mimesis, this is a terrifying but divine dream."[78] In the barely thinkable un-moment where the divine becomes present, graspable, material ("ehe sie der gegenwärtige Gott ergreift"), the sacred and the terrible are one, and as the real becomes ideal, artistic mimesis turns into a dream—an appropriate term for the imitation of the unreal. Mimesis proper—the imitation of the real—ceases. Just as the historical caesura must truly be thought of as non-time, the caesura of tragedy marks tragedy's discontinuation. As Hölderlin says in the "Annotations to Oedipus," in a series of remarks pertaining to tragedy as such, the succession of ideas (Vorstellungen) in tragedy tends to the point where "Vorstellung itself" emerges. In so far as Vorstellung is precisely that which is not yet Darstellung, this is the presentation of the unrepresentable:

> In the rhythmic succession of representation wherein transport presents itself, there becomes necessary what in poetic meter is called caesura, the pure word, the counter-rhythmic rupture; namely, in order to meet the onrushing change of representations [Vorstellungen] at its highest point in such a manner that very soon there does not appear the change of representation but representation itself.[79]

Vorstellung, apart from signifying 'representation', 'idea', 'concept', and 'imagination', is also performance. The end of the quotation, then, can also be translated as following: "so that there does not appear the change of representations anymore but rather performance itself." For tragic transport itself "is empty and the most unbound" ("[d]er tragische *Transport* ist nämlich eigentlich leer, und der ungebundenste" [618]). The "pure word" is the tense silence of the caesura where only theatricality itself remains present, as its own metaphor (metaphor, in this case, literally understood as transport).

While Antigone's madness preserves the *possibility* of Geist, not Geist itself, the tragic caesura preserves only the *conditions* of time and space: "Within the utmost limit of suffering, nothing remains but the conditions of time or of space."[80] In other words, tragic anti-time and tragic madness constitute the condition for the perpetuation of Geist and a definable historical time and place during the suspension of all three—so that there will be no gap in the course of the world.

This concept of *Aufhebung* is decidedly a break with Hegel, for whom everything significant happens *within* historical time, where Geist is always at work, and where the "blank pages" of history are the happy days, not the ones of deepest suffering. For Hölderlin, time itself betrays the human mind when it "turns around categorically and beginning and end do not rhyme with each other anymore."[81] Hölderlin's choice of a poetological metaphor here (*reimen*) emphasizes again that the summit of tragedy ultimately escapes its language, or, more precisely, that tragic language moves towards the silence of the unspeakable which it presents and contains.

The encounter between God and man draws its unspeakable power from its incestuous quality, for Hölderlin's tragic god is always the Father-God Zeus, and the "representation of the tragic" centers on the "monstrous coupling of god and man," an "unlimited becoming-one" that "purifies itself" in an equally "unlimited differentiation."[82] Thus, the second main task of tragedy is to represent the establishment of the eternal *difference* between god and man, a difference that is so all-pervasive that it tends to be forgotten and needs violent reaffirmation.

Language is the medium and the token of this difference. In Hölderlin's translations and annotations, the sensualization of cognitive processes is striking, and it is especially the status of the word and the sign that sensual perception is linked to. Steiner remarks that "the late Hölderlin has a hauntingly sensory concept of the spell of abstract and analytic thought," and that he is "gambling, as it were, on the archaic resources of a more immediate, bodily condition of human utterance."[83] The body is throughout associated with the word, the sign. In Hölderlin's reading of Sophocles, Antigone's crime gains its meaning from this substitution, for her self-given task is the burial of her brother's dead body, the corpse that marks the desert. Antigone's religious deed emerges as a desire to erase the sign, to recreate the desert as unmarked space, to become one with the Geist of "the eternally live unwritten wilderness and the world of the dead" ("Geist der ewig lebenden ungeschriebenen Wildnis und der Totenwelt" [671]). Whereas Creon wants to establish the body-sign as the mark of differentiation (between friend and enemy, political loyalty and treason, good and evil), Antigone longs for the purity of the desert, in the image of which she finally recognizes her fate.

> I hear that desertlike became
> the Phrygian one, full of life.
> [. . .]
> Like that one, a ghost takes me to bed.[84]

Antigone recasts her impending wedding night, substituting a ghost (Geist; the Greek original has daimon) for Haimon's body. Her obsession with death, her erotic desire for [the] Geist, and her project to erase the mark of the corpse are manifestations of the same metaphysical drive. Thus, she clashes with the Father-God Zeus, of whom Hölderlin says that "his character is, against the eternal tendency, to turn the strife from this world into the other one into a strife from the other world into this one." "This one" is the world of language, body, and difference, "the other one" the divine "unwritten" realm.[85] Zeus's role, according to Hölderlin, is to reverse this tendency, to reestablish the sign as the signature of eternal difference, "to be present in the form of death." As Hölderlin adds immediately, the role of Zeus is related to the question of representation: "For we have to represent the myth in a more ascertainable way."[86] Zeus, "father of time" and God of law, presides over the representation of myth in tragedy; tragic representation, as the materialization of the divine, constitutes the body of the incorporeal sacred. Thus, tragedy is the opposite of philosophy's metaphysical drive towards metalingual knowledge, for the transcendence of signs is also the ancient desire of (Platonic) philosophy where the sign, especially in its most privileged form, i.e., language, contaminates the knowledge of pure being. Where philosophy moves towards the incorporeal undiscursive realm, tragedy creates "the solid letter" of the closing lines of Patmos.[87] In the physicalization of the sacred, the divine betrayal of man appears, a betrayal because it breaks through the border between secular materiality and sacred immateriality that defines the life of man and polis.

Oedipus, too, is a sacrifice; he, too, transgresses against the gods on the gods' behalf so that they may be remembered and difference be established once again. His transgression, however, is of quite a different nature than Antigone's act. As a tale of patricide and incest, the mythos of Oedipus exemplifies lawlessness per se. Hölderlin, however, in a move startling especially to post-Freudian readers, but not necessarily "prudish silence,"[88] pays little attention to Oedipus's more scandalous offenses. His interpretation is, in fact, most peculiar. In his annotations to Oedipus, Hölderlin comments:

> The intelligibility of the whole rests primarily on one's [ability to] focus on the scene where Oedipus interprets the oracle too infinitely, and is tempted

into nefas.[89] Namely, the oracle ... could mean: maintain, in general, a severe and pure court of law [*Gericht*], maintain good civil (*bürgerliche*) order. Oedipus, however, right afterwards speaks in priestly fashion.[90]

This passage resurrects several crucial terms of the introduction to the annotations: "infinitely," "general order," "*Bürgerlichkeit*." The socio-aesthetic theory *in nuce* that prefaces Hölderlin's interpretation is not merely a method which he applies to *Oedipus*; in his reading, the mythos reenacts the very tension of particular meaning and general law that the tragic poet must resolve. Oedipus is guilty of overinterpretation, of a reading that rashly moves out of the political into the metaphysical realm. Oedipus misdetermines the relation between particular meaning, i.e., the oracle, and general law, i.e., good civic order. Becoming "priestly" too readily, he arrogates the voice of the gods, already forcing the catastrophic encounter between the divine and the worldly that is the content of tragedy. In his quick dismissal of *Bürgerlichkeit* and law, he emerges, in the context of Hölderlin's text, as the anti-poet.

This is important, because it determines the relationship of poet and tragic madness. As record and performance of the gods' betrayal, tragedy perhaps is divine, but certainly not mad. For all the intimacy (*Innigkeit*) between tragic poet and tragic hero, they do not, indeed must not, converge. Hölderlin insists on both the necessary intimacy and the necessity to conceal it in "Der Grund zum Empedokles":

> Thus, the divine which the poet senses and experiences in his world is also expressed in the tragic-dramatic poem; for him the tragic-dramatic poem, too, is an image of life which is and was present to him in his life; yet to the extent that this image of intimacy [*Innigkeit*] always denies and must deny its ultimate foundation, to the extent that everywhere it approaches increasingly the symbol, the more infinite, unspeakable, the closer that intimacy is to the *nefas*, the stricter and colder the image separates man and his felt element in order to contain the sensation [*Empfindung*] within its boundaries, the less the image can express the sensation in an immediate manner; it must deny it with regard to form as well as to subject matter; the subject matter must be a more daring and foreign parable and example of it; the form must bear more the character of the opposition and separation.[91]

Lacoue-Labarthe reads this passage as a "paradoxe sur le dramaturge" ("The Caesura of the Speculative," 78), but it is perhaps rather a dialectic, recasting for the tragic poet the dialectic between national character and aesthetic form that Hölderlin explains in the Böhlendorff letter. The intimacy Hölderlin speaks of is based on experience and observation, not on identity, an experience, moreover, that must be further alienated, if this Brechtian term be allowed, so that the distance between the poet and his material may be maintained. In the fragmentary hymn "Wie wenn am Feiertage," Hölderlin again insists on the necessity of distance and the dangerous mistake of

collapsing it. Readers of Hölderlin have been prone to perform this false integration, as, most prominently, Heidegger's reading of the passage in question
shows. The following pages offer a short excursion into Heidegger's reading,
since it exemplifies the implications which the relationship between poet and
tragic hero has for the theory of poetic madness.[92]

Heidegger equates Hölderlin and Oedipus at the end of his essay
"Hölderlin und das Wesen der Dichtung" ("Hölderlin and the Essence of
Poetry"): "To *Hölderlin* himself applies the word which he said . . . of Oedipus:
'King Oedipus has one eye too many, perhaps'."[93] Earlier on, Heidegger asserts forcefully but also rather vaguely that "the poet's own fate says everything."[94] I have said above that any theory that makes sense of Hölderlin's
madness is seductive, and Heidegger's suggestions in this regard are perhaps
the most seductive ones, precisely because they remain mere suggestions
within a larger philosophical agenda and do not pretend to produce a certifiable reading according to the questionable standards of *Literaturwissenschaft*,
a business for which Heidegger had, at least on the surface, nothing but disdain.[95] Moreover, there is unquestionably some evidence in Hölderlin's
work—and life—that lends itself to Heidegger's interpretation. It might well
be outweighed, however, by the numerous passages Heidegger ignores, passages that testify to the contrary and often occur in the immediate vicinity of
the ones he bases his analysis on. Thus, Heidegger quotes the following lines
from a stanza from the fragmentary poem "Wie wenn am Feiertage":

> But it is our part, under God's thunderstorms
> You poets! to stand with our heads bared,
> To grasp the father's lightning, him himself, with our own hand,
> And to bestow the heavenly gift
> Wrapped in song to the people.
> (Doch uns gebührt es, unter Gottes Gewittern,
> Ihr Dichter! mit enblößtem Haupte zu stehen,
> Des Vaters Strahl, ihn selbst, mit eigner Hand
> Zu fassen und dem Volk ins Lied
> Gehüllt die himmlische Gabe zu reichen.)

Evocatively, Heidegger continues: "And a year later, after Hölderlin has
come back into the mother's house as someone struck by madness . . . "[96] He
does not quote the stanza's remaining lines, which continue:

> For if we are only of pure heart,
> like children, if our hands are without guilt,
> [then] the father's lightning, the pure one, does not burn it,
> And deeply shaken, compassionate with the suffering of the
>   stronger ones,
> the heart, in the high-rushing storms
> of the god, when he nears, remains firm nonetheless.

(Denn sind wir nur reinen Herzens,
Wie Kinder, wir, sind schuldlos unsere Hände,
Des Vaters Strahl, der reine, versengt es nicht
Und tieferschüttert, die Leiden des Stärkeren
Mitleidend, bleibt in den hochherstürzenden Stürmen
Des Gottes, wenn er nahet, das Herz doch fest.)

Clearly, the speech is of the tragic poet whom Hölderlin explicitly distinguishes from "the stronger ones," i.e., the tragic heroes. The poet's heart will remain firm, unless . . . This sentence must end with an ellipsis just as Hölderlin's unfinished poem ends elliptically, with fragmentary evocations of an unnamed danger:

But woe is me! if from

Woe is me!

And even if I say,

I had come to see the heavenly ones,
They themselves, they throw me deep amongst the living,
the false priest, into the dark, so that I
will sing the warning song to the learned ones,
There

(Doch weh mir! wenn von

Weh mir!

Und sag ich gleich,

Ich sei genaht, die Himmlischen zu schauen,
Sie selbst, sie werfen mich tief unter die Lebenden,
Den falschen Priester, ins Dunkel, daß ich
Das warnende Lied den Gelehrigen singe,
Dort)

This passage does not, as Heidegger's reading would suggest, speak of "the essence of poetry," but of poetry gone wrong, of the poet who turns, like Oedipus, into a "false priest." As so many of the passages treated so far suggest, the main limitation of poetry is that it must impose limits, on others as well as on itself. Poetry can sing of the ones who approach the gods, but it cannot approach them itself. Hölderlin's image of the poetic process is that of the hand that grasps the lightning; the metaphor designates poetry as a work of the hand, *Handwerk*, i.e., craft, *technê*. Poetry is an act of containment, not of fusion. Lightning caught by the hand and wrapped in song is not lightning anymore. The poet's task, then, even though it cannot be performed without divine interference, attends to the solidification of the swiftness of time for which the image of the lightning stands. These verses echo beautifully with the passages from Hölderlin's theoretical texts quoted above: the poet, if he does not want to turn into a false priest, must not leave himself or abandon earthly labor, for while he delivers the "terrible and divine dream" of tragedy, it is a dream "*within* free artistic mimesis" ("*in* der freien Kunstnachahmung ein furchtbarer aber göttlicher Traum" [emphasis added]). *Freie Kunstnachahmung* is the realm of technique, consciousness, and freedom, and must thus contain the terrible and sacred moment of Zeus's lightning within it.

Hölderlin's Oedipus is one of the "stronger ones," not only alien to the poet, but, as I have said, an anti-poet. He is also, or rather *as* such, a figure of philosophy. Lacoue-Labarthe has commented on the emergence of Oedipus as the figure of the philosopher in the late eighteenth century:

> Oedipe y aurait été pensé comme le héros philosophique par excellence, celui en qui ou dans le destin duquel, symboliquement, vient se rassembler tout le sens intime de l'aventure spirituelle de l'Occident; il y aurait été reconnu comme le héros initial ou le héros tutélaire et exemplaire de notre histoire et de notre civilisation.[97]

I would like to suggest a modification: Hölderlin's Oedipus, philosopher-figure that he undoubtedly is, is not necessarily philosophy's *hero*, not a figure of its "achèvement," but also, on the contrary, the figure of its hubris and its failure. The image of Oedipus the blind King looms in the background of Hölderlin's fragment about the "wise ones" who differentiate "with their mind alone." Oedipus prides himself on his intellect, and, mocking the seer Teiresias, boasts that he solved the riddle of the sphinx "with the mind, not taught by birds" (579). Oedipus, in Hölderlin's reading of his *nefas*, does not differentiate sufficiently: " . . . the saying of the oracle and the story of Laius's death, not necessarily related to it, are brought together."[98] In not distinguishing between general law and particular crime, Oedipus initiates his downfall: "In the sentence immediately following, Oedipus's spirit states in angry presentiment, knowing all, the *nefas* itself by resentfully interpreting the general injunction in particular terms and applying it it to a murderer of Laius, and then also taking the sin as infinite."[99] The particular will take its revenge, the revenge that Hölderlin's ellipsis at the end of the fragment hides, in the form of madness, "because knowledge, once it has torn through its barrier—as if intoxicated in its wonderful harmonious form, which can remain, after all, for a while—incites itself to know more than it can bear or contain."[100] Thus, "in the end there primarily dominates in the speeches the insane [*geisteskrank*] questioning for a consciousness."[101]

"Consciousness," here, must be read as self-consciousness, not only but also because the questions Hölderlin cites are all directed towards Oedipus's identity. In the context of Fichte's determination of subjectivity as well as of Hegel's and Schelling's writings to which Hölderlin's thought on tragedy belongs,[102] tragedy is largely read as the manifestation of the will to be a subject. For Hölderlin, the question of subjectivity asserts itself most significantly in the moment when divine interference most threatens subjective self-determination (the "sich-fassen-können" [674] of the annotations to Antigone).

In the beginning, Oedipus's questions are quite specific, and they are all questions for the father. The following passage is the one that Hölderlin himself emphasizes in his annotations:

Oedipus: "What do you say? Did Polybus not plant me?"
Messenger: "Almost something like one of us."
Oedipus: "How so? a father who is similar to no one?"
Messenger: "A father it is. Not Polybus; not I."
Oedipus: "How then that that one calls me the child?"[103]

The desire to know one's parents, of course, is not, in itself, hubristic. If Oedipus's quest is an "insane" one, speaking, literally, of a sickness of mind or spirit (*geisteskrank*), then it can hardly be the quite reasonable search for the biological father. It is only "in the end" that Oedipus's desire to know his origin sickens his spirit. The turning point, I suggest, is the moment when Oedipus's questions for a father are inverted into an assertion of his fatherlessness:

But I will not be dishonored,
Taking myself to be a son of fortune,
The well-endowed one, for she is my mother. And great and small
The co-born moons encompassed me.
And thus conceived, I will not perish
Without exploring fully what I am.[104]

At the same time that Oedipus avows his willingness to "explore fully what he is," he also claims to know already. The quest for the particular turns into a declaration of universality. It is in presenting himself as the son of fortune, as cosmic progeny, that Oedipus becomes the "wise one" of the fragment, someone who erroneously believes that he has distinguished sufficiently between this world and the other one. Thus, he opens himself to the revenge of his nature and "the lowest grade of reality." At the moment when he thinks to transcend the materiality of his descent, the pure biological fact of his genealogy catches up with him and "lets his mind [*Geist*] be defeated by the coarse and simplistic language of his servants" (623).

Oedipus's insane quest constitutes the heart of tragedy, for when he declares himself the son of a goddess and the brother of the moons, he enacts the tragic fusion of human and divine realm in his body: " . . . the monstrous [event in which] the god and man mate and the power of nature and that which is innermost to man boundlessly become one in wrath comprehends itself when the limitless becoming-one purifies itself through limitless differentiation."[105] Oedipus, who thought to transcend the body by the force of mind alone, is thrown back into the coreality of his sexual and murderous encounters: "O Light! I see you for the last time now!/They say I was conceived by what [sic] I/should not have been, and cohabitated where I should not have, and there/where I was not allowed to, I have killed."

Like *Antigone*, *Oedipus* centers around the status of the word; but where Antigone attempts to supercede the sign, Oedipus trusts the sign—or his ability to read it—completely: "for all words I espy" ("denn alle Worte späh ich"). Through Hölderlin's syntax, Oedipus's interpretative obsession, unquestionably already noticeable in the Greek, is emphasized throughout. Oedipus is a maniacal reader of signs, and all signs refer back to him— in Oedipus's speech, the words "ich," "selber," "mir," and "mich" are almost always placed at privileged places in the verse, the beginning or the end (an ingenious device, seeing that the answer to Oedipus's question will, indeed, be: "I").

It is this obsession with "Worte spähen" that constitutes Oedipus's insanity: all his questions will be thrown back at him if "I" is the only possible answer, and the image he conjures will blind him. In Hölderlin's eccentric reading, Oedipus's *nefas* is *not* related to the murder of Laius but to an interpretative fallacy: Hölderlin claims that the words of the oracle may not call for the atonement of Laius's death but merely for *bürgerliche* order. Oedipus's mistake consists in an overreading, he reacts in "too priestly a fashion," he reads "too infinitely" and "too particularly" at the same time, and his excessive speculative desire for the infinite leads him more surely into particularity and alienation. This, of course, is the law of tragic consciousness: the infinite uniting of God and human has to be purified in infinite differentiation (*Scheiden*). There is no *Aufhebung*.

Purification, of course, is always also related to the Aristotelian catharsis; Lacoue-Labarthe, in fact, argues that Hölderlin's Sophocles annotations perform a "catharsis of the speculative"—a catharsis, I would like to suggest, that works through a spectacle of madness at/as the far end of a process of self-recognition. "King Oedipus has one eye too many, perhaps"—an excess of insight, surpassing man's limitation in self-reflection, turns into blindness. Too much light, Hölderlin has always stressed, is a catastrophe[106] because it makes differentiation impossible and would thus create the "gap in the course of the world," since history and its representation are possible only in the alteration of light and shadow, of marking and unmarking: Antigone, who erases the sign of the corpse and thus risks creating the absence of all meaning in a desert of pure light, must substitute her own body as the mark of historicity.

Oedipus's madness can be read as the sacrifice he himself asked for ("through which purification . . . "), a sacrifice even in the Bataillean sense, an expenditure reconstituting community. The absence of history constituting the possibility of history corresponds to "*that which is called the caesura in metrics, the pure word*" ("*das, was man im Silbenmaße Zäsur heißt, das reine Wort*" [619]). The pure word is a silence, a non-word, but it centers the order of metrics. Metrics, *Silbenmaß*, is measure, *Maß*, and as such stands for order, reason, language, and history.[107] All of these things are sustained only by their interruption which is the very condition of their appearance.

Whereas Antigone is "soul rather than language," Oedipus is *Geist*, but *Geist* diseased by language, by signs. It is an illness of thought, of deliberating and differentiating reason, and thus, ultimately, a sickness of philosophy. Hölderlin's Fichte critique (1795), his warning to "the wise ones" (1799), and his reading of Oedipus (1802) speak of a continuous and growing suspicion of philosophy's claims to absolute knowledge. The reservations expressed in the Fichte letter and "The Wise Ones" inscribe themselves into Hölderlin's translations. Steiner observes that "[w]hat is evident in Hölderlin's exegesis and in his text is the inference of a violent imbalance or even rupture of harmonic relations between spirit and matter, between the transcendent freedom of the totally spiritual, a concept highly suggestive of Hegel and of Schelling, and the adversative 'object' . . . ."

A letter to Sinclair, dated December 24, 1798, expresses Hölderlin's involvement with the tragedy of thought:

> The passing and alternating quality of human thoughts and systems has struck me as almost more tragic than the fates which man usually alone calls the real ones, and I think it is natural, for when man, in his most proper, freest activity, in independent thought itself, depends on foreign influence, and if he even there remains modified by circumstance and climate, as it shows itself uncontradictably, where then does he still have mastery? It is good, too, and even the first condition of all life and all organization, that no power is monarchic in heaven and on earth. Absolute monarchy everywhere cancels itself [*hebt sich selbst auf*], for it is objectless; in the strict sense, there has never been one, either. Everything is meshed and suffers as well as it acts, and thus also the pure thought of man, and taken in all sharpness, an a priori philosophy, fully independent from all experience . . . is as impossible [*ein Unding*] as a positive revelation where the revelator does everything and he who receives the revelation may not even move when he receives it, for otherwise he would have added something of himself already.[108]

Here, Hölderlin's critique of a philosophy of self-consciousness is explicitly linked to tragedy and the question of divine inspiration, and Kantian and post-Kantian philosophy are alluded to in the catchword *a priori*. Certainly, this letter, in its sweeping generality, does not and cannot mean to present an assessment of Kantian philosophy and German idealism. Idealism, however, is certainly its frame of reference, a frame that Hölderlin carries into his Sophocles annotations. Oedipus, as Lacoue-Labarthe demonstrates, has become the "figure" of the philosophy of subjectivity as self-consciousness. As such, Oedipus can become philosophy's hero in Schelling's *Letters* and, to a certain extent, in Hegel's philosophy of history. For Hölderlin, however, Oedipus appears as philosophy's anti-hero when "the quest for a consciousness" starts to disease [his] *Geist*.

If, as Hölderlin suggests, ancient philosophy attempted to transcend the world and modern philosophy to transcend consciousness, then Antigone and Oedipus indeed stand to each other like Greece and modern Germany, and both appear in their failure. Oedipus's quest for consciousness echoes with Antigone's quest for unconsciousness, her rebellion against the sign with his unqualified trust in the sign.[109] Both are thrown back unto the body that cannot and must not be transcended, and both lose what they sought to gain: an absolute identity without difference, be it in Antigone's attempted fusion with the "eternally live unwritten wilderness," the undiscursive realm of the metaphysical desert, or in Oedipus's quest to inscribe himself into the cosmic realm.

Antigone's sacrifice, however, forfeiting self-consciousness to the *possibility* of *Geist*, preserves the possibility of historical conciliation, and Greece, to Hölderlin, is the *promise* of reconciliation, the founding of its condition, not its realization. Antigone, thus, remains the most Greek of tragedies, while the mythos of Oedipus emerges as the most modern one, since the philosophy that falters and fails in *Oedipus* is the philosophy that has only fully come into its own in modernity, in the wake of the Kantian crisis of metaphysics. Modernity is characterized by the sickness of *Geist* brought on by the absence of the divine as that which constitutes humanity in its difference, and thus in its identity.

Hölderlin's Sophoclean tragedy is always a tragedy of philosophy, indicting the longing for a transcendence of either world or self that is ultimately a mere abandonment. Losing its foundation in the vastness of the empty space that the mind thus creates for itself, it hurtles upwards into the abyss above.

CHAPTER THREE

NIETZSCHE: THE
MARKETPLACES OF MADNESS

INTRODUCTION: NIETZSCHE'S MADNESS
AND THE FEAR OF CONTAMINATION

Well then, I continued, do you realize the sort of danger to which you are
going to expose your soul?

—Plato, *Protagoras*

Hölderlin may have been Germany's last great poet of the divine, that is to
say, the last great poet for whom the presence or absence of the gods was not
a matter of cultural and historical idiom but a question of the utmost urgency, one that pervaded his poetics and his aesthetics, his mode of living in
the world as a poet. Far from being mere commentary on the last great quarrel between the ancients and the moderns, his work was this quarrel's site,
the realm in which the divine withdrew, reappeared in a flare, and was lost.
Nietzsche, in his turn, was surely not the first to discover, mourn and celebrate this loss, but he was the one who not only understood but found a new
articulation of its gravity.

For Nietzsche, the loss of the divine—or the death of God, to use the
more familiar formula—entails the reformulation of human history and possible human futures in their entirety, a process of reconfiguration that—again,
according to Nietzsche, but he is very persuasive in this regard—may have
barely begun. The revaluation of all values he projects concerns first of all the
revaluation of human reason—its history or geneaology, its function and its
limits, its manifestation in the enigmatic "truth drive," its dialectics, and,
finally, its negation, i.e., madness.

Nietzsche, as we will see, makes some extraordinary claims on behalf of
madness, but he is also deeply skeptical of any praise of folly. Nietzsche's

madmen raise their heads throughout his oeuvre, but their faces are all different, and they duck again quickly. If there is a red thread in his thoughts on madness and the mad, it is the *moral* relevance of madness, or rather the relevance of madness in various systems of morality. Before we get to Nietzsche's madmen, however, we have to linger for a while with Nietzsche the madman. In some respect, it is deeply ironic that Nietzsche, champion of radical reason, has so often and so quickly been seen to embody the fate of mad philosophy. After all, as I will argue, Nietzsche's writings mean nothing less than the *end* of madness as a category of epistemic privilege—the death of God is, by necessity, the death of divine madness. His madness, then, can no longer be the madness *of* inspiration—if anything, his madness would have to *be* this inspiration (provided that he was, indeed, mad while he still wrote). Of course, as with Hölderlin, the biographical speculation works two ways—if Nietzsche didn't think the way he did because he was mad, perhaps he went mad—and silent—because of the thoughts he thought. Can philosophy drive you crazy? Nietzsche's answer is ambivalent, as we shall see.

To go mad by poetry would not be the same as to go mad by philosophy; the story of the mad poet and that of the mad philosopher, for all they have in common, are different stories, and Nietzsche's madness opens some questions utterly different from those that Hölderlin's madness poses. Certainly, like Hölderlin, Nietzsche is nothing less than a legend of insanity, and even though their afflictions were quite different in appearance, their fates have raised similar questions about the nature of radical thinking and have given rise to similar speculations about, to put it simply, the dangers inherent in too much reflection. Like Hölderlin, Nietzsche's mad persona encompasses work and writer alike; as the name of Hölderlin stands not merely for the mad poet but for mad poetry itself, so the name of Nietzsche conjures not merely the vision of a mad philosopher but one of mad philosophy.

Yet there remains an important disparity in the ways Hölderlin's and Nietzsche's descent into silence have influenced and shaped critical encounters with their work, a disparity that touches directly on the difference between poetry and philosophy. Even though this distinction has become notoriously difficult to delineate, in many regards we are still operating under the Socratic legacy that I have outlined in the first chapter of this book: to Platonic poetic madness, solitude is central, but both the mode and the telos of philosophical madness are communication and dissemination.

Mad philosophy, and mad poetry therefore, initiate different critical responses. Since criticism, as the first chapter suggests, is complicitous with philosophy rather than with poetry, it is open to contamination by mad philosophy in a way in which it cannot be threatened by mad poetry. The critic of poetry operates in a genre entirely different from his subject, in marked contrast to the philosophical commentator. Poetry does not aim to convince or convert; philosophy, traditionally, does. Writing about poetry does not recreate poetry; writing about philosophy often does, or at least makes the attempt. In consequence, the critic of poetry is protected by the dissimilarity between the genre of his own writing and the genre of his subject—the critic of philosophy is not, or not to the same degree. Hölderlin's madness, ultimately, begins and ends with him, even if it were intimately connected to his poetry. If Nietzsche's madness, in contrast, were engendered by his ideas, an abyss might silently open every time we try to paraphrase, follow, or think his thoughts.

In Plato's *Protagoras*, Socrates points out that we can examine food without eating it, but we cannot examine an idea without thinking it:

> When you buy food and drink, you can carry it away from the shop or warehouse in a receptacle, and before you receive it into your body by eating or drinking you can store it away at home and take the advice of an expert . . . . But knowledge cannot be taken away in a parcel. When you have paid for it, you must receive it straight into the soul.[1]

In this regard, Nietzsche's madness appears to be a more urgent issue than Hölderlin's madness. Hölderlin's influence on modernity, while monumental in some areas, is closely circumscribed in the end; Nietzsche's work may not even have begun to exert its full force. If, as the critic Christoph Türcke has recently argued, Nietzsche's madness is the "logical consequence of his passion of reason [*Vernunftpassion*],"[2] then his works could act, as it were, like a hallucinogenic drug, and we would do well to ingest them with the utmost caution. The study of Nietzsche, in this case, would put each and every reader at the risk of contamination.

At the same time, critical conjectures along these lines tend to have a somewhat self-celebratory ring to them. If Nietzsche's work posed a very real threat of driving us mad, philosophical commentary would be quite a thrilling project. Hermeneutics would turn into an enterprise in which the reader can put her very self at stake. Nietzsche interpretation would become an epic struggle starring the critic, that usually so singularly unheroic figure, as the hero in the quest for, as we will see, nothing less than the very survival of civilization. And once again, criticism becomes victory—the mad Nietzsche's reader emerges as someone who surpasses Nietzsche's achievements, thinking the thoughts he thought, but bearing what he could not bear. In simultaneously surrendering to and resisting Nietzsche's thought, the critic rises to a position above and beyond the text from which he derives his livelihood, an accomplishment all the more meaningful the more vividly its threat is painted. If, on the contrary, Nietzsche simply suffered from syphilis, our only achievement in avoiding a similar fate will have been a certain prudence in sexual, medical, or hygienic matters, and who could be proud of *that*?

Despite those caveats, it seems to be a concern of some gravity whether Nietzsche's work stands in an intimate relation to his mental breakdown in 1888–1889, even though it should be clear that such relation can hardly ever be argued decisively, much less proven beyond reasonable doubt. Surely, biographical issues are always and irreducibly different from the issues of the text. And yet, Nietzsche himself seems to endorse inquiries along biographical lines when he notes, in *Beyond Good and Evil*, that there is nothing impersonal in philosophy.[3] In the *Gay Science*, he suggests that "perhaps the sick thinkers are the majority in the history of philosophy—: what will become of the thought itself that is brought forth under the *pressure* of illness?" His conjectures on the mental well-being of Socrates and the Christians are infamous. Looking back on his work, Nietzsche spoke of it as an instrument of doom (*Verhängnis*)[4]—why not wonder, then, whether his thought did not bring his own doom upon him, and whether doom, in the form of madness, may not strike anyone who approaches Nietzsche without the necessary intellectual chain mail?

Speculation along these lines, then, appears to be a legitimate intellectual enterprise, certainly legitimated by Nietzsche himself, who often warned of the dangers of thinking, especially his own thinking. This granted, however, we may ask from these speculations, biographical or otherwise, that they be plausible where they cannot be conclusive, that the liberty they take with their subject be not an excuse for losing sight of it altogether. In other words, we ought to be persuaded that Nietzsche's thoughts really are mad in a significant and profound sense—and not merely mildly pathological in the sometimes grandiose mode of their delivery. Measured against the tradition of classical reason, Nietzsche is, of course, deeply deviant—certainly in style, and perhaps in substance. He signs himself as "the Antichrist," he speaks in the voices of the hermit on the mountains or the fool in the marketplace, he polemicizes, lyricizes, fragments, and rhapsodizes. Nietzsche is a figure too heterogeneous to fit into an intellectual landscape divided into little workshops of mental labor where scientist, sociologist, prophet, critic, priest, composer, poet, and philosopher coexist in mostly peaceful isolation. With him, philosophy expands to lose its established identity, and his polyvalent persona encompasses a great many of the traditional and contemporary mad roles: the raving preacher, the hermit who speaks to animals, the megalomaniac, the maniac, the melancholic, the antisocial, the compulsive, and the obsessed.

The very excess of his work has surely helped turn Nietzsche into a model of the mad philosopher, the personification of a world headed into chaos. Ideally, perhaps, the texts would speak wholly for themselves, without recourse to "Mr. Nietzsche." Ideally, but ideally only, Nietzsche's work would be either pathogenic or not, whether he died from thought or from syphilis. This is what Gottfried Benn suggested when he wrote, fifty years ago: "That illness, its genesis and its essence, today do not appear significant anymore. If Nietzsche had died of a heart attack or of blood poisoning, his work would remain the same."[5] The same Gottfried Benn, however, had argued twenty years earlier, and probably with greater justice, that Nietzsche owed much of his fame to his fate.[6] Lange-Eichbaum, in 1947, claimed with great certainty that "only the *psychosis* with all its aspects of fame generation, made us pay *attention* to Nietzsche; *this* has elevated him to the high plateau on which only *then* the throne of genius erects itself."[7]

While Lange-Eichbaum may overstate and oversimplify his case, it is quite true that the reception of Nietzsche's work has been strongly influenced by the various attitudes his madness provoked; thus, a considerable part of Nietzsche interpretations, both sympathetic and hostile ones, contain elements of pathography. "Our" Nietzsche, for better or for worse, is the Nietzsche who went insane, and while it is, of course, possible to disregard this knowledge in any encounter with his texts, the tradition of Nietzsche readings will most likely continue to influence even those studies that could not care less whether the man ended his days in progressive paralysis or blissful communion with higher powers.[8]

To be sure, Nietzsche's madness can serve, and has served, as a pretext to dismiss what he wrote long before his collapse. Nietzsche's antagonists, in fact, have openly suggested that the final breakdown only corroborated a madness that had been evident in his earlier writings for any perceptive reader to see. In this scenario, it is not his work that drove him mad, but his madness that drove his work. Max Nordau, for example, a once highly influential though by now rather infamous cultural critic, pictured Nietzsche as a "maniac" who

> with glittering eyes, wild gestures, and a foaming mouth spouts forth a deafening swill of words, intermittently breaking into insane laughter, interspersed with obscene invectives and curses . . . . To the extent to which the endless stream of words lets us make any sense of it, its main elements are a series of ever recurring delusions based on hallucinations and pathological organic processes.[9]

This passage is curious not so much for the vehemence of its denunciation—Nietzsche elicits strong passions—but rather for the way it appears to enact the very traits it seeks to denounce. Nordau's rhetoric itself might with some justice be thought to foam at the mouth, and his monumental *Degeneration* is nothing if not an almost endless stream of words loosely structured by a handful of recurrent motifs that are repeated with an intensity that one may be tempted to call obsessive (provided that one is willing to operate within these terms).[10] This is not to say that Nordau should be judged by the taxonomy he introduces into the debate; the significance of Nordau's style lies in the strange affinity one of Nietzsche's most vociferous critics shares with the object of his disdain. Nordau's language, as well as the overall argument of his major work, seems to point to the fear of a contamination that may have already progressed beyond control.

George Bataille, arguing from a position that could hardly be more radically removed from Nordau's, may yet be admitting to a similar fear of contagion when he says, in *Sur Nietzsche*, that "motivating this writing—as I see it—is fear of going crazy."[11] This opening remark may be read in a general fashion—"I am writing a book in order not to go mad"—but Bataille talks about *this* writing, his writing on Nietzsche. "I am writing *on* Nietzsche to avoid being *like* Nietzsche." Bataille does not say this, but it could be shown, I think, that the central enterprise of *Sur Nietzsche* is indeed the attempt to reintroduce a teleological project into a world that Nietzsche has voided of all absolute *teloi*.

A fairly recent study of Nietzsche, *Der tolle Mensch* by Christoph Türcke, confronts the anxiety of contamination explicitly. Türcke's book, a nuanced commentary on section 125 of *Gay Science*, the famous "Death of God" passage, is representative of modern Nietzsche pathography. Türcke addresses many of the assumptions that latently but importantly inform a considerable number of Nietzsche studies, and his Nietzsche figure is an allegory of late modernity:

> [Nietzsche] could not bear himself. This would not have to concern us any further if the way in which he did not bear himself did not precariously resemble the way in which the modern world does not bear itself. [. . .] It is not yet clear whether Nietzsche's fate anticipates the fate of a whole epoch, whether he is perhaps more significant than even glowing Nietzscheans would like him to be, whether there is more truth in the megalomania of his last days than he himself knew. Now, however, is still the time to prevent all this.[12]

"All this," presumably, is the "whole epoch" going mad. But what does it mean for an epoch to go mad? It is hard to believe that this epochal madness would resemble Nietzsche's silence during the last twelve years of his life. In general, Türcke's urgent rhetoric of analogy appears impossible to concretize. He mentions the dropping of the atom bomb, but do Hiroshima and Nagasaki really resemble Nietzsche's later life and death in any meaningful sense? Certainly, none of the violent twentieth century events that are often called 'mad' these days appear to be inspired by Nietzsche's critique of morality, none of them can be traced to " 'totalized' self-reflection in the name of rationality."

It is this self-reflection that Türcke fears enough to consider a "thought prohibition (*Denkverbot*)"[13] against it. At the same time, he claims that Nietzsche interpretation "belongs to the most significant indicators of the state of the intellectual force of resistance without which the worst cannot be averted."[14] We have to be careful not to "drown in the abysses that Nietzsche opens, not to go mad from the irritations into which he plunges," but we also have "to ruthlessly open ourselves to them [*sich ihnen schonungslos zu öffnen*]."[15] Can you open yourself to an abyss? Isn't it the abyss that opens? How do we resist and study Nietzsche at the same time? What good are generalized warnings against "the permission to think everything possible in the name of the critique of reason"?[16] Is there any reason to believe that we can censor our thoughts without thinking them first? Can thoughts be stopped? How and by whom? Which convictions could shield us from the very critique of conviction?

Türcke writes:

> What if the unreserved turn of reason against itself, from which Aristotle had expected the highest human happiness, would in truth inevitably lead to the self-destruction of reason as it is pre-delineated in Nietzsche's passion of reason? If unreserved self-reflexion were only the noble philosophical form of a raging against the self with which mankind has made its survival more than questionable?[17]

"What if" won't do. There is, after all, very little reason to assume that Nietzsche's reason "self-destructed," and much reason to assume that his madess was somatic. Certainly, it is most Nietzschean to ask whether self-reflection, or reflection *tout court*, is *useful*, but nothing in Nietzsche's work *or* life absolves us from the task of thinking dangerously. What if, to borrow the phrase, Nietzsche wasn't "thinking too much but much too well," as Harold Bloom said about Hamlet?[18]

I will suggest that Nietzsche's critique of reason is, almost *always*, and most fundamentally, a critique of moral reason, and thus, on Nietzsche's terms, a critique of unreason, of the complicity of morality and reason that compromises rather than embodies reason. In *Ecce Homo*, Nietzsche returns to this one point again and again: it is the critique of morality, not the critique of the truth drive, that makes him into a "force majeure"[19]—not the "self-destruction of reason," but the "self-defeat of morality out of truthfulness."[20] It is significant that Türcke mistakes the one for the other when so much of Nietzsche's thought is devoted to distinguishing them, to forcing apart the ancient amalgamation between morality and truth drive. Nietzsche, paradoxically, marshals the dying force of morality to erase itself from the reason = morality equation. As long as being truthful is a moral imperative, "the self-overcoming of morality out of truthfulness" is "the self-overcoming of the moralist"—and it is here that Nietzsche truly parts company from not just from Platonic and Aristotelian thought but from the enlightenment and its nineteenth century legacy.[21] It is not the will to truth that expires in this self-critique, but morality: "what sense would *our* entire existence have if not that in us that will to truth becomes conscious *as a problem*? . . . From this coming-to-self-consciousness of the will to truth, from now on—there is no doubt about this—morality will *perish*."[22]

Passages like the one just cited make it abundantly clear that Türcke's epochal anxiety has its roots in much of what Nietzsche himself wrote. The perishing of morality, Nietzsche continues, will be a "great spectacle in a hundred acts which will be saved for Europe's next two centuries, the most terrible, most questionable, and perhaps also the most hopeful spectacle of all . . . "[23] It is of utmost importance to note, however, that the demise of morality is *not* the same as the end of moral behavior as hitherto understood:

> It goes without saying that I do not deny—unless I am a fool—that many actions called immoral are to be avoided and resisted, or that many actions

called moral are to be done and encouraged—but I think the one [should be encouraged] and the other [avoided] *for other reasons than hitherto.* (KSA 3: 91–2)

Nietzsche's distrust of conventional goodness is amply borne out by the fact that the most heinous acts of the century have been committed in the name of various moralities. In this regard, it is somewhat surprising that, a hundred years after Nietzsche, immorality and madness are still fused together in the minds of those who think themselves the champions of critical reason,[24] and there is an insidious element in the attempt to enlist Nietzsche's own work in support for a thesis that denounces his thought as either pathological or pathogenic, or both.

It is true, of course, that Nietzsche would be the last to deny causal links between a thinker's soma and his work. First of all, however, we don't really know what Nietzsche's somatic state was. Second, the mad Nietzsche didn't write. Without any work, however, there is no clear connection between work and madness; or, conversely, madness and work, as Foucault has argued, do exclude each other, at least in Nietzsche's case. If, on the other hand, we are meant to believe that Nietzsche's final breakdown was not truly a break but only the finalizing moment in a long process of deterioration, then his critics should be able to sustain this claim by pointing to specific passages, by saying: this sentence here, this thought, this contradiction is either mad or must lead to madness. It is surely not enough to rely on metonymical substitutions where self-critique equals self-destruction, and the critique of reason, however radical, the absence of reason.

Nietzsche's own speculations about the physiology of thought suggest complexities far beyond easy surface analogies. Most importantly, Nietzsche argues that philosophers are precisely not what they seem, that the trust in moral reason itself is "a symptom of illness [*Krankheitssymptom*]" (KSA 12: 202) rather than a mark of sanity. When Nietzsche talks about the "brain maladies of sick cobweb weavers [*die Gehirnleiden kranker Spinneweber*]" (GD, KSA 6: 76), he thinks prominently of Socrates, the very model of controlled rationality, quite possibly the West's most exemplary man of reason. It is true that Nietzsche counted himself amongst the "machines that can burst" [*Maschinen, welche* zerspringen *können*]"[25]—he also claimed, however, that, despite all his physical afflictions, "[a]ll pathological disturbances of the intellect, even that semi-numbness which follows on a fever, have remained utterly foreign to me" (EH, KSA 6: 265). He may or may not have been right about this: all that these passages tell us is that we cannot rely on Nietzsche to provide his *own* diagnosis. We may, however, inquire whether Nietzsche's critique of moral reason does not carry enough weight to resist and defy its pathologization.

In the end, Nietzsche's own answers to all these questions remain, as so often, ambiguous. Both reason and madness emerge as objects of celebration and censure, but, more importantly, they appear as *historical* objects within specific constellations that continuously change their valences. This chapter will analyze the role Nietzsche assigns to madness in some of the most important of these constellations. To this purpose, I propose to study not Nietzsche's madness but Nietzsche's madmen, a handful of mad figures scattered through his writings. They are the artist-fool of *Truth and Lie in the Extramoral Sense*, the mad thinkers who have defied the "morality of mores [*die Sittlichkeit der Sitte*]" in *Daybreak*, the footloose dancers of the mind in the *Gay Science*, and the maniac in the marketplace, also in the *Gay Science*. In reading the relatively few passages in which Nietzsche addresses madness directly, madness emerges as an ambiguous intellectual force that is, indeed, at times complicitous with philosophy: Nietzsche's philosophy, but also philosophy in general. At the same time, I will suggest, Nietzsche's reevaluation of reason implies a revaluation of insanity due to which all traditional conceptions of madness (including, incidentally, traditions that are active in some of the contemporary discourse on Nietzsche) collapse. Thus it becomes possible to say that, yes, Nietzsche's work would be the maddest of all works—if it were not for this work itself. I will try to make a case for this paradox, but doing so will involve a number of digressions: from considerations of physiology and metaphysiology to an investigation of morality and mad metamorality to the surreal—but by no means mad—figure of a dancing cow, ending, with Nietzsche, on a little island of reason.

NIETZSCHE'S MADMEN (1): THE ARTIST IN THE DITCH, OR FROM METAPHYSICS TO METAPHYSIOLOGY

A nice folly, this speaking: man dances across all things with it.

—Also sprach Zarathustra

Traditionally, the idea of a mad truth depends on a sometimes tacit, sometimes explicit distinction between low and high madness that operates along the same line that separates the body from the soul. Socrates' discrimination between divine and nosological madness in the *Phaedrus*[26] is prototypical of this operation, which sustains the very possibility of a condition that is simultaneously irrational and meaningful. The two types of madness, and their various sub-classifications, correspond to the classical dichotomy of existence in its many philosophical manifestations: apparent and true, physical and spiritual, human and divine, body and soul, transitory and eternal, etc. At the same time, the relationship of insanity to divine madness is not simply an instance of these metaphysical dualities; to use a Platonic metaphor, divine madness does not relate to insanity as the idea of the bed relates to the actual bed. There can be no idea of divine madness, only a mad path to the ideas. Divine madness, more precisely, is always only an appearance of madness, revealing itself as an instrument of reason or order in retrospect—through an act of interpretation. Madness is always in need of critical intervention in order to reveal itself as what it is. Divine madness and insanity share exterior characteristics that may be deceiving: the divinely mad and the pathologically mad body can look and act alike, and as far as speech is thought to be both a corporeal and a noncorporeal act, the speech of the mad may or may not be in the service of reason. While the physician diagnoses the mad body, the metaphysician interprets the mad text. Ideally, both perform acts of restoration: of bodily health, of reasonable meaning.

In Nietzsche, metaphysician and physician begin to merge. The unprecedented expansion of the natural sciences during the nineteenth century, their growing influence and ever more ambitious scope had certainly prepared the ground for a radical reevaluation of the mind-body dichotomy; but literature and philosophy, with only a few exceptions like the brilliant writings of the physician Georg Büchner, had been rather slow on the uptake. Nietzsche often reprimands what we call the humanities for their neglect of scientific thought,[27] and he liked to envision a new type of philosopher, the "philosophical physician."

Nietzsche's physiological excursions are, at this point, vastly unpopular, not only because his scientific information is seriously outdated.[28] Terry Eagleton, even though he lauds Nietzsche as a "full-blown materialist," finds "more than a smack of vulgar Schopenhauerian physiologism about him,"[29] and Arkady Plotnitsky notes, more cautiously, that many of Nietzsche's connections "between the mental and the physical may be problematic." Nonetheless, Plotnitsky continues,

> Correlations between physical and theoretical—or artistic—symptoms are by no means impossible . . . . Such matters are far from discountable, either in Nietzsche's case or in general, although we are far from knowing how to account for them. While Nietzsche himself may at times rely on a dubious physiology, the relation itself of the *philosophical* spirit to the *body* is a crucial part of Nietzsche's *psychology*—and the *physiology*—of philosophy, as part of his critique of the *philosophy* of philosophy.[30]

In the spirit of this remark, I will ignore Nietzsche's specific physiological conjectures—some suggestive, some merely preposterous. Instead, I will concentrate on some of the implications that follow from Nietzsche's insistence on the primacy of the body, implications that bear, although often indirectly, on the nature of artistic production, recasting some of the fundamental arguments that have made the privilege of madness possible from Plato on. This line of inquiry leads us not so much into specific biological speculations, but to the *fact* of physiology, of thinking bodies both sane and insane, or 'healthy' and 'unhealthy'. These terms, even though very Nietzschean, may be deceptive. While Nietzsche utilizes concepts of health and sickness quite frequently to various argumentative and polemical ends, including insinuations of insanity, he by no means consistently privileges the healthy body; nor, conversely, does he suggest that the healthy body provides the norm at all times. In the *Gay Science*, he asserts that "there is no health in itself, and all attempts to define such a thing have failed miserably."[31]

Certainly, some of his most virulent attacks on Socrates and Christianity are framed in terms of health and illness. He dismisses much of philosophy summarily as "brain maladies of sick cobweb weavers" (GD, KSA 6: 76), evaluates "Greek philosophy from Socrates on as a symptom of illness and accordingly preparation of Christianity" (KSA 12: 202), and says of Socrates himself that "ugliness is often enough expression of an inbred development, *inhibited* by inbreeding" (GD, KSA 6: 68).

In *Ecce Homo*, however, Nietzsche portrays himself as the result of a certain "inbreeding". The section is titled: "Why I am so wise,"[32] suggesting that Nietzsche's own brand of wisdom is not unrelated to the antithetical heritage of which he portrays himself as the offspring. And in the second preface to the *Gay Science*, Nietzsche talks of his own serious illness with gratitude:

> One will guess that I do not part from that time of severe infirmity without gratitude; I have yet to fully exhaust its gain for me: as I am in general well enough aware of how my changing health puts me at an advantage to all coarseness of mind. A philosopher who has made and makes again and again his way through many [forms of] healths, has gone through as many philosophies: he *cannot* but transform his condition into the most intellectual [*geistigste*] form and distance every time—this art of transfiguration *is* what philosophy is. We philosophers are not free to distinguish between soul and body . . . . And what concerns illness: would we not be almost tempted to ask whether it is dispensable to us?[33]

In light of Nietzsche's virulent invectives against "physiologically weak" moral philosophers and theologians, this passage has a self-serving ring to it. Nonetheless, there is a decisive difference between the sickness of moral philosophy and the sick philosopher of the *Gay Science*. The latter moves back and forth between health and illness, or various illnesses and healths; his thinking body is a body subjected to acute changes of condition, and thus to divergent modes of thinking that will yield divergent results. While Nietzsche declares himself free of all "pathological disturbances of the intellect,"[34] nothing in Nietzsche's praise of illness excludes madness as a potentially creative affliction—as long as it does not inhibit the "art of transfiguration" that transforms physiological ailment into intellectual argument.[35]

It is the plurality of the single body, as a legitimate and important plurality that, feeding the multiplicity of thought itself, undermines the ambition of traditional philosophies to be the *one* possible philosophy that would construct its truth as unconditional. Illness, then, is simultaneously at the root of traditional metaphysics and provides a lever for its dislocation. The body that falls sick and convalesces is a metamorphosing body, and it produces philosophy as metamorphosis that escapes dialectical *Aufhebung*[36]: sickness can be more than a negation of health, just as madness can be more than a negation of reason. In the many gradual transitions from health to sickness and back, the thinker of changing physical and therefore mental fortune achieves a devious advantage over both "decadent" and coarsely common thought. In this recurrent change of perspective, reason itself appears contingent on the material conditions of thought that are subject to biohistorical change. Nietzsche extends this argument to a general paradigm when he says that

> I still expect that a philosophical *physician* in the exceptional sense of the word—one to follow the problem of overall health of people, time, race, mankind—will have the courage one day to radicalize my suspicion and to dare to say: with all philosophizing to date it was not a matter of 'truth', but of something else, let us say health, future, growth, power, life . . . .[37]

Needless to say, Nietzsche himself poses as nothing less than the founder of this new discipline. Since, however, he attacks the very premises by which any condition could be identified as a transhistorical optimum, his diagnosis renders the very terms 'health' and 'sickness' problematic as normative or evaluative concepts. While he at times appears to privilege a certain type of robust bodily health over others, he will also argue, in an ironical (and rather unfair) aside against Darwin, that physical vigor is a disadvantage when more often than not the strong perish at the hands (or rather the minds) of the weak, and that, conversely, weakness is an advantage in the struggle to survive because it fosters intelligence: "the weak ones always defeat the strong ones—because their number is greater; they also are more intelligent."[38] In the play of forces, physical vigor or mental hardiness is hardly ever the most important one.

More radically, Nietzsche at times contends that there may be no longer such a thing as an absolute weakness, i.e., no activity, no condition, no way of thinking that would not *in some way* benefit the survival of the species, "for nothing is older, stronger, more relentless, more invincible [*nichts . . . ist älter, stärker, unerbittlicher, unüberwindlicher*]" (FW, KSA 3: 369) than the instinct of species survival:

> I do not know any longer whether you, my dear fellow human and neighbor, *could* at all live to the disadvantage of the species, i.e., 'unreasonably' or 'badly'; whatever could have harmed the species, may have died out many millennia ago and now belongs to those things that are not even possible with God anymore.[39]

Under this comprehensive view, then, there may be no sickness, and, by extension, no madness, that would not be healthy or "reasonable" in some way. The "astonishing economy [*erstaunlichen Oekonomie*]" (FW, KSA 3: 369) of life always appears to offer at least one perspective that allows any apparent loss to be booked as a gain (the whole history of divine madness, of course, is a case in point here): "Even the most harmful man may perhaps be the most useful of all."[40] So great are the repossessive powers of life as it "now" is—and in the spirit of evolution in which Nietzsche writes, 'now' would refer to all of known human history—that no unreason would be absolute. The breakdown of the economy might be, at this point, inconceivable.[41]

And yet, the body remains important, and not all strategies of survival are equal. Since physiology can only describe the body norms and their deviancies, not evaluate them, it can be no more than a subdiscipline of philosophy; philosophy must go beyond the normative descriptions that physiology, or any of the natural sciences, can offer. Philosophy has to be mindful of, but more than, physiology: a metaphysiology, a philosophy not of the body, but of the body's meaning, and of the various entangled histories of this meaning.

While the reasoning mind will not yield any insight of permanence, human reasoning itself seems to be a permanent event—reason may have "come into the world" "in an unreasonable way, by accident"[42]—but it is unlikely to leave this world as far it is of any concern to us: "*Rational thought is interpretation according to a scheme that we cannot cast off.*"[43] While the image and the ideological significance of the body rapidly change, there will always be a body. And while there is a body, it will influence, in uncountable and unaccountable ways, the way thought happens, and happens to reflect on itself. It is the interplay between the permanence of the body as a given (perhaps *the* given) and the variance of thought that is, I think, at the center of Nietzsche's famous essay *On Truth and Lie in the Extramoral Sense*.

On the surface, Nietzsche's project in "Truth and Lie"[44] is to deconstruct the postulate of a transparent or even adequate language of representation. Naturally, this endeavor inscribes him into an ancient philosophical tradition: Plato's doctrine of the forms had already implied that all representation, be it verbal or cognitive, implies distortion, and in the history of philosophy, object perception is hardly privileged as a superior mode of recognition.[45] Clearly, the significance of Nietzsche's achievement in *Truth and Lie* lies elsewhere. The wide attention this essay has received during the past decades has been justified by Nietzsche's *angle de visée*; the focus of critical inquiry has been Nietzsche's assertion that all language is figurative, or rhetorical. The best-known reading along these lines is probably Paul de Man's justly famous study in *Allegories of Reading*.[46]

In his insistence on the rhetorical nature of all language, Nietzsche erases the line that has traditionally separated philosophers and poets. At the same time, the essay reestablishes a similar distinction, the one between "stoic" and "artist." Both are subject to the "metaphorizing drive," "that fundamental drive of man"; it is not the use of metaphor that divides them, but their attitudes towards metaphor. "Reasonable man" and "intuitive man" fulfill different roles in different times. The artist, in deceiving openly, provides happiness for a species that has an "invincible inclination to be deceived

[*unbesiegbaren Hang, sich täuschen zu lassen*]" (888). He is "free and emanci-
pated from his usual servitude as long as he can deceive without *doing damage*
[*so lange frei, und seinem sonstigen Sklavendienste enthoben, als er täuschen kann,
ohne zu* schaden]" (888). Stoic man, on the other hand, draws his strength
from metaphors as well, but from metaphors petrified into concepts,
schemata, abstractions. He, too, deceives, actually "delivers a masterpiece of
deception" during calamities when artistic man is reduced to "screaming loud
and having no consolation [*schreit laut und hat keinen Trost*]" (890).

In appearance, it is certainly the artist who seems mad, who "falls again
and again into the same ditch into which he fell before" [*immer wieder in
dieselbe Grube fällt, in die er einmal gefallen*]" (890). He is said to "confuse
metaphors and move the cornerstones of abstraction." He does not see "the
principle needs" and "only takes life for real if it is displaced into appearance
and beauty."[47] In this description, the artist does seem to emerge as the antithesis of every sort of reason that is built on stable conceptualizations and
abstractions. As soon as all conceptual systems are seen as metaphoric constructions whose truthfulness is a general conviction enforced by convention
rather than on any adequate representation of the real, however, the stoic is
no less mad than the artist, no less under the sway of illusion or delusion. It is
only under the perspective of an abstraction that has repressed its genesis that
the artist can appear as mad—whether we take the word in a weak or a strong
sense. The madness of the artist is in the eye of the stoic, and there only.

To read Nietzsche's essay exclusively in terms of its critique of language
is to neglect another of its key concerns, its preoccupation with physiology.
Nietzsche insists that our trust in the order of the perceivable world is due to
the physiology of perception humans share as a species. It is this shared machinery of perception that is at the basis of man's capacity to name and clas-
sify that which is external to him, not any power of transcendent recognition
on which man may pride himself. Reason, then, in this most generic sense, is
first of all a function of a body that conforms to the necessary extent to the
bodies of other reasonable beings:

> If we had, each of us, a different mode of perception, if we could only per-
> ceive once like a bird, once like a worm, once like a plant, or if one of us
> saw the same stimulus as red, the other one as blue, if a third one even
> heard this stimulus as a sound, then nobody would talk about [the] lawful-
> ness of nature but would grasp it as a highly subjective creation.[48]

The question of madness inserts itself here silently; it may indeed be
possible that certain forms of madness either produce, or are the result of, a
deviation in this homogenized "mode of perception"—not enough to achieve
the perspective of bird, worm, or plant, but sufficient to throw into question
the perceptual consensus on which the collective enterprise of reason, of
which empirical science is only a privileged mode, rests.[49] The term that I
have translated as 'creation,' is *Gebilde*, translatable also as 'product', 'work',

'formation', 'form', 'vision', 'image'.[50] The prefix Ge- designates the outcome of an activity, a product of construction. Incidentally, *Gebilde* also evokes *gebildet*, 'educated', 'cultivated', 'civilized'. In this context then, the term comprises the major theme of the essay: the "laws of nature," for the nineteenth century (and much of the twentieth) the paragon of objective truth, are the accomplishment of an essentially artistic activity of image production the output of which is culturally, or collectively, transmitted. This is not to say that these laws are not valid *within* the limits imposed by man's apperceptive machinery, limits that can be known, but not superceded in any immediate sense. Between man and the object world, as Nietzsche had said earlier on, there can be only an "*aesthetic* correlation [*ein ästhetisches Verhalten*]" (884), a phrase that implies distance and negates immediacy of experience. As Nietzsche argued in the roughly contemporary essay on the *Use and Abuse of History for Life,* the act of original, or more narrowly artistic, creation, however, depends on an act that cuts the subject loose from the history of *Gebilde,* to the extent to which this is possible.[51]

To the extent to which reason (or truth drive) would be that mode of thought that conforms to both the physiologically determined and the collectively transmitted or enforced forms of seeing, any act of creation would necessitate a *certain amount* of madness—if we think of madness, schematically, as a violation of or a deviance from reason. This line of argument is indeed a rather common modern cliché, as Nietzsche's laconic remark in *Daybreak* acknowledges: "While it is suggested to us again and again today that a genius, instead of a grain of salt, has received a grain of mad herb [*Wahnwurz*], all earlier men were much more prone to think that everywhere where there is madness, there is also a grain of genius and wisdom" (KSA 3: 27). This presupposes, of course, that the element of madness remains a minor ingredient if the cultural recipes are to be palatable to the community. The artistic type in *Truth and Lie* is by no means a profoundly aberrant character, and if he is allowed to play with the truth in happy times, he may do so only as long as he stays within the rules.[52]

In his attack on the lawfulness of nature and the truthfulness of law, Nietzsche seems to cancel the distinction between artificiality and authenticity in the field of representation. The lawful and the true, however, are not simply superannuated by their assumed contraries, the accidental and the artificial. The obvious objection against Nietzsche is that his text is structured like Eumenides' liar paradox. It seems that this text claims as truth that all texts lie. If all distinctions along the lines of true/false and artificial/natural were to fall away, the category of art would itself become obsolete, and with it all forms of knowledge; in other words, Nietzsche's essay would self-destruct. In essence, this is what Paul de Man's very suggestive reading sets out to demonstrate.[53] De Man reads Nietzsche as a theoretician of rhetoric, and rhetoric only. Surprisingly enough, while de Man seems to indicate that he merely applies Nietzsche's theory to itself, his analysis operates from an assumed beyond of the text. Thus, de Man writes: "The lie is raised to a new figural power, but it is nonetheless a lie. By asserting in the mode of truth that the self is a lie, we have not escaped from deception. We have merely reversed the usual scheme . . . ."[54]

De Man implies that Nietzsche's text is hopelessly aporetic because it claims to "escape deception" (to be true) while simultaneously demonstrating that deception (lying) is the fundamental necessity of every text. De Man thus suggests that Nietzsche poses as one who has broken free, while he really is only rattling the chains that bind him. That is to say that, in falling victim to the snares of language he himself points out, Nietzsche ultimately *fails*, albeit necessarily, unavoidably, even brilliantly.

De Man's approach presupposes that Nietzsche thinks it desirable to "escape detection," to tear down the wall of language that encloses, in all its perpetually changing variety, what reason is meant to be at any given time. Nietzsche's project, however, might be a wholly different one, much closer to the first section of *Beyond Good and Evil*, which questions the very value of truth. His operations are paradoxical only as long as the terms *truth* and *lie* are meant to designate opposite actualities, as if one referred to an absence and the other one to a presence—and it is precisely this claim that Nietzsche refutes. Besides, as the title of his essay shows, Nietzsche does not concern himself with the truth/lie distinction *in general* but predominantly with the moral implications it has come to hold. If he proposes to write about "truth and lie *in the extramoral sense*," he indicates that this distinction might still be legitimate once we move "beyond good and evil," as it were.

Nietzsche locates the genesis of 'truth' in the necessity of societal accord:

> [S]ince man, out of need and out of boredom, wants to exist socially and herd-like, he needs to make peace and tries to achieve that at least the roughest bellum omnium contra omnes disappear from his world. This peace carries with it what looks like the first step in the acquisition of that enigmatic truth drive.[55]

This hypothesis would explain why the fool, as soon as his play threatens to cross the lines within which it is allowed to operate, can so often appear as a deeply immoral figure. As Nietzsche will demonstrate at greater length in his later works, that which develops into morality is at first nothing but the aversion of harm;[56] the true/false distinction as linguistic convention is thus at the basis of the self-preservation of the species as a cultural one. If the conventions of language called "truth" secure the peace, then the break with this convention—and madness is always, at bottom, a break with convention—is a return to the discomforts of war; and war, to be sure, must not be understood as the local wars that break out within society at large, but a war that would mean the end of society altogether. To preserve peace, that is to say to preserve society and the advantages it offers to its members, liar and madman must be ostracized as soon as their delusion, or rather their deviance, threatens harm. But what precisely does it mean to lie?

To say the truth, according to Nietzsche, *originally* meant to use the word the collective agreed upon *to designate a perception, not a thing*. As we have seen above, this process is made possible by the relative uniformity with which humans as members of the same species perceive the world of objects. As a consequence, to lie was to "willfully interchange or even reverse names" (877–8), an act *originally* to be condemned only if harmful: "[Men], at this stage, basically do not hate deception but rather the adverse, hostile results of certain categories of deception." Nietzsche implies that "at this stage" society is still somewhat aware of the mediated quality of all language, which it will deem "deceptive" only once the ideology of *adequatio rei atque linguae* is firmly established. According to Nietzsche, the assumption of transparent language is a symptom of a progressive forgetfulness (881) or repression.

There are two points here that I think have been underestimated in the critical debate on this piece. On the one hand, Nietzsche develops his argument in a quasihistorical framework; although linguistic units are shown to be necessarily transformative of what they allegedly seek to represent, Nietzsche's critique is not aimed at a transhistorical delusion but at its naturalization through history. Nietzsche insists on the progressive character of this process. Thus, he situates his critique of recognition in a historical time that is characterized by the fact that it has forgotten its genesis. The second point, an obvious one, is the fact that at this point Nietzsche disputes only language's claim to truthfully represent a world of *objects* that is allegedly extrasubjective as well as extralingual. In this light, his argument does not go all that far beyond Kant. In order to assess the uniqueness of Nietzsche's contribution, we have to look at his description of the representative act:

> What is a word? The portrayal of nerve stimuli in sounds. . . . [The creator of language] designates only the relation of things to men, and to express these relations, he avails himself of the boldest metaphors. First, he translates a nerve stimulus into an image! That is the first metaphor. Then, the image is reshaped into a sound! The second metaphor. And each time there is a complete overleaping of the sphere—smack into a wholly different and new one.[57]

It is crucial that, here and all through the essay, Nietzsche stresses the role the "nerves" play in the process of representation. His commentary mainly concerns traditional assumptions about the move from perception to language. In his insistence on the physiological aspect of representation, he suggests that it is in human anatomy that the gulf between subject and world opens. Certainly, Nietzsche proceeds to point out the insufficiency of language to achieve adequate representation of the world of things, but the deficiency of language is an epiphenomenon of limitations we might almost call carnal, of the accidental nature of the perceptual apparatus. The "metamorphosis of the world in men [*die Metamorphose der Welt in den Menschen*]"

(883) is *primarily* due to these limitations which banish the extra-human world into inaccessibility. In this, Nietzsche's world of things is as radically removed from recognition as, for example, Lacan's "real," albeit for somewhat different reasons. The original object of recognition remains on the other side of the gulf over which the perceiving subject must leap in order to articulate its experience. When Nietzsche demonstrates that human life is exiled from the world surrounding it, he does not assume a position outside of the edifice that is at once our prison and our home.[58] There is no escape, neither for the stoic nor for the artist (and Nietzsche is quite capable of assuming both roles). Although the concepts have lost their absolute (metaphysical and metalingual) claims, one can still speak of truth and lie:

> If someone hides an object behind a bush, then seeks and finds it there, there is not much to be praised in this seeking and finding: but that is the way it is with the seeking and finding of 'truth' within the sphere of reason.[59]

One can still speak of truth and lie—indeed, as we have seen above, one must continue to do so due to the necessities of communal life. The rules of playing hide-and-seek, however, are flexible, and they accommodate the artist as well as the stoic, madman as well as philosopher. After all, in happy times man loves to lie and to be lied to, that is to say to cheat and to be cheated at the game. In such friendly times, poet and harmless madmen can play the role of a welcome fool, uprooting the bushes and replanting them elsewhere, stealing the objects or interchanging them with each other. It is only in redrawing the topography of the playground that man realizes that he *is* playing, "enchanted with happiness" (888).

Truth drive and fiction drive exist simultaneously, and they both aim at pleasure: in the one case at pleasure as the absence of pain, in the other as a presence, as the fulfillment of the quest for that enigmatic condition happiness. Nietzsche personifies these drives in the figures of the stoic and the artist; whereas in happy times the artist, mad or not, is in charge of the game, the stoic and his morality of reason take over in unhappy times. It is important to note that both of them are masters of "dissimulation/displacement [*Verstellung*]" (890). Although Nietzsche clearly privileges the artistic mode of "intuition" of the particular over the scientific mode of erasing difference in abstraction, he by no means implies that stoic and artist are not removed from the world of objects by the same gap, or that either of them may escape the game that confines us. Although the rules are flexible—under favorable conditions, that is—they do not provide an escape to Cartesian certainty (which is another dream to be dreamt).

De Man's assessment refuses to acknowledge a certain cheerful resignation that marks this essay. Nietzsche's work may very well "resemble the endlessly repeated gesture of the artist 'who does not learn from experience and always again falls in the same trap.' "[60] So what? To fall into the same ditch again and again is a mode of living, as Nietzsche tells us, and it may not be inferior (or superior) to the mode in which de Man writes. De Man's concluding sentence speaks about the necessary resignation to the hardship of philosophy: "The hardest thing is to confess that this allegory of errors is the model of philosophical rigor."[61] Thus, de Man simulates Nietzsche's stoic, his text "walks away under the rain with slow strides,"[62] so to speak. But if it is possible to fall into a pit again and again, it is also possible to climb out of it again and again. This pit is no abyss, and this mode of living, while "unreasonable [*unvernünftig*]" (889), is far from mad; rather, as Nietzsche quite succinctly says, it is a product of "the intellect, that master of deception [*[d]er Intellekt, jener Meister der Verstellung*]" (888), an intellect that, for Nietzsche, is at the heart of every successful culture (889).

Madness, in the full severity of the term, ultimately does not enter into this constellation of competing forms of reason. Again, Nietzsche suggests that it is the very nature of reason to leap over the limitations established by the nature of perception and, consequently, the nature of language. Madness, accordingly, may be absolute only when it falls into the gap this leap spans. It is true that Nietzsche's essay evokes a deep menace, an unreason that would be more than a lie, one of those " 'truths' that are of a wholly different nature than scientific truth [*die der wissenschaftlichen Wahrheit ganz anders geartete 'Wahrheiten'*]" (886). It is not, however, the menace of rhetorical aporia, as de Man wants us to believe. To be caught in a paradox also means to be sustained by its poles; if two horses of equal strength pull a rope in opposite directions, you can dance on it . . . . Nietzsche's paradoxes and contradictions might actually serve precisely this end, achieving the balance created by suspension. Just as the different games stoic and artist play allow for different forms of steadiness—after all, repetition is a form of stability as much as the hierarchic architecture of the pyramid of concepts—Nietzsche gains and loses balance in the force field he himself creates.

If all these operations sketched above are cognitive strategies aimed at self-preservation, we must ask under what terrible threat the subject operates: what kind of consciousness would be, as Nietzsche put it in the *Gay Science*, truly "unreasonable" or "bad"? This question finally leads us back to anatomy:

> Does not nature keep nearly everything secret from [man], even about his own body, in order to ban him and lock him into a proud, delusional consciousness, detached from the windings of his entrails, the swift flow of his bloodstream, the intricate quivering of his fibers! She threw away the key; and woe to the fatal curiosity that ever succeeded in peering through a crack out of the room of consciousness and downward, now surmising that man, in the indifference of his ignorance, rests on the merciless, the greedy, the insatiable, the murderous, as if he were clinging to the back of a tiger in dreams.[63]

Nietzsche here tells us that the greatest of horrors were to be found once man succeeded in gazing out of the "chamber of consciousness," one more metaphor of enclosure. Consequently, the ultimate peril, a madness that would go beyond any artistic folly, lurks neither in the moral nor the extramoral conception of truth and lie but rather in the possible truth of an extramural sensation beyond the walls constituted by the limits of self-perception. Any deviance that stays within the circumscribed field of recognition is ultimately harmless. No lie, invention, fiction, or madness would upset the balance of the original deception to any significant degree as long as it plays by the rules that govern discourse itself.

The "secret" that man cannot decipher concerns the nature of his body. Nietzsche's writing dissects this body like a pathologist; in dividing it into particles, he dismantles the illusion of the body as a stable unit serving as the locus of the individuum. In this regard, Nietzsche does not so much deconstruct the self as de Man suggests, but rather establishes a distinction between subject and individuum (in the literal sense as the individed). The subject consolidates itself at the price of the unmediated knowledge of its material condition: in the employment of terms like *winding, flow, quivering*, Nietzsche evokes the fundamental instability of the physis. When we read this passage together with his other references to anatomy, the nerve stimuli involved in the production of images and concepts, it appears that our fundamental incapacity concerns the perception of perception. (The fact that Nietzsche is able to point to the processes he says we cannot perceive only shows once more that signification and perception are fundamentally different procedures.) The text also emphasizes that this incapacity is a blessing, for without it, we would not be able to leap over the spheres into the dream of reason. The perception of perception (a self-conscious awareness, say, of firing neurons) would lead us into infinite regress, a self-consciousness without a self to govern it. The metaphysiology of thought is essential to life: language and its indispensable benefits rest on the oblivion of the body producing them, at the cost of an alienation we can only dimly be aware of [*ahnen*]. Thus, we dreaming things are protected from the full realization of our nature by the same token by which the "real," or nature in general, becomes inaccessible.

Nietzsche evokes the threat of this other world in strong terms—*Woe!, fatal*—but he never identifies the danger. There is a beast of prey prowling out there, but Nietzsche, very much contrary to his usual figurative practice, stresses the fact that his tiger image is a simile: *gleichsam*. We never get to know what it is a simile of; thus the tiger appears as the metaphor of that which must not and cannot be said. If speech preserves us in alienation, the only real menace to life lies in an immediacy of self-recognition that the whole structure of our consciousness serves to prevent. It is interesting to note, in this context, what Reich said about schizophrenics: "What belongs specifically to the schizophrenic patient is that . . . he experiences the vital biology of his body."[64]

This perspective constitutes an interesting reversal of the traditional conception of the reasonable and the mad mind—the alienation from the self, long thought of as a fundamental characteristic of the mad, is what makes reasoning possible. Borrowing from Lacan, we might say that for Nietzsche, the *conscious* is structured like language, not only inescapably but beneficially so. The secret that "nature" keeps from man is the secret of the physiological basis of (mis)representation. Even though science might tell us about the labor of our nerves, we will never be able to translate science into experience. For Büchner's Danton, this is a melancholy insight—"Go, our senses are crude. To know each other? We would have to crack open our skulls and tear the thoughts out of each other's brain fibers," Danton says to his wife, Julie, in the first scene of *Dantons Tod*. For Nietzsche, it is a blessing. If self-knowledge could be complete, we would be sucked into a mad spiral of perception of perception of perception.

So the Delphic imperative, the most distilled formula of philosophical reason, is finally canceled. Not self-knowledge, but self-ignorance becomes the condition of possibility of any knowledge in general. Does the tiger still prowl? We are left with an apparent tautology: outside language lies the menace of a world without language. To know still means to know primarily through language, to leap over the materiality of self. But, as Nietzsche suggests in the *Gay Science*, this process is irreversible. His concept of the self changes from a metaphysical into a metaphysiological one, but the self is still a valid category (that is to say, no less valid than others). Reason, whatever form it takes, strictly precludes any immediacy of its own experience as physical—the madness that would spring from full self-recognition, a chaos of unrepression, would be absolute: "it might be a basic characteristic of existence that those who would know it completely would perish."[65]

The artist of *Truth and Lie*, then, is a mad figure only in a very limited sense; under the perspective of the essay, 'unreasonable' does not easily translate into 'mad', unless we were to assume the perspective of the stoic which Nietzsche effectively deconstructs. The essay is, in this regard, no exception; throughout his oeuvre, Nietzsche pays little attention to the concept of poetic madness, not least because his perspective on the history of mad privilege is so broad that the madness of the poets appears like a mere footnote to his general appraisal of the immense tensions under which more or less fragile and tenuous concepts of reason have operated.

Even though the general thesis of *Truth and Lie* does not offer much illumination in regard to poetic madness, it is, nonetheless, crucial for understanding Nietzsche's position on the role and value of madness in the history of philosophy, which is, for Nietzsche, always also the history of morality. In a later fragment, Nietzsche asserts that "Since Plato, philosophy has been dominated by morality. Even in his predecessors, moral interpretations play a decisive role . . ." (KSA 22: 259). *Truth and Lie* suggests that the complicity of reason and morality, a central Nietzschean theme, is not limited to any specific ideology or historical period, but coincides with the very birth of language and civilization. In the next two sections, I will attempt to analyze how the significance, the value, and the role of madness emerge from this nexus of reason, morality, and culture.

NIETZSCHE'S MADMEN (2): META-MORALITY, OR THE MADNESS OF NEW THOUGHT

"Und diess ist selber Gerechtigkeit, jenes Gesetz der Zeit, dass sie ihre Kinder fressen muss": also predigte der Wahnsinn.

—Also sprach Zarathustra

If all reason, as Nietzsche suggests, is historically entangled with morality, then madness, as far as it is reason's antithesis, relates to immorality: between them holds a relationship not necessarily of identity, but of at least potential kinship. In *Madness and Civilization*, Foucault, probably inspired by Nietzsche, has analyzed the association of crime and insanity in and around the Age of Reason.[66] Nietzsche's theory, however, suggests that the link between immorality and madness cannot be relegated to specific historical periods, even though different periods, of course, will shape and conceive it differently.

I will argue in this section that Nietzsche's writings on what presumably might be called prehistory suggest that the relationship between crime and madness constituted, for a long time, a strange paradox where they were at once virtually identical and diametrically opposed to each other, distinguished by an act of judgment that would rule not on the substance or the quality of an act or a thought, but on the nature of its conception. Foucault argues that the pre-Enlightenment world had a relationship to madness that was characterized by an essential openness to the realm of unreason. In contrast, Nietzsche, who senses a similar openness, suggests that madness found an audience exactly to the degree to which it was seen to represent reason itself, in its highest, divine form.

Nietzsche develops this train of thought predominantly in the first sections of *Daybreak*, where he speculates on the age of *Sittlichkeit*, a term that, even though it is often indiscriminately translated as 'morality', does not mean the same thing as *Moral*. *Sittlichkeit*, briefly, is the reign of rigid conventions that minutely codify action and behavior in all realms of life in the name of "tradition," a tradition to be feared as "a higher intellect" (M, 22). The morality of *Sittlichkeit*, in contrast to the *Moral* of the post-Socratic and Christian ages, is rigidly anti-individual and punishes any aberrance from its established laws of conduct, exerting on its subjects a "terrible pressure" to obey and conform to a degree that, Nietzsche asserts, is barely imaginable to the sons and daughters of *Moral*.[67]

And yet it is precisely the strictures of an unforgiving system of coercion that allow madness to create, for a brief, terrifying, but perhaps glorious moment, a space of freedom that makes "new thought" possible. This space, to be sure, is closely circumscribed; the liberation of thought is fleeting, and its price is high:

> If in spite of this terrible pressure of the 'morality of conventions' [*Sittlichkeit der Sitte*] under which all communities of mankind lived, for many millennia before our time and the same way all in all until the present day (we ourselves live in the small world of exceptions and in the evil zone, as it were): if, I say, nonetheless new and deviant thoughts, judgments and drives broke forth, then this happened under a dreadful accompaniment: almost everywhere it is madness that prepares the way for the new thought.[68]

This is a strong statement, delivered with few qualifications. It suggests that, up to the point where *Sittlichkeit* transmutates into *Moral* (on that later), the progress of thought (one is almost tempted to call it *Geist*) owed "almost" everything to madness. What is it that Nietzsche calls madness here? How does it relate to pre-Socratic, pre-Christian forms of reason, and how does it differ from post-Socratic, post-Christian ideas of madness? Is it at all the same thing? Can it be? Who are these madmen who made history move on in these ancient, barely imaginable times? In *Institution and Interpretation*, Sam Weber observes that

> if there is a social decision . . . to attribute the origin, the mode of organization, the self-understanding, and the cultural accomplishments of a society of whatever magnitude . . . to gods conceived of as inhabiting a distinct ontological realm, then this decision represents a desire and a determination to split the society from its first causes in such a way as to make the latter inaccessible to human intervention or tampering, as the many tales of woe befallen to those humans who have tried attest.[69]

If madness, as Nietzsche suggests, constitutes the only venue of "human intervention" in such a society, and if then the age of *Sittlichkeit* owed all its transformations to the mad, was its final transformation into *Moral* the work of madmen as well?

In the *Gay Science*, elaborating the survival theme of *Truth and Lie*, Nietzsche distinguishes between "basic" and "ancillary" errors. The erroneous "basic endowment of the species," to be questioned only "very late," "proved to be useful and helped to preserve the species," and the errors that constitute it are nearly impervious to reasonable doubt:

> all higher functions [of our organisms], the perceptions of our senses and every kind of sensation worked with those basic errors which had been incorporated since time immemorial. Indeed, even in the realm of knowledge these assertions became the norms according to which 'true' and 'untrue' were determined—down to the most remote regions of logic. Ergo: the *power* of insights [*Erkenntniss*] lies not in their degree of truth, but in their

age, their incarnation, their character as a condition of life. Where life and knowledge [*Erkennen*] seemed to be at odds, there was never any real fight, but denial and doubt were simply considered craziness [*Tollheit*].[70]

"Simply craziness," then, used to be everything that shattered the very foundations of civilization as such, the basic, universal errors that, in the argument of *Truth and Lie*, provide the conditions of minimal peace, i.e., the conditions of communication. Since these basic errors form the foundation on which *all* systems of truth and reason in the age of *Sittlichkeit* are erected, the craziness of fundamental doubt cannot be incorporated into any specific, local or historical, system of faith that does not privilege the truth drive over the forces of tradition.[71]

In the age of *Sittlichkeit*, therefore, madness can be heard only as long as its protest remains within certain limits, as long as it accommodates, on a fundamental level, the system which it calls into question.[72] The first book of *Daybreak* analyzes the degree to which even the most rigid ideological landscape of *Sittlichkeit* is structured in a way that allows madness to alter it. In a long section, entitled "The Meaning of Madness in the History of Morality," he suggests that madness was—and perhaps remains—a powerful agent in the necessary unrepression that moves history.

Since obedience toward tradition is the highest value in the value hierarchy of *Sittlichkeit*, any assertion of individual independence is a deviance from the law, and therefore, a crime: "The free man is immoral [*unsittlich*] because he will depend in everything on himself and not on a tradition" (M, 22–3). Since compliance with the laws of *Sittlichkeit* is mandatory in almost every realm of life, however—"originally . . . everything was *Sitte*"[73]— any act of irregularity will assert the individuality of its perpetrator. Madness gains its extraordinary power because it is the only state that simultaneously allows for eccentric behavior and exculpates the eccentric from the suspicion of individual motive: "[s]omething that so visibly carried the sign of total involuntariness, like the convulsions and the foam of the epileptics, which appeared to designate the madman as mask and spokepiece of a divinity." Paradoxically, madness clears a space of independence precisely because it is, to all appearances, a state of utter unfreedom. Divine madness—or rather, any madness that performs as if divinely inspired—is the only state of intellectual autonomy that escapes the collective's sanctions against individual aberrance, precisely because it appears as the ultimate negation of autonomous thought.

Under the reign of *Sittlichkeit*, any act of intellectual freedom, unless it is divinely dictated, and hence unfree, is evil: "it is impossible to calculate what especially the rarer, more exceptional, more original minds must have suffered throughout history from the fact that they were always perceived to be the evil and dangerous ones."[74] "New thought" can prevail over the power of tradition only as divine madness—because all traditions legitimize themselves by taking recourse to a higher authority, a divine prescriptor. Every given system of *Sittlichkeit* is, on some deep level, fundamentally arbitrary and must, in order to stay authoritative, deny its arbitrariness at all cost. *Sittlichkeit* cannot exert its terrible force without that "fear of a higher intellect"; tradition is powerful only if it operates within a religious perspective, and "whoever wanted to rise above conventional morality [*Sitte*] had to be legislator and medicine man and a kind of demigod" (M, 22).

While it seems plausible that there would have been other ways to achieve this position of power, Nietzsche goes as far as to suggest that madness was indeed the *exclusive* legitimization if it came to "breaking the yoke of any *Sittlichkeit* and to give new laws," mandatory to the degree that all innovators, "*if they were not really mad*, had no choice but to make themselves mad or to pretend to be mad." Frustratingly but perhaps wisely, Nietzsche refrains from providing any ontological definition of madness. Madness, it would appear, is simply the contradiction of *Sitte*, and everything that contradicts *Sitte* is at least potentially mad. Madness, then, would be defined exclusively by the conventions it departs from—and all convention is, in the last analysis, arbitrary. Nietzsche's formulation, however, is not one of bleakly rigid relativism. Certainly, some of the mad legislators had only "to pretend to be mad," clever strategists who exploit the conventions that would restrain them. Others would "make themselves mad," suggesting that they conceived their thought in sanity. Some, however, must have been "really mad," and whatever Nietzsche has in mind when he speaks of the "really mad," he does seem to credit the novelty of their thought to their madness; even if there was nothing mad to their thoughts, the very articulation of "new thought" is, in his scenario of extreme compulsion a perhaps truly mad act.

Nietzsche's portrait of the voluntary madman suggests that madness is the only solace for the free thinker, that he needs it to bear himself:

> 'Oh, give madness, divine ones! Madness, so that I will finally believe in myself! . . . Doubt is eating me, I have killed the law, the law frightens me like a corpse frightens the living man: if I am not *more* than the law, then I am the most wretched man of all. The new spirit that is in me, from where does it come if not from you? Prove to me that I am yours; madness alone will prove it to me.'[75]

This is moral man speaking, a legislator ultimately as involuntary as the true madman, as much in need of self-legitimization as of communal sanction. This passage, once again, stresses, in the proximity of crime and madness, the complicity of reason and morality. "The law" is always both descriptive and prescriptive of the established rules of *Sittlichkeit*, and its provisions are always meant to embody both reason and morality, that which should be thought because it is true and that which ought to be thought because it is good. The free thinker is always guilty, for "man has given everything there is a relation to morality [*hat der Mensch Allem, was da ist, eine Beziehung zur Moral beigelegt*]" (M, 19), and the profound unfreedom of madness is the only possible remedy for the freedom of thought. Madness is not a disease but a cure, and the means employed to invite madness closely resemble esoteric medical procedures, "a secret teaching of techniques and dietetic hints."[76]

Sittlichkeit would be an inalterably static system if it did not contain, in its very structure, a provision that allowed for the transmutation of crime into reform. Every system of belief that presents its own truths as dependent on a higher authority includes the possibility of their mad revision. The divinely mad legislator exculpates himself from the crime of individuality because he speaks against *Sitte* from the only locus that is superior to *Sittlichkeit*: the locus of its imaginary origin. Nietzsche proposes that, for the longest time, *all* revision came into being as an act of divine interference that would materialize in the body of the madman, since, in Nietzsche's picture of *Sittlichkeit*, the law is valid *only* as long as it can establish its provenance from this higher source, and since madness is the only way new thought can disguise itself as divine thought.

In a sense, everybody capable of escaping the rigorous demands of *Sittlichkeit* is mad, and Nietzsche's distinction between real, voluntary, and pretended madmen is almost a minor subtlety: the deviance, however, is a real one in each case. Yet, every transgression that establishes its divine origin at that very moment ceases to be a transgression, and since *Sittlichkeit* always acknowledges a higher authority, the act of mad revision itself becomes, as a ritual of deviance, another *Sitte*. The mad legislator, then, in overturning conventions, has to overturn them in the conventional way—as every Old World Catholic knows, the apparent freedom of the carnival follows its own rules. In the end, it is more important to conform to the established image of madness than to be "really" mad. Not all madness can accredit itself as divine: its recognition always depends on the critical authority of moral reason to verify it.

Naturally, then, none of Nietzsche's mad legislators is mad under the long perspective, for as soon as his madness is deified, it defines new reason, new truth. Madness, while calling specific provisions of *Sittlichkeit* into question, is not fundamentally immoral. On the contrary: in taking recourse in the very authority that is deemed to establish the laws of *Sittlichkeit*, the ideology of divine madness merely enforces its general structure, which turns every newfound freedom into the law to come. Madness is an anticonventional force in the service of convention.

Nietzsche, saluting them, or some of them, as superior men, pays homage to the madmen of history; he does not, however, glorify the system that produced their rare victories. Unlike Foucault, he indicates that madness owed the voice it had to the most ruthless repression of any voice that was not mad, or not mad in the right way. If the powers of *Sittlichkeit* listened to the thoughts of madness, then they did so only because they drove thought mad. While madness promised a refuge from guilt and shame, the odds were stacked against the thinker who sought justification in the secret practices of loneliness, special diets, or sexual abstinence that promised madness:

> at that time where Christianity proved its fertility of saints and desert hermits most abundantly and meant to thereby prove itself, there were in Jerusalem great asylums for hapless saints, for those who had given their last grain of salt.[77]

Thinking madly, thinking amorally, thinking against the law in anticipation of a law to come, is a hazardous enterprise, perhaps even some thinkers' ultimate gamble.[78]

Nietzsche's speculative reconstruction of *Sittlichkeit* suggests that *any* change, i.e., the possibility of history itself, was— "originally"—wholly dependent on madness. This is a strong claim, and one that seems to rival other Nietzschean histories, as in the *Genealogy of Morals* where Nietzsche does not explicitly concern himself with the role of madness in the moral reevaluations effected by the twin event of Platonism and Christianity ("Platonism for the people"). These various accounts, however, are not necessarily in conflict with each other; they rather represent a shift in emphasis. In the terms analyzed so far, Socrates and Christ, the two great reevaluators, are fundamentally mad figures. In the *Daybreak* passage cited above, Nietzsche explicitly includes the early Christians in his history of madness; in *Götzendämmerung*, he refers to "those auditory hallucinations that, as 'Socrates daimonion,' have been interpreted religiously."[79] More importantly, in regrounding virtue in individual conscience, both Christ and Socrates are, to the sentiment of *Sittlichkeit*, exemplary criminals:

> Those moralists, however, who, like those who stepped into the Socratic footsteps, recommend the morality of self-control and abstinence to the *individual* as his own *advantage*, as his personal key to happiness, *make the exception*—and if it appears differently to us, that is because we have been educated under their influence: all of them walk a new path under the highest disapproval of all proponents of the *Sittlichkeit der Sitte*—they step out of the community, as *Unsittliche*, and are, in the deepest sense, evil. Similarly, every *Christian*, who 'strived first for his *own* blessedness,' seemed to be evil to a virtuous Roman of the old sort.[80]

Nietzsche's interpretation of the history of madness and morality sounds less fantastic, then, if we remember that both Socrates and Christ indeed were executed as criminals, not least because they failed to convince their tribunals that they were divinely inspired—by the *daimonion* and the Judaic God, respectively. In this respect, they were failed madmen, convicted of being *individuals*, hence lawbreakers, hence doomed to die. In consequence, it is the very failure of their mad gamble that has conditioned us to think of them as neither mad nor criminal. Under the perspective of *Sittlichkeit*, they were rightly convicted, for their teachings mark the beginning of all modern ideologies of individuality, the old madness and the new reason that appear at the watershed in the history of morality:

> All things that live long become so saturated with reason that their genesis in unreason becomes improbable. Does not every story of origin sound paradoxical and heretical to the sentiment? Does the good historian not *contradict* all the time?[81]

In the light of this remark, Nietzsche's theory of historical madness—and of madness as the once propelling force of history—appears as the improbable, paradoxical, heretical account of the good historian, a story that sounds quite unbelievable to our ears because the story of madness itself is always saturated with reason in retrospect—or forgotten and unknown.

Nietzsche suggests that the introduction of individual *Moral* into the world-historical scene marked the beginning of the end of *Sittlichkeit*; as such, it necessarily also marks the beginning of the end of a certain ethos of madness. Certainly, the praise of folly has never quite subsided, but in a world that privileges individual conscience, individual deviance does not need to legitimize itself through the rituals of madness. The break between *Sittlichkeit* and *Moral*, however, is hardly an absolute one. In its institutionalized form, Christianity has certainly retained the principles of *Sittlichkeit* to a strong degree—hence, perhaps, the predominance of Christian madmen at times when Christian dogma was the most rigid. Conversely, Plato's *Phaedrus* can still celebrate madness as a path to absolute truth, but his narrative of knowledge nonetheless is the first in a long history of stories that will ultimately make mad intuition obsolete. The Platonic moral revolution that distills itself in the formula "virtue = reason = happiness" differs from the old formula "obedience = virtue = reason," mostly because it takes all higher authority out of the equation. Thus, it weakens the distinction between human and higher reason on which any theory of true madness depends. Socrates can grant privileges of knowledge to the mad precisely because he still acknowledges this distinction to a certain degree: the divine soul in the *Phaedrus* sees clearer than the human soul. But—and this is finally more important—they see the same thing, so that their reason is only quantitatively different, not qualitatively.

In a world where reason is not subordinated to a highest authority but itself becomes that highest authority, madness can no longer hold any privilege. This also means, however, that madness continues to be, if to a lesser degree, a potentially subversive mode of thought as long as *Sittlichkeit* and *Moral* overlap.

Nietzsche's writings do not make it easy to assess how long the twin reign of mores and madness lasted. In *Daybreak*, Solon, a pre-Socratic, is said to live in "milder times [*mildere Zeiten*]" that at best exploit "a certain convention of madness [*eine gewisse Konvention des Wahnsinns*]" (M, 27). At some point in *Daybreak*, Nietzsche asserts that the pressure of mores on individual reason has lessened "astonishingly [*erstaunlich abgeschwächt*]," and that it "might as well be called evaporated [*dass es ebenso gut als verflüchtigt bezeichnet werden kann*]" (M, 21). He also argues that any increase in the "sense of causality [*Sinn der Kausalität*]" will bring about a decrease in the "sense of *Sittlichkeit*" (M, 24), so that the triumph of scientific thought will eventually end its rule.

In section 14 of *Daybreak*, however, Nietzsche writes that the constraint of mores exerts itself "all in all up to the present day," even though he adds an important qualification, in parenthesis: "(we ourselves live in the small world of exceptions and in the evil zone as it were)." It is difficult to decide whether this is a world-historical 'we', referring to the age of science, or an authorial 'we', referring to Nietzsche's own world, or to the world of philosophy which he repeatedly calls "evil" (M 291, AC 179). Certain is only that Platonism and Christianity emerge as the climactic events in the history of mad privilege, changing the ideological landscape in ways that have weakened the authority of madness to the point where it is only a faint echo of its former power:

> Where it is still suggested to us, again and again, that a grain of mad herb [*Wahnwurz*] accompanies genius, all earlier men were much more prone to the thought that everywhere where there is madness, there is also a grain of genius and wisdom—'something divine,' one used to whisper.[82]

The modern concept of the genius, of course, is the ideology of the superior *subject*, in contrast to the ancient ideology that deemed virtuous or superior only those whose singularity could be presented as anything but the result of individual agency. Even the contemporary vocabulary calls the madman him who is not himself, besides himself, possessed: that is, one whose madness is not his own. Within an ideological context that celebrates the individual, however, madness ceases to be a privilege, remaining significant only to the extent to which the *Moral* of individual agency has not entirely superceded the old laws of *Sittlichkeit*.

The sentiment of *Sittlichkeit* will decrease, Nietzsche argues, "to the degree to which the sense of causality increases." The triumph of science as the master discourse of the late nineteenth century, then, would eventually destroy *Sittlichkeit* altogether—if the belief in reason that underlies the belief in science were not itself "a moral phenomenon." Since it is, however, even secular society operates under the legacy of *Sitte*, as an unpublished fragment suggests:

> Out of being *used to unconditional authorities*, at last a strong need for *unconditional authorities* has developed:—this need is so strong that, even in a critical age such as Kant's, it proved itself superior to the need for criticism and was, in a certain sense, able to *subordinate* the *entire work* of critical reason and put it to its own uses.—It proved its superiority once again in the following generation, which was necessarily drawn by its historical instinct toward a relativity of all authority, by pressing into its service even the Hegelian philosophy of evolution, history re-baptized philosophy, and presenting

history as the progressive self-revelation, self-surpassing of moral ideas. Since Plato, philosophy has been dominated by morality. Even in his predecessors, moral interpretations play a decisive role . . . . (KSA 12: 259; WP, 222)

In this sense, the pre-critical age of *Sittlichkeit* and the critical age of *Moral*, despite all important disparities, are not entirely distinct, but historically intertwined and still complicitous. The moral imperative creates its own conventions, its own arbitrary judgments, its own "unconditional authority."

The postulate of an extraneous absolute authority may have weakened, but it is far from extinguished as long as the idea of individual freedom is checked by the moral imperative under which it is proclaimed. As long as the idea of freedom is a moral idea, however, it can be arrogated by madness,[83] even if the only thing that madness *can* still claim to be is individuality itself.

The long decline of true madness, then, would come to a close only with the death of all unconditional authorities that are not pure reason. Nietzsche's thought, however, ultimately leaves it open whether the complicity of reason and morality can ever be undone. Certainly, science has arrogated for itself the privilege of revising established truth, once the domain of the mad. Science and *Sitte*, however, continue to compete for the soul of culture, since *Sitte*, as Nietzsche stresses again and again, is a life-preserving force that cannot be discarded without peril. While Nietzsche is habitually, and not incorrectly, associated with an attack on all religion, all "superstition," all morality, he is acutely aware of the life-preserving, stabilizing cultural force that the old and even the new religions, or all the ideologies that function like religions, provide. Nietzsche's modern man has not yet reached the stage where the truth drive has turned suicidal, but may stand on the brink:

The thinker: that is now that being in which the drive to truth and those life-preserving errors fight their first fight, after the drive to truth has *proven* itself to be a life-preserving power as well. In relation to the importance of this battle everything else is insignificant. (WL, KSA 1: 885)

In the next section, I will try to assess the extent to which madness plays a role in this all-significant battle.

NIETZSCHE'S MADMEN (3): THE LAST MADMAN
ON THE MARKETPLACE

Wenn Götter sterben, sterben sie immer viele Arten Todes.

—Also sprach Zarathustra

In section 76 of the *Gay Science*, Nietzsche returns to the question of madness in the scientific age—a question still to be posed in relation to the battle between truth drive and *Sitte*. It is here that Nietzsche finally gives a definition of madness, not as *Wahnsinn*, however, but as *Irrsinn*: "the eruption of arbitrariness in feeling, seeing, and hearing, the enjoyment of the mind's lack of discipline, the joy in human unreason."[84] The shift in vocabulary is important, since *Wahnsinn* implies *Wahn*, i.e., hallucinations, delusions, deliriums: necessary ingredients of all ritual madness that does not lay claim to the techniques of reason. *Irrsinn*, in contrast, suggests not only error, as in *Irrtum*, but a wandering mind, one that strays from the path: *irren*, to drift, to stray, *sich verirren*, to get lost. *Wahnsinn*, then, implies a vision that constitutes a belief—be it an erroneous delusion or an inspired divination. The ideology of divine madness is always a theory of *Wahnsinn*, relying on the possible substitution of one sense [*Sinn*] for another—*Irrsinn* implies a dynamic and unlimited deviation, like travel in an unmarked desert, a failure to walk the established paths of reason as well as to create new paths: a failure to arrive.

In a world ruled by ultimately arbitrary value judgments, Nietzsche's madness as *Irrsinn* constitutes both the exemplification of a truth drive freed of its moral moorings, and, as the title of the section proposes, "the greatest danger":

> *The greatest danger.*—If there had not always been a majority of men who considered the discipline of their minds—their 'rationality'—their pride, their obligation, and their virtue, feeling insulted or embarrassed by all fantasies and excesses of thought, as friends of 'healthy common sense,' humanity would have perished long ago! Above it has always hovered, and still hovers, as its greatest danger, the eruption of madness [*Irrsinn*]—which means the eruption of arbitrariness in feeling, seeing, and hearing, the enjoyment of the mind's lack of discipline, the joy in human unreason. Not truth and certainty are the opposite of the world of the madman, but the universality and the universal binding force of a faith; in sum, the non-arbitrary character of judgments.[85]

This passage echoes Nietzsche's arguments in *Truth and Lie*, where the complicity of reason and morality, or, as he says here, "rationality" and "virtue," emerge as a conceit of survival. All the great debates of political theory tend to focus on the distinction between natural right and convention: Nietzsche, however, no friend of natural right theory, argues for the indispensability of thinking about convention *as* natural right. To phrase it differently: while he frequently and forcefully argues that morality is, to use the current shortcut phrase, socially constructed, he also suggests, as the earlier reading of *Truth and Lie* argues, that morality itself has been an inextricable part of what humans are.[86] More importantly, he insists that the distinction between reason and morality that underlies the debate about natural right vs. convention is a late invention, anachronistic when applied to any but the most recent period of time.

As we have seen, the true/false dichotomy that is part of all conceptions of reason carries both prescriptive and prohibitive force from the beginning, if originally only in the sense of communal pressure to use "the right name"[87] to designate a perception and to refrain from the wrong names—unless it be as part of a game. While this accord does not, in itself, represent a genuine truth drive, it is nonetheless the first moment in the truth drive's genealogy. And for all the accidents, reversals, and contingencies of its later development, this truth drive has not fundamentally deviated from its original purpose, i.e., the fundamental deception about the totality of life before "its metamorphosis in man."

In Deleuze's paraphrase, "the concept of truth describes a 'truthful' world. Even in science the truth of phenomena forms a 'world' distinct from that of phenomena themselves." And

> he who wills the truth always wills to depreciate [the] high power of the false: he makes life an 'error' and this world an 'appearance.' He therefore opposes knowledge to life and to the world he opposes another world, a world-beyond, the truthful world. The truthful world is inseparable from this will, the will to treat *this world* as an appearance. Thus the opposition of knowledge and life, the distinction between worlds, reveals its true character: it is a distinction of moral origin, an *opposition of moral origin*.[88]

Deleuze treats this problem in connection with the ascetic ideal: "knowledge, morality and religion; the true, the good and the divine as values superior to life. All three are connected: the ascetic ideal is the third moment, but also the sense and value of the other two moments."[89] Deleuze is right to single out asceticism as a specific constellation of morality, truth, and religion; Nietzsche, however, sees the connection between knowledge and morality by no means only in various forms of asceticism (understood as a strategy by which the weak preserve themselves). As *Truth and Lie* as well as much of Nietzsche's later work suggest, the complicity of truth and morality rather seems inherent to the functioning of communicating language itself, even though it can, of course, take different forms and serve different purposes.

To divest reason, or truth drive, from all forms of morality is one of the most important, and perhaps ultimately impossible, tasks of the genealogist. It certainly seems to be his most dangerous undertaking, for the morality of reason that characterizes life long before its specific ascetic—Socratic or Christian—configurations, is as much a life-serving concept as it is a life-negating one, or possibly even more so. The moral component is essential as a homogenizing agent of reason:

> And man's greatest labor so far has been to reach agreement about very many things and to take on a *law of agreement*—regardless of whether these things are true or false.[90]

Without this "greatest labor," the labor of accord that constitutes the moral category of law, mankind would have perished long ago. This accord, always sustained simultaneously by an idea of reason and an idea of morality, operates under the threat of *Irrsinn*, a threat so strong that "essentially one may talk with little faith about the future of mankind [*dass man im Grunde von der Zukunft der Menschheit mit wenig Vertrauen reden darf*]" (FW 76, KSA 3: 431–2).

While those that pride themselves on the virtue of their rationality sustain the relative stability of life, it is now the "the most select minds" who "continually strain against this obligatoriness [*sträuben sich gerade die ausgesuchtesten Geister gegen jene Allverbindlichkeit*]"—and "the explorers of truth lead the way! [*die Erforscher der Wahrheit voran!*]" (ibid., 432). The history of the truth drive has finally reached the point, then, where the moral idea of rationality and the amoral desires of the truth drive part company. The truth drive has evolved into lust [*Lüsternheit*, ibid.], a lust of *Irrsinn* as a lust of speed, "for madness has such a gay tempo [*weil der Irrsinn so ein fröhliches Tempo hat!*]" (ibid.).

Despite its almost apocalyptic scenario, this passage ends on a lighthearted note, right after Nietzsche includes himself among the fast-paced forces of *Irrsinn* that threaten the slow dance of the masses which he both acclaims and ridicules:

> we need *virtuous stupidity*, we need those who unshakably drum the beat of the *slow* mind so that the faithful of the great universal faith stay together and continue their dance. *We others are the exception and the danger*—we always need defense!—Well, there really might something be said in favor of the exception, *as long as it never wants to become the rule*. (ibid.)

This atmospheric reversal seems to suggest that Nietzsche, gay scientist and fast-footed madman, finally trusts the staying power of the conventions of sanity more than he suggests earlier on; simultaneously, this about-face embodies the full paradox of a writer writing not to be read, not to be understood, not to be heeded. If this is madness, then it is a madness that understands itself, and understands itself to be saner than reason as we know it, and yet as being more dangerous than any criminal ever was to *Sittlichkeit*. The virtue of rationality, in the end, differs from the virtue of *Sitte* in that it has no defenses against the madman whose affliction is not a delusion but a delirium of truth. While Nietzsche, in the end, seems to trust that only the few will succumb to this lust, there can ultimately be no certain way to contain it.

I have argued earlier in this chapter that the idea of a mad truth depends on the faith in a higher authority that would send it and endow it with meaning; Nietzsche's portrait of the gay madmen among whom he counts himself seems to contradict this claim. The truth they proclaim, however, is not the truth of a system or belief, and they are mad not as the old visionaries were mad. Madness under the reign of *Sittlichkeit* is beholden to an idea of truth that would bind everyone into a universal faith—the new madmen rave against faith itself. In canceling the contract between knowledge and faith, however, their truth is *Irrsinn* itself—the truth of no arrival. It is at this very point where the truth drive finally liberates itself from its erstwhile purpose to serve the stability of culture, however, that it must call itself into question. Earlier, Nietzsche speaks of the all-important battle between truth drive and life-preserving errors—in the lustful *Irrsinn* of Nietzsche's truth-loving madmen, this battle has been fought and won by a desire whose superior value is, after all, far from established.[91] Nietzsche suggests that the desire for truth will turn into a suicidal force if it is not held in check by those who, albeit perhaps unknowingly, love the law more than the question of true and false.

Nietzsche conjures a historical moment where the truth of *Irrsinn*, or *Irrsinn* as truth, could effect the end of civilization itself—unless the truth drive turns against itself once more. In the first reversal, the truth drive would eliminate the moral sentiment that brought it into being, sustained and nurtured it. In the instant where the truth drive discovers the truth about truth, namely: that it is not, it is paradoxically still motivated by the love of truth. In the second reversal, the truth drive would have to abandon *itself*, it would have to start asking the questions that open *Beyond Good and Evil*:

> We asked about the *value* of this will [to truth]. Supposed that we want truth: *why not rather* untruth? And uncertainty? Even ignorance?...And should one believe it that it may finally appear to us as if that problem has never before been posed—as if it was seen by us for the first time, focused on, *dared*? For there is daring in it, and perhaps there is no greater daring.[92]

To question the value of truth is not only a great, perhaps the greatest daring—it seems that there is no more important undertaking. Nietzsche pretends to wonder that he is the first to ask the question about the value of truth, but his own work suggests that it did not *have* to be asked earlier, since it was never before a matter of truth alone, since there never was any truth independent of moral imperatives, imperatives always stronger than the imperative to know.

The death of God, this most famous of Nietzsche's formulae (even though it had been employed long before Nietzsche), may from now on serve as a shorthand for the threatening split between morality and reason—a split that has not yet occurred, and perhaps, or even probably, never will. It is still impossible to tell whether the truth of God's death will ever, as Nietzsche has it, "arrive"—and yet, he mourns it in section 125 of the *Gay Science*, mourns it in the voice of a madman.

This madman is no dancer; there is not a trace of gaiety in this passage, which represents a somber counterimage to the ironic undertones of the earlier one. This shift in attitude is, again, marked by a shift in vocabulary. The madman who mourns the death of God is *der tolle Mensch*, where *toll* connotes not only madness but a frantic, furious, and destructive quality: a dog with rabies is *toll* (English uses 'mad dog' in much the same way, but the implication is much stronger in the more specific German term *toll*).

Once again—and possibly, I will suggest, for the last time—mad truth arrives like the madness of old, as the truth to come. The madman on the marketplace occupies the same ambivalent position that circumscribed the moral madness of *Sittlichkeit*:

> 'I have come too early,' he said then; 'my time is not yet. This tremendous event is still on its way, still wandering; it has not yet reached the ears of men. Lightning and thunder take time, the light of the stars takes time, deeds, though done, still require time to be seen and heard. This deed is still more distant from them than the most distant stars—*and yet they have done it themselves.*[93]

While the madman, classically, appears as a solitary figure, facing a crowd of unbelieving spectators, he is yet part of it: " 'Whither is God?' he cried; 'I will tell you! *We have killed him*—you and I! All of us are his murderers!' " (FW, KSA 3: 480–1).[94] His madness, however, is not a revelation anymore, but an anticipation of the effects of an act already committed. He is a genealogist of the future, a precipitate reader of events who precedes his time, born too early, a prototypical subject of "untimely meditations,"[95] to be heeded, like Cassandra, only after his death.

Nietzsche himself has come to be so closely associated with the death of God that the temptation to read the madman *as* Nietzsche is strong. In essence, this is what Christoph Türcke suggests when he claims, without qualification, that Nietzsche "represented [the madman] in order not to become like him,"[96] a gamble that, for Türcke, proves to have failed when Nietzsche breaks down.

In order even to begin to unravel the complexities of Nietzsche's moves in this short text, however, we have to take more seriously than Türcke does that Nietzsche's madman is a narrative persona, a fictional voice in which Nietzsche, the master of many voices, writes—and that he is introduced by another fictional voice, a narrator who frames his appearance. It is this narrator, not an implied authorial—Nietzschean—voice that presents him as a madman. Certainly, the maniac delivers part of his soliloquy in a tone resembling the high style of the prophets, similar to Zarathustra. Thus, he may be said to stand in the tradition of divine madness—but is this not, at least potentially, a masterfully ironic device rather than the desperate self-protecting, self-concealing confessional that Türcke reads in it? Can we say with any confidence that Nietzsche represents the maniac as someone he tries not to be? Does this specific passage offer insights that Nietzsche conceals elsewhere? The madman's soliloquy is not dissonant with those parts of Nietzsche's oeuvre that are spoken in the sane voices of argument and logic; God has always died in Nietzsche's writing, and the announcement of God's death does not seem to be in itself a mad event. In what sense, and from whose perspective, then, is the man on the marketplace mad?

These questions necessitate a closer look at the dim figures of the "bystanders" who watch his performance. These bystanders, it is said, "do not believe in God," and they are baffled and amused by the urgency with which the man searches for God—and he does, indeed, search for God before he starts to mourn his death. God, then, dies in the moment of this search, the death of God is enacted precisely here in this text, in the encounter with the atheists who do not understand that God was once alive. Thus, the maniac subjects himself to a historical moment, or, more precisely, he condenses what is really a historical process into a moment to be experienced. The man, if mad, is a mad historian, mad, perhaps, because he introduces a historical dimension into the question once (and still) deemed the most ahistorical of all: the question of God's existence. He asks (and, to a certain degree, answers) this question not as a historian of the past, but as a historian of the present, as someone aware of a precise historical instant he finds himself in. It is a deeply paradoxical moment, reminiscent of those animated cartoon moments where a rabbit, having run across the edge into an abyss, can keep running in thin air as long as he does not realize that he has left the firm ground behind. It is not the madman, however, who thus runs over open space, but the bystanders "who do not believe in God," but do believe that their world is not affected by an event they did not know happened. These "mere faithless [bloß Glaubenslosen]," as Martin Heidegger calls them in his comment on this passage, have not realized "nihilism as the fate of their own history [Nihilismus als Geschick ihrer eigenen Geschichte]."[97]

God, to put it in Nietzsche's bluntest formulation, has always been "an error [Irrthum]," but like many Nietzschean errors, it constituted historical reality. God exists, or has existed, in the same way that metaphysics exists: possibly, or probably, as a delusion, but as a delusion that creates cultural reality in the widest sense. In the Gay Science, Nietzsche argues that "believed motives" are far more important than actual motives:

> The inner happiness and misery of men has been imparted to them according to their faith in this or that motive—not, however, by that which really was motive! All of the last is of secondary interest.[98]

The former belief in God as a force that creates both reality and our perception of it, then, is far more important than the shallow insight of the bystanders who do not realize that they are still living by the very effects of the faith they do not hold. They are, in a Nietzschean formulation that Heidegger picks up, "incomplete nihilists" who "may well replace the previous values with other ones, but [they] place them in the old space which is quasi held free as the realm of the metaphysical [des Übersinnlichen]."[99]

Nietzsche's madman, in contrast, knows that the center does not hold anymore. In powerful metaphors of a post-Copernican apocalypse, he asks:

> What did we do when we unchained the earth from its sun? Whereto is it moving now? Whereto are we moving? Away from all suns? Are we not

falling all the time? And backwards, sideways, forwards, to all sides? Is there still an above and a below?[100]

If the answer to these questions is no, then all orientation, and with it the possibility of all moral and intellectual hierarchy is lost. Even the term *vertigo* would not do justice to the implications of this loss; without an above and a below, there cannot even be an abyss anymore. There is no "whereto," and there is, strictly speaking, no fall, only the endless space of *Irrsinn* that used to be circumscribed by the virtuous rationalists, who are, of course, the same people as the bystanders. And yet, Nietzsche's madman's lament turns into a tribute before his monologue is over: "There never was a greater deed—and whoever will be born after us will, by force of this deed, belong to a higher history than all history has been hitherto."[101]

It is true that a whole world collapses in Nietzsche's writings, a collapse engendered by the death of God thought in all its severity. "God," Türcke rightly points out,

> does not simply stand for a higher being in which one may believe or not, but for the essence of metaphysics, and that means: if God falls, then the whole immaterial spiritual being falls that lends the physical world form, coherence, recognizability [*Form, Zusammenhalt, Erkennbarkeit*].[102]

It is, of course, the very assumption that "form, coherence, recognizability" exist by timeless, supernatural dispensation that collapses here. If there is form, if there is coherence, then they have come into being as a deeply human achievement—and the "immaterial spiritual being" that sustains them is both part of the same creative act and one of these "cobwebs of millennia" which Nietzsche diagnoses as "brain maladies." The death of God is both an overdue necessity and a catastrophe whose consequences cannot be foreseen. God has never lived, and God cannot yet die. Like the end of morality, God's death is always a dual event, deliverance and disaster, a terrible and a hopeful spectacle. Most of all, however, it is a *historical* event of the greatest magnitude, one that defines both the past and the future. "God is dead" means, in Heidegger's reading, "the fate of two millennia of occidental history."[103]

As such, however, it does not, by itself, mean the end of *Erkennbarkeit*, as Türcke suggests, only the end of a certain kind of *Erkennen*, perhaps even the very beginning of recognition. The anticipation of a reversal of this magnitude does not, at least not in this reader, produce any positive visions; it is impossible to tell, in Weber's paraphrase of a similar conundrum, "whether at the end of this tremendous development entirely new prophets will arise, or whether there will be a great rebirth of old ideas and ideals, or, if neither, mechanized petrification, embellished with a sort of convulsive self-importance."[104]

Heidegger seems to suggest that the madman's truth leads us to renew the search for God which, for him, is synonymous with thinking (as opposed to mere reason). Heidegger argues that the bystanders "cannot search for God anymore, because they do not think anymore." And, later: "The maniac, in contrast, is unambiguously [*eindeutig*] according to the first sentences, even more unambiguously according to the last sentences of the piece, the one who is searching for God by screaming for God." And, lastly: "Thinking only begins when we have experienced that reason, glorified [*verherrlicht*] for centuries, is the most tenacious opponent of thinking."[105]

This is a suggestive reading, but one, I fear, that is not borne out by the text. It seems at least doubtful whether the madman is *at the end* still "searching for God by screaming for God." The madman's words are unambiguous: "God is dead! God remains dead! [*Gott ist todt! Gott bleibt todt!*]" (FW 125, KSA 3: 481) It is not even clear, I think, that reason [*Vernunft*] emerges as the antithesis of thinking. Heidegger himself says that the maniac has only "fully moved into [*eingerückt*] the predestined essence of previous man, to be the animal rationale."[106] As such, he speaks from the culmination of reason, but not, or at least not yet, its self-termination. The maniac may very well mark the end of Enlightenment reason, of "incomplete nihilism," of a moral reason that thinks it can claim its secularity within a nonsecular metaphysical structure. The madman's last deed is the destruction of the institutions that are sustained by a principle that no longer applies:

> One tells that, on the same day, the madman invaded several churches and there started to sing his requiem aeternam deo. Led out and questioned, he only answered: 'But what are these churches now if not the tombs and the gravestones of God?'

The requiem may be eternal, but it is a requiem to a dead God that will not rise from the dead this time: "God remains dead." The search is over.

The madman's madness, to repeat, is not defined by his knowledge of God's death, but by the knowledge of all that follows from this death, as well as by his determination to mourn it. Heidegger proposes that this man is "*toll*" because he is "*ver-rückt*." *Verrückt*, one of the German terms for mad, literally designates a displacement, comparable to the English 'deranged'. For Heidegger, "he has moved out of [*ausgerückt*] the realm of previous man, within which the ideals of the supernatural world, having become unreal, are presented as the real while their opposite realizes itself. This mad [*verrückte*] man has moved beyond [*herausgerückt*] previous man."[107] Deeply deviant in regard to "previous" humanity, however, he is also the only one in this scene who is not *verrückt*—the only character who is aware of, or rather who *lives* his own historical moment. While the bystanders operate within a delay during which the structure of their thought still holds while its foundation has crumbled, the maniac has actually arrived in the present—even though he is, like Nietzsche, "born posthumously *unzeitgemäß* precisely because he knows his time, because he does not experience the delay with which all present truth unfolds.

Is the madman the same as Nietzsche? He certainly looks like him, in a certain light, from a certain angle. Nietzsche, however, does not mourn, and *der tolle Mensch* may very well be philosophy's last madman. The madness of truth has always needed a God to sustain it—Nietzsche sees this perhaps more clearly than the modernists who follow after him. He is not in the business of rehabilitating the insane, and he has more than one snicker for the tradition of reverence for the mad:

> All experiences used to have a different glow, for a God shone out of them; likewise, all decisions and anticipations of the far future: for one had oracles and secret clues and believed in prophecy. 'Truth' was experienced differently, for the insane could be accepted formerly as its mouthpiece—which makes *us* shudder and laugh.[108]

God's death, then, is the last event that can send off a mad truth, the last event to shatter reason from within. Since God is both dead and not dead, his wake is a song both mad and truthful, and as long as we do not know whether his death ever will arrive, mad knowledge has not and may never fully become obsolete. The Nietzschean philosopher who knows about the death of God certainly has nothing to gain from madness as *Wahnsinn* anymore—but he might be the privileged voice of *Irrsinn*.

THE HYPERBOREAN: LA VACHE QUI DANSE

This is not to say that philosopher and madman are one and the same, even though Nietzsche's philosophy operates in a paradoxical field in this regard. As we have seen, Nietzsche raises the question of madness as genealogist, as evaluator, and, in a category that needs explanation, as Hyperborean philosopher. The Hyperboreans, figures from Pindar's poetry, are mythical creatures: "Neither by sea, nor by land will you be able to find the way to the Hyperboreans," Pindar says. Nietzsche, however, in a posthumous note titled "We Hyperboreans," claims to have arrived in their impossible place:

> Beyond the north, the ice, the hardness, the coldness—*our life! our happiness!* We are Hyperboreans. We know the road, we have found the exit out of whole millennia of labyrinth. Who else has found it?[109]

After Nietzsche, the question of an *absolute* madness might perhaps be raised only from this perspective—the unthinkable, unreachable perspective of one who has moved beyond morality, out of the labyrinth of reason defined and confined by moral presuppositions. As Nietzsche's work itself suggests, it is indeed an impossible position to assume in all its purity, or for longer than a split second. Perhaps Nietzsche has found the road—that does not yet mean that he traveled it often, or that he settled beyond the North wind for any length of time.

From the Hyperborean perspective, there can be no madness, because any accord that would allow us to declare anyone or anything mad is fragile. To be sure, this space is part of Nietzsche's philosophy, and to inhabit it is one of the demands he poses to anyone whom he would accept as a fellow philosopher. From any other viewpoint, however, the Hyperborean perspective is itself the quintessentially mad perspective, since it is outside the jurisdiction of all accords but its own—a perspective considerably *more* fragile than all moralities.

If Nietzsche alone has found the way, if he is the only Hyperborean—"I say 'we' out of politeness"—then he speaks from a place that is, for all the rest of us, not merely eccentric or marginal but experipheral: *arbitrary* not in the sense of capricious, unjustified, or inconsistent, but in the sense that he established in the *Gay Science* as *"beliebige"*: "Not truth and certainty are the opposite of the world of the madman, but the universality and the universal binding force of a faith; in sum, the non-arbitrary character [*das Nicht-Beliebige*] of judgments."[110] His philosophy, then, would be deeply, necessarily, irrevocably mad—"the greatest danger." This danger, as we have seen in the previous section, is contained as long as it remains the exception among the majority of the "friends of common sense":

> We others are the exception and the danger—we eternally require defense.—
> Well, there is something to say in favor of the exception, *given that it will never desire to become the rule.*

Nietzsche, detractor of the herd, nonetheless finds kind words for mediocrity, as perhaps only elitists can:

> How may one spoil mediocrity for the mediocre! I do, as one will see, the opposite: for every step away from morality—this is what I teach—leads *to immorality!*[111]
> Hatred against mediocrity is unworthy of a philosopher; it is almost a question mark to his *right* to 'philosophy'. Precisely because he is the exception, he has to protect the rule, he has to maintain mediocrity's good courage to itself.[112]

But nothing can guarantee that the drive for unreason will not spread, a danger not merely to morality or moralities, but to the very survival of the species. Under the threat of insanity as *Beliebigkeit*, "one may basically speak with little faith of the future of mankind."[113] And while, in the age of God's death, the force of *Sittlichkeit* recedes and the will to truth increases, we may indeed near an age of *Beliebigkeit*:

> Continuously, the image of things is shifting; and from now on perhaps more and faster than ever; continuously, especially the choicest of minds struggle against that universal obligation [of accord]—the explorers of *truth* lead the way![114]

So the explorers of *truth*, philosophers surely among them, might lead the way into madness, a road they share with the artists and poets said to cherish madness chiefly for its "gay pace," a pace suitable no less for a gay science, a dancing philosopher. But if Nietzsche is singing the praise of *allegro* thought, he has more often declared his taste for the *lento*.[115] Even though he here ridicules "the slow pace which the commonplace belief demands of all mental processes" as "this imitation of the turtle which is accepted as the norm,"[116] he will sing the praise of the cow in *Beyond Good and Evil*. On the whole, I think, Nietzsche comes down on the side of deceleration, against the madmen of all times: "The heroes, martyrs, geniuses and inspired men are not quiet, patient, refined, cold, slow enough for our taste."[117]

The philosopher can never be *simply* a madman, for the gay pace of madness is but one mode of existence, and not the one Nietzsche cherishes most. Even if, and especially if, it still carries prophetic power, it is only the convention to come, in an oscillation between yesterday's madness and today's reason that allows Nietzsche to say, in *Beyond Good and Evil*: "Madness is rare in individuals—but in groups, parties, peoples, and times, it is the rule."[118]

And since it is the rule, we find ourselves with a dubious heritage: "Not only the reason of millennia, also their madness breaks out in us. It is dangerous to be an heir."[119] If Nietzsche is correct, then we are heir to all kinds of madmen, and, in a sense, to madmen only. Nietzsche writes under the enormous tension of someone who has taken up the burden of morality's *Selbstaufhebung*, a project that, as he himself suggests, always operates under the risk of amounting to reason's self-annihilation. The risks we take, however, do not necessarily fail us, and I do not think we can know for certain that Nietzsche's gamble was an impossible one.

Morality can only deny itself in Nietzsche's thought because he so relentlessly uses its own vocabulary against it; reason only enters its most precarious state because Nietzsche unmasks its sustaining concept of truth as self-contradictory, in arguments as rigorous as any defender of the truth of logic might wish for. And even though Nietzsche wanted to think of himself as a great affirmer, his affirmations may already have proven to be less vital than his negations. If reason and truth and morality are not what they present themselves to be, and if madness always stands in an antithetical relation to reason, truth, and morality, then there is either nothing but madness, or there is no such thing as madness. The relation between madness and reason parallels the relation between true and apparent world as Nietzsche formulates it in *Twilight of the Idols*: "We have abolished the true world: which world remains? the apparent one perhaps? . . . But no! *together with the true world, we have abolished the apparent one as well!*"[120]

Nietzsche himself, in any case, never says that madness—with or without God—holds any potential that would go beyond a disturbance of local reason, local truth, local morality. It certainly provides no escape from

Hegel's dialectical machine. There is not a single passage in Nietzsche that unambiguously celebrates madness, but there are quite a few passages that either present madness as a danger or poke fun at the "certain convention of madness."

This is not to say that the the idea of madness has become obsolete for anyone but the Hyperborean philosopher—even Nietzsche lived beyond the North wind only for moments. To be a philosopher of Nietzsche's ambition, "one must speak several languages and produce several texts at once."[121] In Nietzsche's case, more specifically, this entails a language that dances and a language that chews the cud, vulgar and decadent language, the language of philologist, psychologist, scientist, historian, and logician; the language of affliction and the language of recovery. Madness loses its privileges along the same way on which reason, God, and morality lose theirs. Perhaps, Nietzsche has indeed made mad language—the speech of true, voluntary, and feigned madness—one of the languages of philosophy, but they are subjected to reason throughout. In the end, his most powerful image might be his most humble one—not the summit or the mountaintop, but its opposite, the island of *Daybreak*:

> In the midst of the ocean of becoming, we awake on a little island that is no larger than a dinghy, we adventurers and birds of passage, and we look around for a short time: as quickly and as curiously as possible, for how fast can a wind blow us away, how fast can a wave wash over the little island, so that nothing of us will be left. But here, in this small space, we find other birds of passage and hear of former ones—and so we live for a delicious moment of recognition and solved riddles, among a gay fluttering of wings and twittering, and we venture out onto the ocean in our minds, not less proud than the ocean itself.[122]

Zarathustra's triumph is not the "freedom of meaninglessness," but the creation of meaning. The title of the last chapter is "The Sign," and Zarathustra's triumph reads: "Am I striving for my *happiness*? I am striving for my *work*!" But this might very well be the same thing, for when "the sign comes (KSA 4: 406)," it comes in the same image of fluttering wings that Nietzsche evokes on the little island, a space of reason under the unremitting threat of wind and surge, but of reason nonetheless.

CONCLUSION

LOGOS AND PALLAKSCH: PAUL CELAN'S "TÜBINGEN, JÄNNER"

theos ê tis anthrôpôn?
("A god or one of the humans?")

—the first four words of Plato's *Laws*

ANACHRONY

If supreme madness has a guiding trope, it is anachrony. The madness of both poetry and philosophy is defined by the ways in which time misbehaves—be it in Cassandra's transgressive knowledge of the future, Socrates' palinodic memories of an unknowable past, Hölderlin's speculations about the tragic subversion of human time itself, or Nietzsche's portrayal of a maniacal recognition of a truth that cannot be assimilated in, or to, the present. When Socrates speaks of divine *mania* as a 'complete change' of all that is customary and familiar, this change concerns an intense transgression of the limits of bodies in time. For Hölderlin, the shattering encounter between human and divine, i.e. tragic madness, creates a space where beginning and end do not 'rhyme' anymore because time itself has turned. Nietzsche's madman, announcer of the greatest catastrophe ever to befall human culture, has not only come 'too early,' he is speaking of an event that has both already happened and not yet arrived. This most 'untimely' of all Nietzsche's characters is, as I have argued, the last divinely inspired madman, messenger of a death that also marks the end of a mode of speaking.

The anachrony of supreme madness is mirrored in the anachronisms of the book. The distinction between poetry and philosophy is hard to maintain in the wake of poststructuralism, and yet it is at the heart of the discussion. To study madness without reference to the history of the asylum may appear historically naive or politically retrograde, not just in view of Foucault's work and its enormous impact, but, more importantly, in light of the appalling conditions that still characterize the streets and the institutions where today's mad live. The very term of madness has become superannuated by the concept of mental illness with its thousand diagnoses. And last, the notion of the divine, which grounds the division into high and low madness that is crucial to this study, has long ago lost its intellectual force and aesthetic legitimacy.

And yet, this is not the history of a metaphor or a record of its death, or at least not exclusively. The image of madness relates to the history of poetry like a watermark—much of the time, it is so faint that it can barely be distinguished from the blank page, but at a certain angle, in a certain light, it appears suddenly as prominent as the writing itself—and much harder to erase. Poetry has long lived in the tension between *technê* and *mania*[1]—as the form of speaking and writing that is both most rigorously formalized and quintessentially unteachable, as the most as well as the least individual voice, as the most hermetic and yet the most archaic form of speech, as that which guards the particular in constituting community. In this sense, it is perhaps not surprising that the figure of the mad poet is still prominent at a time when poetry itself—or the literary in general—cannot always be clearly distinguished anymore from other forms of writing, and when the very term of madness has become all but obsolete in its generic vagueness.

These days, the mad poet of the cultural imagination rarely invades philosophy or literary theory, but rather makes his appearance in psychology and related disciplines. There exists a voluminous 'science of creativity'[2] to which, more often than not, a poem is one symptom among many—be it of extraordinary mental health (whatever that may be to any given author) or of deep psychical affliction. Often, psychological and psychiatric studies of creative psychopathology begin or culminate in lengthy lists of long-dead famous writers,[3] all mad or at least alleged to have been mad, as if they could testify to the sure grasp of a scientific or quasiscientific stance to which the gods have always been as dead as they can be. This gesture, whether psychological, anthropological, medical, or neuroscientific in approach, is as a rule linked to a both unapologetically ahistorical and aggressively secular intellectual gestus. Even Dodds, whose fifty-year-old study on *The Greeks and the Irrational* remains one of the best monographs written on his subject, reproaches fellow scholars for "ignor[ing] the evidence of anthropology and abnormal psychology,"[4] as if contemporary psychology or anthropology did not belong to a specific historical moment that closely circumscribes what validity they possess. The madness of creation (i.e., of *poiêsis*, 'making'), however, has its roots in a universe divided by a line between the sacred and the secular; its very possibility has depended on this line—or, more specifically, on crossing it.

In the secular world of quantitative science, despite its habitual and at times fascinating flights into theoretical speculation, the relationship between mental illness and creativity remains forever restricted to correlation, and Leon E. A. Berman laconically sums up the dilemma of the field when he says that 'we are continually vexed by the fact that not all creative artists are mad, and not all mad people are creative.'[5] Much of this vexation, I would argue, stems from the fact that the sciences cannot, *qua* science, engage in criticism;[6] in other words, while science can distinguish between ever so many forms of mental illness, it cannot, on its own terms, tell one poem from the next. But it is only the theoretical possibility of such distinctions (no matter how problematic in practice) that would allow us to ask whether a specific kind of madness is (or may have been) involved in a specific kind of writing or speaking. The link between *this* madness and *this* making, however, is not simply ancient but rather properly *belongs to* antiquity and the pre-modern—as Nietzsche argued in *Daybreak*. In this context, the madness of the poets is not the same as mental illness,[7] and the distinction is the more important the more uncannily close their resemblance may be at times.

Many of the ways in which metaphysical madness and mental illness oppose each other are obvious: Mental illness, say in the articulation of the current *Diagnostic and Statistical Manual for Mental Disorders* (DSM-IV), is an attribute of the individual, and it resides in his body or mind; divine madness, descending from above, manifests itself through works from which all traces of individual provenance have been erased. Psychiatry and psychology ultimately seek to ground themselves in the methods of the natural sciences, but the idea of divine madness is irreducibly metaphysical. The categorization and catalogization of mental illnesses, their symptoms, and putative etiologies are a quintessentially modern project of progressive analysis to which the notion of divine madness cannot submit, but which it also cannot withstand without becoming something entirely different. Contemporary madness is a matter of the *physis*, as it was even and perhaps especially in Freud, who to some appears most removed from today's psychiatric theory and practice; ancient madness, in contrast with the now prevalent concept of the cultural or historical other, conceptualizes a realm of more radical alterity—an otherness that was yet, at times and unpredictably, porous.

When Augustine talks to his God, the medievalist Catherine Brown writes in a wonderful essay, he is

> addressing his other, probably the most Other being a late antique or medieval Christian believer could imagine. He speaks the foreign-country metaphor: he is far away in a land of unlikeness (*regio dissimilitudinis*, translated here as 'a land where all is different from your own') where they do things differently from God, cut off by a divide that feels 'like an impassable abyss.'[8]

And yet, this 'impassable abyss' is, or can become, a space of interaction, even though such encounters carry tremendous risk at times, a risk to which both Nietzsche and Hölderlin are attuned, if in different ways. It is only in Plato that the interaction between the divine and the human seems at times curiously serene—perhaps precisely because the revelatory moments of the soul concern the philosopher as well as the poet, so that *logos* must remain human.

Secular modernity has changed the ways in which we can conceptualize the interaction between humans and that which is not human, without, needless to say, ridding us of all phenomena other eras could with some assurance ascribe to the divine.[9] The divide between the human and the divine could account for the seemingly sudden generation of beauty, form, and meaning precisely because it was both profound and bridgeable. The divine could be imagined and observed, at least in its effects, and it could, above all, be experienced—in religious ecstasy, in the delicious shudder at the sight of a beautiful boy, in the apparition of a poem or a thought that did not originate in a mind one could confidently call one's own. By contrast, Hölderlin's era—to the extent to which he represents it—is still open to the idea of the divine, but the divine no longer generates its own experience, only betrayal's empty spaces in the observable world.[10] In consequence, Hölderlin is at a double remove from the gods, for the most part deciphering their bygone effects in the recorded words and gestures of others—but the divine is not yet a purely historical category, not yet nothing but an idea whose time has gone. The gods are, in his famous words, absent, but they have left material traces, solid letters, that can be read. And they still generate poetry, even if it is now written in defiance.

Nietzsche's ambiguous formulation of the *death* of God acknowledges the same traces, but they become the signs of a tremendous (if tremendously productive) error. With his work, or rather the developments that culminate and crystallize in his work, the idea of the divine truly becomes history,[11] joining the realm of eternal and immutable forms, geocentric universes, and inorganic demons, and as we have seen, the idea of a wisdom acquired through madness (which has already become insanity, mental illness) makes him "shudder and laugh."

At the same time—and nobody has spoken about this with more urgency than Nietzsche—God's death leaves a vacuum, the need to conceptualize an other that is not merely culturally or historically different from the self-contemplating subject. Over the past decades, we have come to think of the other as that which both threatens and serves to consolidate what the self is or wants to be. Nietzsche's fin de siècle is certainly densely populated by such others: the female, the black, the oriental, the Jew, the homosexual, the psychotic, the child, and the animal (even though Rilke is probably the only one who has given adequate expression to the otherness of the last one). As numerous as these various figures of alterity may be, their otherness is of a status different from that of the departing divine, and they cannot take the place of a hypothetically absolute power that has become vacant—a power that could, among other things, account for the most complex enigmas of either poetic or philosophical creation.

In the end, the twentieth century found its powerful other nowhere else but in the human body, in that "intricate quivering of fibers" Nietzsche spoke of in *Beyond Truth and Lie*, forever removed from the man's "proud, delusional consciousness, detached from the windings of his entrails, the swift flow of his bloodstream, the intricate quivering of his fibers!" If the divine is that which can be experienced but not explained, the new microphysiological body that began to emerge in the nineteenth century and is now (or again) rapidly becoming the dominant model of the human can be explained but not experienced. The more precise scientific theories have become, the more removed they are from phenomenological awareness—you cannot experience your serotonin uptake or contemplate in the mode of self-knowledge your mitochondrial DNA.

It is a commonplace that the most durable definition of madness concerns deviance from an idealized norm, be it behavioral, moral, perceptual, or neurological. In a world where man was suspended between animal and angel, there was always the chance that a decline would turn out to have been a disguised ascent, but in the post-Darwinian world we inhabit, such reversals are far between. If madness and creation coexist now, they do so by accident,[12] for our appreciation of the new and the original may at times still privilege what is unheard-of. But it will be rare, for it is, unavoidably, the very nature of diagnosis to rely on that which has been seen before. It striking that in the twentieth century, the standard list of mad creators consists mostly of the melancholy and the suicidal, and while I believe that the medical model of depression and manic depression has merit, I am not yet ready to accept that we ought to medicalize quite so rashly despair, euphoria, and the desire for death—and *their* relation to writing is, I think, a different matter altogether.

In *Literature and the Gods*, Roberto Calasso writes that "literature is never the product of a single subject. There are always at least three actors: the hand that writes, the voice that speaks, the god who watches over and compels."[13] This may have been true for the longest time, but if anybody is watching these days, either his eye sockets are empty, or he is watching through a microscope.

APPROPRIATION

The Gods have become diseases

—C. G. Jung

If the madness of the maker and the madness of the asylum are profoundly different, they still share a name, and while it is imperative to distinguish between them, it may be just as important to trace what they have in common. There is indeed one element that ties together the most abject madness of the streets, i.e., severe psychosis, and the madness of epistemic privilege. That is the idea and the experience of a radical solitude—a loneliness beyond social isolation, obsessions and compulsions, or the intense inwardness of both mourning and melancholia. To hallucinate is to see or to hear what no one else can see or hear—to *know* it in the same mode of sensual certainty Hegel identified as the lowest form of consciousness. And even if our immediate awareness of what is here and now—"now, it is night," "this is a tree"[14]—disappears as soon as the night is over or we turn our back, it is still the mode of knowing we most readily assume we share. Now, it is night for all who are around us, this is a tree for all who look this way. Certainly, the *this* or *there* might be in deep shadow, and perhaps darkness descended during the day, but such doubts and uncertainties neither affect the certainty of perception itself nor the habitual assurance that others perceive as we do. For the Nietzsche of *Truth and Lie*, it is this commonality of perception that makes the world intelligible and language possible.[15]

Like the phantom pain of amputees, hallucination and sensory delusion cut through that primal bond, that first certainty, and expose as a radically interior construction our most basic and seemingly most reliable awareness of the external world and our own body. In *Phantoms in the Brain*, the neuroscientist V. S. Ramachandran describes an encounter with a partially paralyzed patient:

> I gripped a woman's lifeless left hand and, raising it, held it in front of her eyes.
> 'Whose arm is this?'
> She looked me in the eye and huffed, 'What's that arm doing in my bed?'
> 'Well, whose arm is it?'
> 'That's my brother's arm,' she said flatly. . . .
> 'Why do you think it's your brother's arm?'
> 'Because it's big and hairy, doctor, and I don't have hairy arms.'[16]

While the experiences of Ramachandran's patients invite various potentially intriguing speculations about selfhood and the physiology of self-awareness in general, they remain firmly anchored within the realm of pathology and appear to have little in common with the history or theory of divine madness. They serve well, however, to underscore the possibility of a profoundly solitary certainty that is the hallmark of the more exalted forms of nonreason. At its most powerful extreme, madness produces not the radical doubt of the modern philosopher but a knowledge that is both absolutely sure and absolutely singular. 'I foretold my countrymen all their sufferings. . . . I persuaded not one person of not one thing (*politais pant' ethespizon pathê. . . . epeithon ouden' ouden*).'[17]

The nameless woman's afflictions make her the object of anecdote, research, and therapy, but nobody will ever believe her about that arm. For Cassandra, having suffered a different kind of stroke, there is, of course, no cure, but her loneliness has a different quality. Apollo's cursed gift ensures that Cassandra's knowledge will arrive; in the *Agamemnon*, this arrival almost immediately succeeds her exit, and prophecy and the prophecied for once almost coincide: "the time is full (*chronon pleô*, 1299)." The future perfect of prophecy flashes into the dramatic present, but only after her speaking, which encompasses the whole range of mad utterance, has progressed from the moaning nonarticulation of *otototoi popoi da* (1072) to the intelligible order of *rhêsis* (dramatic speech, declaration, tale). Her predictions become increasingly accessible, and in her last speech, she insists that she is speaking for herself: "This one time I want to give a speech, or a funeral song of my very own [*hapax et' eipein rhêsin ê thrênon thelô emon ton autês*]" (1321–2). Her presence on stage thus recapitulates the passage of mad utterance into event or work, a movement I would like to call appropriation. Appropriation here means the process of recuperating mad speech as one's own—a return to subjectivity, if you will—as well as making it appropriate, i.e., acceptable to the community, bound into a system, and hence comprehensible. This movement, which emerges in Plato's *Phaedrus* as philosophy's most crucial event, always and everywhere marks the end of madness, or, to paraphrase Foucault, the presence of the work. Which is not to say that those works could have been possible without the moment of extreme unreason in which they originate.

The abyss that separates dead writers from their gods affects another gap, that between those writers and their contemporary reader. The older the texts are, the more their intellectual or spiritual center recedes out of sight, and the stronger the urge gets to translate their terms into a contemporary vocabulary. In this study, I have tried to resist this temptation, to let the terms unfold in their original constellations—tried and without doubt failed, since it is, of course, impossible not to invade any text one reads. Like Benjamin's angel of history, reading cannot resist the winds of its contemporaneity. It is once again a poem that, for me, exemplifies the struggle of reading madness carefully, mindful of both its historical moment and its anachronic particularity, Paul Celan's "Tübingen, Jänner."

ANAMNESIS

Writing about poetic madness is always a project of demystification and remystification. It is demystification because it tries to comprehend and formalize precisely that which presents itself as resisting understanding; any attempt to define madness loses the essence of its elusive power and appeal. Madness demystified is not madness anymore—it becomes either strategy or disease. Talking about madness, then, at the same time necessitates remystification, the creation of a space for madness apart from its critique, an elsewhere that always runs the risk of being only emptiness, mere negation without force. The following reading will trace the movement of de- and remystification in "Tübingen, Jänner," a text that denarrativizes (and thus retells) the stories of madness that surround Hölderlin's years in the tower.

Since Hölderlin remains the legendary figure of the quintessential mad philosopher's poet, at least in the German (and quite possibly the French) context, any poetic encounter with him will be an encounter with the *mythos* of poetic madness. Celan's poem is unmistakably a poem that speaks on Hölderlin as well as on his madness; I will argue that it does more: it speaks of the danger of this specific legend, of the veil it draws over Hölderlin's words. It is a meditation both on madness and on a specific gaze on madness, a poem on reading and blindness, and, lastly, not on the power of madness over poetry, but of poetry over madness.

> Tübingen, Jänner
>
> Zur Blindheit über-
> redete Augen.
> Ihre—'ein Rätsel ist Rein-
> entsprungenes'—, ihre
> Erinnerung an
> schwimmende Hölderlintürme, Möven-
> umschwirrt.
>
> Besuche ertrunkener Schreiner bei
> diesen
> tauchenden Worten:
>
> Käme,
> käme ein Mensch,
> käme ein Mensch zur Welt, heute, mit
> dem Lichtbart der
> Patriarchen: er dürfte,
> spräche er von dieser
> Zeit, er
> dürfte
> nur lallen und lallen,
> immer-, immer-
> zuzu.
>
> ("Pallaksch. Pallaksch.")[18]

There is little need to establish the Hölderlinian facets of this text. "Tübingen, Jänner" mentions Hölderlin by name, it evokes the carpenter and the tower, it quotes from his hymn "Der Rhein," and it closes with mad Hölderlin's sunken word "Pallaksch"[19]—or almost closes, for its last mark is a closing parenthesis. It is also, with equal force, a poem touching on madness. Its imagery is hallucinatory—swimming towers, visits of drowned carpenters, lightbeards. It is inhabited by voices and figures—by many more voices and shapes than appear on its surface, as the numerous readings of this poem have shown. It moves from what has been conveniently called hermetic imagery towards stuttering, stammering, and babble. It quotes, as I will explain, two 'mad' words, "immerzu" and "pallaksch." Madness is the poem's most persistent theme, but it is not one single madness that is at stake here.

If a human came—and the *if* implicit in the German subjunctive 'käme' is repeated three times—if a human came, and if he were of a certain quality, a quality associated with enlightened, prophetic, perhaps biblical speech, with the "light beard of the patriarchs"—he would not be able, or allowed, to speak at all, he "might only babble." Perpetually: "immer-, immer-/zuzu." Here, the babbling, the *lallen*, already invades the poem. The "perpetually" of *immerzu* falls apart, into "immer-, immer-" and "zuzu." A babbled word, a nonword. Also, in the repetition of "zu," a doubling of closure—for "zu" means 'shut'—and, at the same time, a negation of closure—for "zu" also means 'towards'. It is this simultaneity of opening and closing that seems most significant in this poem's advance towards the madness implicit in its last word, "pallaksch". The "immerzu" already is a mad word, and, like "pallaksch," a quotation, although, unlike "pallaksch," unmarked as such. It refers itself back to Georg Büchner's *Woyzeck*, a play with which Celan is intimately familiar: in his "Büchner-Preisrede," he refers to *immerzu* as Woyzeck's "Wahnsinnswort" ('word of madness'). Woyzeck is haunted by the *immerzu* while he contemplates the murder of his fiancée, Marie.[20] Woyzeck's hallucination, in turn, is itself a quotation: he overheard it when Marie cheered on the officer, her dance partner, "immer zu, immer zu"—"faster," "don't stop," "go on, go on!"

Thus, *immerzu* enters Celan's poem doubly mutated, as a memory of a memory, an allusion to an allusion, changing from innocuous flirtation to an urge toward murder to the perpetuity of a broken language. Celan does more than draw Woyzeck's *Wahnsinnswort* into the poem; the intertextual quality of the poem and the *Preisrede* takes us to Celan's comments on Büchner's "Lenz," a short story that chronicles Jakob Michael Reinhold Lenz's decline into madness. That story begins with another ascent into the abyss: "Am 20. Januar ging Lenz ins Gebirg." January twentieth, however, is also the date of the Wannsee conference. The "Jänner" of "Tübingen, Jänner," emerges as the splintered time of multiple memory.[21]

Rainer Zwibowski justly called the poem "diaphanous." It is not only the title that layers meaning over meaning; a comparable exegesis could probably be given for every single line. There are many memories written into this poem, memories of madnesses of radically different kinds. This condensation of various historical references could itself be read as a mad loss of location, a temporal disorientation, a loss of associative control. Multiple evocation is, of course, a poetic prerogative, not mad by itself, and while the ancient association of poetry and madness may be partially grounded precisely in such parallel discursive practices, the many disorientations of Celan's poem evoke an imposing poetic control rather than its loss. This poetic control in the face of madness, the power of *Rede*, is central to the poem.

"Immer-, immer-/zuzu." Toward what does the stammering language move? The next line after "zuzu" is blank (and the blankness of verse-breaks is never accidental in Celan's poetry, never a mere convention). Toward silence, then? An openness toward nothingness? Not quite, for there is a remainder, even though this remainder of speech is triply qualified: "pallaksch" is not only a non word, it is also not the poem's word, but a quotation from one who stopped speaking, from after poetry; it is doubled—and the madman's quoted nonword appears in parentheses. The *pallaksch*, as it appears in "Tübingen, Jänner," repeats the gesture of opening and closing on another level. For while it does not mean anything by itself, the nonword *pallaksch* which invades poetry (as madness, perhaps, invaded Hölderlin's life as a poet) is also something of a biographical watchword, signaling to Hölderlin readers that it is the late, the mad Hölderlin who is at stake here, the Hölderlin who, as his friend Schwab reported, refused to distinguish between *yes* and *no*.

In probably the most controversial single line of criticism in this century, Theodor W. Adorno asserted that "to write poetry after Auschwitz is barbarous." Perhaps this line is most appropriate precisely in reading Celan, and especially this poem, for the barbarians, originally, are those who stammer or babble, who do not speak the language, foreigners: to speak of this time, Celan, perhaps in a deeper agreement with Adorno, is to stammer and babble, barbarously, like a stranger.

Hölderlin is said to have retreated into "pallaksch" with signs of great distress, under conversational pressure by those who wanted to visit the famous madman and take a memory home, some meaning, some enlightenment. Confronted with these expectations, he retreated: "pallaksch." At Celan's time, "this time," one might have remembered different quotations from Hölderlin, and, more importantly, different quoters. By then, Hölderlin himself had become something of a poetic patriarch, the author of the *Vaterländische Gesänge*, patriotic (patriarchal?) songs, and he had been a popular poet with the National Socialist propaganda machine. Celan's Hölderlin poem answers to those other quotations with a total refusal of anything that could possibly be construed as patriotic rhetoric in the service of nationalist sentiment, or, for that matter, any meaning in any ideological service.

The reflections herein, however, are not foremost concerned with Celan, Germany, or that "this time." At stake in this reading are poetry and madness, the movement between *logos* and *pallaksch*—and "Tübingen, Jänner," speaks to this as well. It speaks in the very act of asking profound questions about the possibility of speaking, of insight, of remembrance. It does not say that no one may speak anymore, only that certain humans could not speak of this time in a certain way: that no patriarchal pronouncements are possible "today," and, by extension, that none may be expected here, in the space of this poem. At the same time, it is important to keep in mind that the patriarchs themselves have, at times, privileged babble over *logos*. Syntactically and phonologically, Celan's poem at the end operates in striking parallelism to a passage in Isaiah: "Jawohl, Gott wird einmal mit unverständlicher Sprache und mit einer fremden Zunge reden zu diesem Volk, er, der zu ihnen gesagt hat: 'Das ist die Ruhe; schaffet Ruhe den Müden, und das ist die Erquickung!' Aber sie wollten nicht hören. Darum soll so auch des Herrn Wort an sie ergehen: 'Zawlazaw zawlazaw, kawlakaw kawlakaw . . . .' (Isaiah 28: 11–12)."[22] Certainly, "('Pallaksch. Pallaksch.')" does not speak of God's presence-to-come. In speaking of Hölderlin, it is always a matter of God's absence, an absence that could hardly be more final than in these words.

While "Tübingen, Jänner" refuses patriarchal speech of a single and familiar tongue, then, it places no prohibitions on speaking in a foreign one, even though it is not the strangeness of God that makes its language so alien. It is still possible to quote the mad Hölderlin, even though only in parenthesis and after poetry has broken down, has started to stammer. The *pallaksch* appears as an intensification of stammering, an even more dramatic loss of language than the "immer-, immer-/zuzu," a final abandonment of the poem's own voice (if there still is, at this point, something like anybody's "own" voice). At the same time, however, the "pallaksch" does not speak of the abandonment of speech alone. While moving from mad imagery to the mad word to the nonword, the poem, in a parallel move, recuperates meaning while abandoning it on the surface. Almost unnoticeably, the "pallaksch" is reinvested with significance by the poem that quotes it, only seemingly negating itself through this act: *pallaksch* picks up fragments of the preceding line, in a condensation of "*Patriarchen*," "*lallen*," and a final sound, "ksch," which might be a code for "kaddish," the ritual prayer of mourning, a cryptic reference to the biblical patriarchs, perhaps, who may not speak anymore, not even to say "kaddish". Or it is the sound one makes to chase away the birds whirring around the tower: "ksch!" In this light, "pallaksch" figures as an open invitation to read, once again, after the silence of the blank line, after speech has been restricted to babbling, after Hölderlin has ceased to write the poetry that made him famous. Thus, while poetry itself seems to collapse under the pressure of "this time," it also reasserts itself as the medium that recovers speaking, that moves, however tentatively, to reunite the solitary words of mad un-language to the fragile structure of poetic speech—a process during which poetry disintegrates into mad babble at the same time as it turns this mad babble back into poetry.

I like the interpretation that reads the kaddish into the pallaksch. Certainly many things still need to be mourned, including the fragmentation of mourning itself, its parenthetical character, its decomposition from ritual high speech into incomprehensible prattle. What would it mean, however, to use a *Wahnsinnswort* in order to say/not say "kaddish"? What does it mean, in a broader sense, to take the mad word and *make it mean*? Like no poet before him, Celan has struggled to simultaneously erase, preserve, and recreate meaning, to let poetry speak and to protect it from an all-too-easy understanding. The great seriousness of this effort perhaps also makes his poetry most suited to touch on madness, for, as Foucault has argued powerfully, the mad as well may need to have their voice both heard and sheltered. Celan, if anyone, can perhaps teach us how to speak of or for the mad without being one of their "best spokesmen" of whom Derrida says that they are the ones who "betray them best."[23]

If "Tübingen, Jänner" has anything to say about poetic madness, then it is not about that sort of madness that is closer to inspiration, a benign inter-ference of an abundance of meaning that, while it cannot be demanded, also does not demand anything back from the poet. It is not Plato's *theia mania*,[24] not even Hölderlin's "insane quest for a consciousness."[25] "Pallaksch" is, to repeat, first and foremost a refusal, a refusal even of itself: a madness that can-not be read, understood, criticized, integrated into a work, or deconstructed.[26] It refuses itself to the *logos*. The madness of "pallaksch," is, for lack of better words, real and final: before it enters Celan's poem, that is. For if we want to continue speaking, then it serves no purpose to simply repeat the "pallaksch." The "words without language" that constitute radical madness are not readily available to either poets or critics, on logical as well as on ethical grounds. As even the most difficult works of modernism and postmodernism show, to speak as poet or as critic is to produce meaning, however polyvalent, unsta-ble, obstructed a meaning it may turn out to be. Not only "philosophy . . . always lives by imprisoning madness"[27]—so does poetry, ultimately. "Tübingen, Jänner"—so sensitively—marks this imprisonment by the brackets that en-circle the "pallaksch," anticipated, perhaps, by the allusion to the seagulls that encircle Hölderlin's tower (as children, we have all drawn seagulls like a pair of round brackets in the air).

"Tübingen, Jänner" is a difficult poem. It would take great patience to read it fully, and there is not enough space to do that here. What remains to be said, however, is that it is itself a poem about attentive reading, about the great effort of attention that it takes to read madness—not the high madness of the patriarchal prophets, but the madness of a raving maniac who had been a great poet.

"Tübingen, Jänner" is written in a mode of multiple displacements, in figures of reflection and inversion: the tower swims, the carpenter who has drowned pays a visit to words that dive into blankness; vision is voided by speech, but speaking is allowed only as babbling. Only some of these tropes can be retranslated into a conventional image:[28] standing at the railing of the tower, looking down at the Neckar, seeing the reflection of the tower and the seagull in the water, frozen water perhaps, because it is January—but even if this accessible image is there, in these lines, it is there only as a remembrance of an image, remembered by eyes blinded by speech: "über-redet," persuaded into blindness, a vision superceded by too much talking. What words can persuade eyes to go blind, not to see? The same diving words that the carpen-ter is visiting? The poem announces "these diving words": but what follows is, again, a blank line. So perhaps it is rather the words that invade the memory of the image: "ihre—'ein Rätsel ist Rein-/entsprungenes'—ihre/Erinnerung".

"Ein Rätsel ist Reinentsprungenes" (without the line break) opens the fourth stanza of Hölderlin's "Der Rhein." Again, a quotation functions as an oblique allusion, for "Der Rhein," too, will later speak about a blinding by words, in the context of Rousseau's divine madness:

> Wem aber, wie, Rousseau, dir
> Unüberwindlich die Seele,
> Die starkausdauernde, ward,
> Und sicherer Sinn
> Und süße Gabe zu hören,
> zu reden so, daß er aus heiliger Fülle
> Wie der Weingott, törig göttlich
> Und gesetzlos sie, die Sprache der Reinesten, gibt
> Verständlich den Guten, aber mit Recht
> Die Achtungslosen mit Blindheit schlägt,
> Die entweihenden Knechte, wie nenn ich den Fremden?[29]

It is virtually impossible to render a syntactically or rhythmically equivalent translation in English. Here is an attempt at a fairly close prose translation, which, strange as it may sound, does not sound nearly as strange as the original: "But to whom, like to you, Rousseau, the soul became invincible, the strongly enduring one, and to whom was given secure sense and the sweet gift to hear, to speak, so that he gives, from sacred abundance, like the wine god, foolishly divine and lawlessly this, the speech of the purest, intelligible to the good ones, but rightly striking with blindness the inattentive ones, the desecrating serfs—how do I name the stranger?"

Celan's image of "eyes per-/suaded to blindness" takes on a different tone when we read these lines together with those to which the poem refers us— the image of a blindness by *Rede* is so extravagant that the connection can hardly be accidental. And yet, as far as I know, none of this poem's readers has picked it up.[30] The oblique presence of Hölderlin's Rousseau stanza, however, lends ambiguity to the blindness of Celan's opening lines, throwing doubt on all the readings that identify the blind eyes with the poem's voice.[31] Reading Celan with Hölderlin, however, suggests that it is not necessarily the poet's or the poem's eyes that have gone blind. It is rather a blindness of inattention, the blindness of those who are ill-disposed to hear and to recognize the language of the purest—Hölderlin's language, for instance, including his "pallaksch."

The blind eyes are the subject of memory, but of a hallucinatory memory invaded by a Hölderlin fragment. The blind eyes, gazing inward rather than paying attention, see nothing but the reflection of a legend—the mad poet in the tower, the carpenter made caretaker. They may only *think* that they remember Hölderlin. In a departure from the usual reverential exegesis directed at them, the first two stanzas' disorienting imagery may perhaps be read as a parody on the culture tourists who pay madness a visit, who remember a famous line, "ein Rätsel ist Reinentsprungenes," or, even more vaguely, the most famous Hölderlin poem, "Hälfte des Lebens." The first stanza of that reads:

> Mit gelben Birnen hänget
> Und voll mit wilden Rosen
> Das Land in den See,
> Ihr holden Schwäne,
> Und trunken von Küssen
> Tunkt ihr das Haupt
> Ins heilignüchterne Wasser.[32]

Debris of this poem pervades the first stanzas of "Tübingen, Jänner." The "trunken" swans turn into "ertrunkene" Schreiner, the diving heads of the swans become the diving words, diving away, perhaps, from the inattentive gaze. While Celan's opening stanzas, at first glance, appear to create a mad imagery, they might also merely play with this expectation of disturbing yet exotic tidbits that the name Hölderlin evokes. Poetry and the legend of the mad poet merge into a jumble of Hölderlin fragments, Tübingen allusions, mythical inventions like the one of a drowned carpenter and romantic stock images. What appears, at first glance, as a poem on madness, might indeed be the opposite: a poem on the blind gaze of reason inhabited by the language of dead patriarchs that no longer means anything.[33] Socrates, too, is present here, after all, again as an unmarked citation, once more from "Der Rhein":

> bis in den Tod
> Kann aber *ein Mensch* auch
> Im Gedächtnis doch das Beste behalten. [emphasis added][34]

The drowned carpenter, then, may well be the carpenter Plato who built the the three beds in the *Republic*, dividing the world into ideal, real, and imitated,[35] and it is Socratic reason and its imperative to recollect the good that would begin to babble and stammer if it returned.

For the remembrance of "Tübingen, Jänner" is hardly a remembrance of what is best, and it is certainly not one that springs forth purely. On the contrary, "Tübingen, Jänner" is a masterful arrangement of contaminations, a highly articulate stammer, a reflection on the impossibility of committing purity to language. Inattentive readers are struck by blindness "rightly," Hölderlin insists, and Celan with him—for inattentiveness is already a form of blindness. In talking of this blindness to and by words, Celan creates another near-invisibility in a language that shields Hölderlin, the poet and the madman alike, from an understanding that would come too quickly.

"Tübingen, Jänner" moves two Hölderlin quotations into play: "ein Rätsel ist Reinentsprungenes" and "pallaksch."[36] The distance between the two seems unbridgeable. And yet, they occur within the same poetic space, one in quotation marks, one in parentheses: tokens of their separateness from the blindness of inattentiveness. Both the mystery of pure origin and the quite different mystery of Hölderlin's madness are set apart, and thus also linked. Both quotations are subtly altered: the "pallaksch" is doubled, the pure origin is cut apart by a line break: "ein Rätsel ist Rein-/entsprungenes." This emphasizes the jump implicit in "ent-sprung-en," the inexplicable suddenness of origin. It also, however, creates a different emphasis, away from purity, towards "entsprungen." And "entsprungen," taken by itself, does not only mean "originated," it also means "escaped," quite specifically in the sense of an escape from jail or from an asylum.[37] Celan thus points us to the mystery of escape, of breaking free, of being lawless, "to have done with judgment," as Gilles Deleuze has put it.[38] For madness, especially a madness like Hölderlin's, remains a riddle. An escape, a pure escape: breaking out, springing forth, enigmatically, irrevocably. Celan's enjambment, however, suggests that it is not an escape into purity, but the opposite: "rein-/entsprungen," escaped from purity, for the only purity there could possibly be is silence. It is silence towards which Celan's poetry is drawn most strongly, and it is silence which it resists at all times. The poet Jacques Dupin has formulated this conflict most succinctly in his eulogy on Paul Celan: "He cannot stop speaking, for otherwise the silence would end."[39]

The only purity there could possibly be is silence, for Celan's poetry as a whole, not just "Tübingen, Jänner," shows over and over again how inescapably language has been contaminated. The only truly uncontaminated words are neologisms, "words without language," *pallaksch*. Hölderlin's non-word may indeed be read as a word of radical purity if we want to understand purity as pure identity. If Schwab was correct, then "pallaksch" (and Celan could read this in Hellingrath's Hölderlin edition) can be understood as the ultimate negation of the double bind of identity as difference:

> one could take it to mean once yes, once no, but usually he meant *nothing at all* by it, but used it when his patience or the remains of his concentration were exhausted and he did not want to go to the trouble of thinking whether he were to say yes or no.[40]

We might transcribe the last line, then, *simultaneously*, as: ("Yes. Yes."); ("Yes. No."); ("No. No."); ("Nothing at all. Yes.") ("No. Nothing at all.")— etc. In this regard, the "pallaksch" can indeed stand as a cipher for "pure origin" if we want, in the metaphysical tradition, to understand "origin" as a radical state of identity preceding any differentiation. But, "Tübingen, Jänner" seems to suggest, this would, indeed, mean "nothing at all," nothing at all. And while the poem moves towards this nothingness, it also brackets it; while it reserves the privilege of the last line for this nothing at all, it also, ever so cautiously, writes a whole history into it: patriarchs, their babble, and, perhaps, a kaddish. Origin and history become undistinguishable, and so do madness and contamination: however, this is not to say that they are the same, only that the oscillation between them can at times be too rapid to allow for their distinction.

NOTES

INTRODUCTION
FUTURE PERFECT

1. P. Vergilius Maro, *Aeneid* (ed. John Dryden), 2.234, www.perseus.tufts.edu. Unless otherwise noted, all citations from Greek and Roman texts will be quoted from *Perseus*.

2. Stephen A. Diamond, *Anger, Madness, and the Daimonic: The Psychological Genesis of Violence, Evil, and Creativity* (Albany: SUNY Press, 1996); Arnold M. Ludwig, *The Price of Greatness: Resolving the Creativity and Madness Controversy* (New York: Guilford, 1995); Kay Redfield Jamison, *Touched By Fire: Manic-Depressive Illness and the Artistic Temperament* (New York: Free Press, 1993); Russell R. Monroe, *Creative Brainstorms: The Relationship Between Madness and Genius* (New York: Irvington, 1992); Albert Rothenberg, *Creativity and Madness: New Findings and Old Stereotypes* (Baltimore: The Johns Hopkins University Press, 1990); *Creativity and Madness: Psychological Studies of Art and Artists*, ed. Barry M. Panther et al. (Burbank: American Institute of Medical Education, 1995).

3. "'Socrates, treibe Musik!'", GB, KSA 1: 96.

4. This claim concerns the popular association of Platonism and *logos* rather than an actual history of the term, which would have to refer to Heraclitus and other pre-Socratic philosophers.

5. References to "Socrates," unless otherwise noted, concern the fictional character of Plato's dialogue, not the historical Socrates. The distinction between "Socrates" and "Plato" serves to highlight the difference between a position Socrates espouses in a dialogue and the position the dialogue as a whole might be read to take; needless to say, the two are not necessarily the same.

6. Cf. the discussion of *Ion*, Chapter One, section II; also the end of the *Symposium* and, for an ironic version, the *Hippias Minor*.

7. *Madness and Civilization: A History of Insanity in the Age of Reason*, trans. Richard Howard (Vintage Books: New York, 1988), x–xi.

8. The most incisive critique of Foucault's claims as they relate to the nature of philosophy can be found in Jacques Derrida's "Cogito and the History of Madness,"

Writing and Difference, trans. Alan Bass (Chicago: U of Chicago P, 1978), 31–63. In the following pages, this essay will be cited as "CHM."

9. *Plato's Phaedrus*, trans. with introduction and commentary by R. Hackforth (Cambridge: Cambridge UP), 1952.

10. The state of supreme madness that Socrates describes in the *Phaedrus* may, of course, also (and perhaps with more justice) be seen as a return of the self to its origins; self-alienation, here, can refer only to the worldly, rational self.

11. *Maladie mentale et psychologie* (Presses Universitaires de France: Paris, 1954). My translation.

12. Louis A. Sass. *Madness and Modernism. Insanity in the Light of Modern Art, Literature, and Thought* (New York: Basic Books, 1992), 1.

13. *Phaidros* (244a), PSW VI: 55.

14. ". . . so fern heiliger Wahnsinn höchste menschliche Erscheinung ist. . ." FA 16: 414.

15. "[F]ast überall ist es der Wahnsinn, welcher dem neuen Gedanken den Weg bahnt." M, KSA 3: 26.

16. Cf. Sigmund Freud, *Psychoanalytische Bemerkungen über einen autobiographisch beschriebenen Fall von Paranoia (Dementia paranoides)*, *Studienausgabe*, ed. Alexander Mitscherlich et al., Bd. VII (Frankfurt/M.: Fischer, 1973), 133–204.

17. Jacques Derrida, *Limited Inc.*, trans. Samuel Weber (Evansville: Northwestern UP, 1988), 117.

18. "La parole soufflée," *Writing and Difference*, 169–195: 193.

19. *Madness and Modernism*, xi.

20. ". . . das geisteskranke Fragen nach einem Bewußtsein. . ." *Anmerkungen zum Ödipus*, FA 16, 247–258: 255.

21. RP, 212.

22. This is not to say that the philosopher might not be privy to incommunicable experiences, merely that Platonic philosophy as an institution and a public practice (as opposed to an institution devoted to shared experience) is restricted to what is sayable and teachable.

23. For a representative essay, cf. Jacques Derrida, "White Mythology: Metaphor in the Text of Philosophy," *Margins of Philosophy*, trans. with additional notes by Alan Bass (Chicago: U of Chicago P, 1982), 207–272.

24. Arkady Plotnitsky, *Reconfigurations: Critical Theory and General Economy* (Gainesville: U of Florida P, 1993), 158.

25. Cf. Liliane Weissberg's analysis of the tension between philosophy and literature in the late 18th century: *Geistersprache. Philosophischer und literarischer Diskurs im späten achtzehnten Jahrhundert* (Königshausen & Neumann: Würzburg, 1990).

26. "Von einem neuerdings erhobenen vornehmen Ton in der Philosophie," *Werke* III, ed. Wilhelm Weischedel (Frankfurt/M.: Insel, 1958), 377–397.

27. Georges Bataille, *L'expérience intérieure* (Paris: Gallimard, 1954), 154, 282–283n (trans. in Plotnitsky, *Reconfigurations*, 20).

28. Rainer Nägele, *Reading After Freud* (New York: Columbia UP, 1987), 16.

29. Ibid.

30. Along with Foucault's studies, the work of Gilles Deleuze and Félix Guattari in *Anti-Oedipus* including their concept of 'schizo-analysis' has been immensely influential. I will not comment on this work, for two reasons. First, since Freud does not figure prominently in this thesis, there seems little need to incorporate Deleuze's and Guattari's critique of Freud either. Second, I suspect that *Anti-Oedipus*, as incisive a critique of Freud as it is, constitutes one of the most flagrant recent instances in the idealization of madness. As such, it raises ethical questions that I am not prepared to discuss here.

31. "*Exergue*," Derrida's translator, Alan Bass, explains, "derives from the Greek *ex-ergon*, literally 'outside the work.' In French and English it has a specifically numismatic sense, referring to the space on a coin or medal reserved for an inscription. In French it also has the sense of an epigraph, of something 'outside the work.' " "White Mythology," 209f1.

32. I have chosen throughout to render the Greek term as 'idea' rather than 'form'. 'Form' might be the more prevalent translation at this point, but since Plato's philosophy postulates the very shapelessness of the ideas, 'form' seems needlessly confusing.

33. Cf. the detailed discussion of "Wahrheit und Lüge im außermoralischen Sinne" in Chapter Three, section II.

34. I borrow this term from Martha Nussbaum's *The Fragility of Goodness: Luck and Ethics in Greek Tragedy and Philosophy* (Cambridge: Cambridge UP, 1986).

35. The best study of Nietzsche's medical condition is probably Pia Daniela Volz's *Nietzsche im Labyrinth seiner Krankheit, Eine medizinisch-biographische Untersuchung* (Tübingen: Königshausen & Neumann, 1990). Volz, fully aware of the ultimately speculative nature of her project, argues, to my lay mind convincingly, that Nietzsche probably suffered from (the much debated and passionately refuted) syphilis.

36. Peter Szondi, *On Textual Understanding and Other Essays*, trans. Harvey Mendelsohn, foreword by Michael Hayes (Minneapolis: University of Minnesota Press, 1986), 13.

CHAPTER ONE
TALKING ABOUT HOMER

1. It should be noted again that all references to "Socrates" here concern Plato's fictional character Socrates, not the historical Socrates.

2. Freud, for all his influence on twentieth century aesthetics, repeatedly stressed that psychoanalysis could not account for artistic creativity. His writings on art leave the notion of Genius more or less intact, even though he throws severe doubt on its conceptual foundation.

3. Cf. Michel Foucault, "What is an Author," *Language, Counter-Memory, Practice: Selected Essays and Interviews* (Ithaca: Cornell UP, 1977), 113–138.

4. Geertz suggests that "[t]he problem with [an] approach to things . . . which extracts the general from the particular and then sets the particular aside as detail, illustration, background, or qualification, is that it leaves us helpless in the face of the very difference we need to explore." (Clifford Geertz, *After the Fact: Two Countries, Four Decades, One Anthropologist* [Cambridge UP, 1995], 40). I am grateful to Andrew Becker, who not only drew my attention to this apposite remark, but provided a generous and immensely helpful reading of a part of this chapter.

5. *The Republic of Plato*, 277.

6. Gadamer, Hans-Georg, "Plato und die Dichter," *Platos dialektische Ethik und andere Studien zur platonischen Philosophie* (Hamburg: Felix Meiner, 1968), 181.

7. Certainly, the charges against him do not explicitly mention poetry as one of the injured parties; however, Socrates' attack on poetry is closely linked to his attack on traditional Greek religion and the forms of religious instruction.

8. Iris Murdoch, to give an example, proclaims that "Plato's . . . view of art is most fully expounded in Books III and X of the Republic." Murdoch, Iris, *The Fire and the Sun: Why Plato Banished the Artists* (Oxford: Oxford UP, 1977), 5.

9. *Ion*, in Allen Bloom, *The Roots of Political Philosophy: Ten Forgotten Socratic Dialogues*, ed. Thomas L. Pangle (Ithaca: Cornell UP 1987), 356–370.

10. Hellmuth Flashar, in his afterword to the *Tusculum* edition of the *Ion*, is one of its few readers to identify the technique of interpretation as an important concern of the dialogue. Flashar, however, concludes, in my opinion too hastily, that "principally, there can be no rhapsodic knowledge [in the sense of *technê*]", and he proceeds traditionally in centering his reading on Socrates' notion of poetry" ("Nachwort," *Ion*, ed. Hellmuth Flashar [München: Heimeran, 1963], 47–63: 56).

11. The second "Symposium Platonicum" under the auspices of the International Plato Society was exclusively devoted to "Understanding the Phaedrus" (Rossetti, 1992). Apart from numerous articles, recent years have seen the publication of several new translations of the *Phaedrus* and several monographs dealing wholly or to a large extent with the *Phaedrus*. Cf. *Understanding the Phaedrus. Proceedings of the II Symposium Platonicum*, ed. Livio Rossetti (Sankt Augustin: Academia Verlag, 1992); White, David A., *Rhetoric and Reality in Plato's Phaedrus* (Albany: SUNY Press, 1993); Rice, A. W., *Love and Friendship in Plato and Aristotle* (Oxford: Oxford UP, 1989); Ferrari, G. R. F, *Listening to the Cicadas: A Study of Plato's Phaedrus* (Cambridge: Cambridge UP, 1987); Griswold, Charles L. Jr., *Self-Knowledge in Plato's Phaedrus* (New Haven/London: Yale UP, 1986); Rowe, C. J., *Plato: Phaedrus* (London, 1986); *Plato on Beauty, Wisdom, and the Arts*, ed. J. Moravcsik and P. Temko (Totowa: Rowman & Littlefield, 1982); Burger, Ronna, *Plato's Phaedrus: A Defense of a Philosophic Art of Writing* (Tuscaloosa: U of Alabama P, 1980).

12. "An Interpretation of Plato's Ion," *The Roots of Political Philosophy*, 371–395: 371, 373; Goethe, Johann Wolfgang, "Plato als Mitgenosse einer christlichen Offenbarung (1796)," *Ion*, 42–46: 43–4.

13. Cf. three fairly recent publications promoting very different perspectives on Plato's work on poetry: Liliane Weissberg. "Einführung: Platons Spur," *Geistersprache*, 1–33; Nussbaum, *Fragility*, 200–235; Bloom, "An Interpretation."

14. Due to the ambiguity of the speech, the reception of the *Ion* roughly divides into two camps: one reads it as a celebration of creative enthusiasm, the other as a denunciation of poetry. To a certain extent, the first school can draw on the *Phaedrus*, but, on the whole, seems informed rather by modern theories of creativity; the latter has the authority of the *Republic* and related passages in other dialogues (*Apology*, *Meno*) behind it. For an overview of the history of the reception of the *Ion*, cf. E. N. Tigerstedt, "Plato's Idea of Poetical Inspiration," *Commentationes Humanarum Litterarum* 44 (1970): 18–20.

15. Goethe uses the same term in the German, "Persiflage" ("Plato als Mitgenosse," 43).

16. Leon Golden and Kevin Kerrane point out that the "claim that [the poet] is protected and inspired by a divine muse, who enables him to please his audience through stories and words that convey a unique kind of knowledge . . . appears explicitly in the writings of Homer, Hesiod, and Pindar." *Classical Literary Criticism: Translations and Interpretations*, ed. A. Preminger et al. (New York: Unger, 1974), 3–4.

17. Critical categories like 'tone' or 'atmosphere' are problematic, and infinitely more so when dealing with a language as foreign as ancient Greek. The following argument, then, might be more reliable to bear out the point that Socrates' theory of inspiration is delivered tongue-in-cheek.

18. Joel F. Wilcox suggests that in this passage Socrates himself is, or presents himself as, inspired, but there is no textual evidence for this claim unless one wants to subscribe every piece of successful *psychagôgia* to divine powers. Cf. "Cross-Metamorphosis in Plato's Ion," *Literature as Philosophy: Philosophy as Literature*, ed. Donald G. Marschall (Iowa City: U of Iowa P, 1987), 155–174.

19. In this passage, the *Ion* already projects the danger of alienation through poetry, an aspect Gadamer identifies as Plato's major ground of objection against poetry (cf. *Plato and the Poets*). The following paragraphs argue, however, that Ion is not as alienated as it is suggested at first.

20. Allan Bloom's interpretation (op.cit.) is an example of such a reading; Bloom extracts a complete Socratic position on Homer, tradition, and the way to lead a happy life out of the dialogue, but in order to do so, he is forced to draw extensively on assumptions tacitly lifted from other Platonic dialogues. In Bloom's reading, the *Ion* thus loses much of its peculiarity, becoming just another showcase for a general Socratism.

21. Nussbaum stresses that "[b]efore Plato's time there was no distinction between 'philosophical' and 'literary' discussion of human practical problems" (*Fragility*, 123). In her analysis of "Plato's anti-tragic theater," Nussbaum diagnoses "the origin of a distinctive philosophical style that opposed itself to the merely literary." However, Nussbaum's very terms *theater* and *merely literary* tend to obscure the force and the rigor of the distinction that a pervasive understanding of Plato will establish for more than two millennia to follow. For an interesting tracing of this heritage, cf. Weissberg, *Geistersprache*, passim.

22. Aristotle, *Poetics* (1447), in Preminger, *Classical Literary Criticism*, 108.

23. Apart from the Romantic poets who favored Plato, Kant's essay "Von einem neuerdings erhobenen vornehmen Ton in der Philosophie" is a case in point. Cf. Introduction.

24. Cf. Robert Zaslavsy, *Platonic Myth and Platonic Writing* (Washington: University Press of America, 1981), 11–19.

25. One passage in the *Republic* might serve to illustrate this possibility, even though it is not spoken by Socrates but by Adeimantus: "Socrates, consider still another form of speeches about justice and injustice, spoken *in prose and by poets* [emphasis added]" (363e). Allan Bloom adds in a footnote to this passage that the "expression for prose is composed from words meaning 'to speak privately' and could also mean what one says in private. Almost all public speech was written in verse []." *The Republic of Plato*, 447n11.

26. *Poetics* (1447).

27. The implications of this statement are too far-reaching to be analyzed in any detail here. It should be noted, however, that the tragic "imitation" Socrates

condemns in Book III of the *Republic* concerns acting, i.e. the imitation of another person's speech, i.e. the imitation of an imitation.

28. The full passage reads: "For the poet is a light thing and winged and holy, and not capable to make poetry until he has become enthused and senseless and *nous* no longer dwells within him. For as long as he holds on to this possession, any man is incapable to make poetry or to speak oracles" (534b).

29. Thus, one can again encounter the analogy between poet/poem and father/son as a relation of possession at the end of the *Phaedrus*, where it sustains Socrates' arguments about speaking and writing.

30. Goethe, for instance, speaks of Ion as "einem Rhapsoden, einem Vorleser, einem Declamator, der berühmt war wegen seines Vortrags der Homerischen Gedichte" ("a rhapsode, a reader, a declamator who was famous for his presentation of the Homeric poems"—"Plato als Mitgenosse," 43.) The editors of *Classical Literary Criticism* footnote rhapsodes simply as "professional reciters of poetry." 236 fn. 1.

31. Gadamer even compares the status of Homer's writing to the status of the Bible in Christian society. "Plato und die Dichter," 186.

32. Sophocles' military position, of course, may play a role in this, but it is hard to determine whether Plato could count on his audience to make this connection.

33. Bloom, *The Roots*, 394.

34. In colloquial Greek, the word means 'sleepy, disinterested.'

35. While this argument disqualifies Ion within the Socratic narrative, obviously it empowers him in other ways. It is Ion's very demagogic skill that renders him a true rival of philosophic *psychagôgia*. Ion might still be a fool, but, commanding large audiences as indeed a general might command an army, he is not harmless. Many readers of Plato make the mistake of underestimating Ion because he would make a lousy philosopher, but Socrates does indeed face a serious rival in this dialogue, certainly one much more powerful in many regards than Socrates himself.

36. This is significant, of course, because Socrates derives his arguments against poetic *mimêsis* in the *Republic* from a posited analogy of poetry to painting.

37. Cf. Jacques Derrida, "Plato's Pharmacy," 66–67 and corresponding footnotes.

38. The Schleiermacher edition in fact lists four sections, but one and four count as introduction and conclusion. The two main sections are entitled "Drei Reden über die Liebe" ("Three Speeches about Love," 230e6–257b7) and "Untersuchung über die Kunst der Rede" ("Investigation of the Art of Speech," 257b8–277a5).

39. Seth Benardete, *The Rhetoric of Morality and Philosophy*, 1.

40. It should be noted, of course, that Socrates is not always as humble when it comes to knowledge; in many of the major dialogues (*Republic*, *Symposium*), Socrates does lay claim to at least limited knowledge.

41. Arkady Plotnitsky, *In the Shadow of Hegel: Complementarity, History, and the Unconscious* (Gainesville: U of Florida P, 1993), 254.

42. *Self-Knowledge in Plato's* Phaedrus, 230.

43. *The Rhetoric of Morality and Philosophy*, 142.

44. The theory of the ideas is never consolidated into a doctrine, and every dialogue concerned with it differs from the next one.

45. *The Rhetoric of Morality and Philosophy*, 141.

46. Ibid., 144.

47. *Self-Knowledge in Plato's* Phaedrus, passim; Jacques Derrida, "Plato's Pharmacy," 69.

48. *Dissemination*, 191.

49. *Reconfigurations*, 168.

50. I am drawing here on Derrida's notion of the *supplément* as both complement and displacement, a concept that eludes the traditional either/or logic of binary thinking.

51. The distinction between *logos* as rational speech and *mythoi* as a fictional narrative structure is to a large extent post-Platonic. In Plato's usage, *logos* seems to be the more comprehensive term by far, including (rational and irrational) speeches, stories, discussions, dialogues. As far as I can see, it *never* means what later readers sometimes project into it, roughly the equivalent of the Latin *ratio*. The word *muthos* may signify any kind of coherent story, possibly with a connotation of historical account (cf. *Platonic Myth and Platonic Writing*, 18–20).

52. To give a few examples, Schleiermacher proposes "göttliche . . . Aufhebung de gewöhnlichen ordentlichen Zustandes," "divine cancellation of the usual orderly state"; Hackforth (*Plato's Phaedrus*, trans. with introduction and commentary by R. Hackforth [Cambridge: Cambridge UP, 1952]) gives "disturbance of our conventions of conduct"; Hellmuth Flashar offers "Herauslösen aus den gewohnten Ordnungen," "taking out of the customary order of things."

53. "In Greek, 'other' is either *allo* or *heteron*. It is *heteron* if one is speaking of either one of a pair; it is *allo* if it is something else that has no other relation to that from which it is different except that it is different." (*The Being of the Beautiful: Plato's Theaetetus, Sophist, and Statesman*, trans. and with Commentary by Seth Benardete [Chicago/London: Chicago UP, 1984], viii.). Benardete proposes that only *heteron* should be translated as 'other.'

54. Cf. Foucault, *Folie et déraison*.

55. Socrates stresses this point when he talks abut the Sybil of Delphi: "For the prophetess at Delphi and the priestesses at Dodone have in madness bestowed much good . . ., in sanity, however, only measly things or nothing" (244a–b).

56. *Plato's Phaedrus*, trans. with Introduction and Commentary by R. Hackforth (Cambridge: Cambridge UP, 1952), 60.

57. Platonic madness, then, may have found its proper literary genre only with the novella, a form characterized by sudden events that initiate violent turns of fortune. The master of this genre is Heinrich v. Kleist, in whose novellas madness plays a crucial part.

58. *Self-Knowledge in Plato's Phaedrus*, 152.

59. Ibid., 151.

CHAPTER TWO
THE ABYSS ABOVE

1. FA 9, 429.

2. *Der kalkulierte Wahnsinn: Innenansichten ästhetischer Moderne* (Frankfurt/M.: Fischer, 1992).

3. *Der kalkulierte Wahnsinn*, 224.

4. It is interesting to note at this point that Nietzsche, in *Daybreak*, does talk about calculated madness, not as a specifically modern but as an almost universal strategy for those engaged in presenting "the new idea." I will comment on this passage extensively in the next chapter.

5. The most noteworthy exception is the Rousseau stanza in the hymn "Der Rhein," where it says of Rousseau that he was given the "secure sense" ("sicherer Sinn") and the "sweet gift" ("süße Gabe") to speak "the language of the purest" ("die Sprache der Reinesten") in the manner of Dionysus, "the god of Wine, foolishly divine" ("wie der Weingott, törig göttlich"). I will not pursue here the difficult questions these verses open up as to Hölderlin's relation to the philosopher-poet Rousseau and to the problem of Hölderlin's concept of the Dionysian in general. It may well be that Hölderlin found in Rousseau, at least for a time, the lone figure to realize the conciliation between enthusiasm and sobriety. As such, however, Rousseau remains a nameless enigma; the stanza closes with the words, "wie nenn ich den Fremden?," "how do I name the stranger?" On the complexity of the Hölderlin-Rousseau connection, cf. Paul de Man, "The Image of Rousseau in the Poetry of Hölderlin," trans. Andrzej Warminski, *The Rhetoric of Romanticism* (New York: Columbia UP, 1984), 19–45.

6. Maurice Blanchot, "Hölderlin's Itinerary," *The Space of Literature*, trans. Ann Smock (Lincoln: U of Nebraska P, 1982), 269–276: 269–70.

7. FA 9, 433.

8. Bettina von Arnim, quoted after FA 9, 488.

9. Roman Jakobson and Grete Lübbe-Grothues, "Two Types of Discourse in Hölderlin's Madness," in *Cognitive Constraints on Communication*, Synthese language library, 18, ed. Lucia Vania and Jaakko Hintikka (Dordrecht: D. Reidel, 1984), 115–136: 127.

10. The different positions can be schematized as follows: His late poetry was bad because Hölderlin was mad; Hölderlin was mad, but his madness left his poetic competence intact; Hölderlin was not mad, but he changed his style; Hölderlin was not mad but he lost his belief in poetry. There has been a passionate debate as to whether Hölderlin was mad in the clinical sense or whether he voluntarily retreated from the world. For the extreme ends of the "mad or not" controversy, cf. Pierre Bertaux, *Friedrich Hölderlin* (Frankfurt/M.: Suhrkamp, 1978); Uwe Henrik Peters, *Hölderlin: Wider die These vom edlen Simulanten* (Reinbeck: Rowohlt, 1982); Gerhard Weinholz, *Zur Genese des 'Wahnsinns' bei Friedrich Hölderlin: Ein Erklärungsmodell aus dem Kontext seines Lebens und seiner Zeit*, Literaturwissenschaft in der Blauen Eule, 2 (Essen: Blaue Eule, 1990). Bertaux argues that Hölderlin deliberately retreated from the world; Peters sees in Hölderlin a clear-cut case of schizophrenia; Weinholz represents a socio-psychological approach.

11. "[. . .] und die Sprache bilde alles Denken, denn sie sei größer wie der Menschengeist, der sei ein Sclave nur der Sprache, und so lange sei der Geist im Menschen noch nicht der vollkommne, als die Sprache ihn nicht alleinig vorrufe. Die Gesetze des Geistes aber seien metrisch, das fühle sich in der Sprache, sie werfe das Netz über den Geist, in dem gefangen, er das Göttliche aussprechen müsse [. . .]." Bettina von Arnim, *Die Günderode* [1840], quoted after FA 9, 490.

12. The passage Jakobson and Lübbe-Grothues quote is a letter by the fictionalized Bettine to her equally fictionalized friend Günderode. It is part of an alleged paraphrase of the mad Hölderlin's deliberations that goes on for several pages, a conglomerate of literal Hölderlin quotes (mostly from the Sophocles annotations), von Arnim's interpretation of these quotes, and her own poetological positions.

13. There has been a lively discussion as to when Hölderlin's madness broke out. Christoph Jamme summarizes the positions in his essay "'Ein kranker oder gesunder Geist'"? Berichte über Hölderlins Krankheit in den Jahren 1804–1806," *Jenseits des Idealismus. Hölderlins letzte Homburger Jahre, 1804–1806*, Neuzeit und Gegenwart; Philosophische Studien, 5 (Bonn: Bouvier, 1988), 279–289.

14. Uwe H. Peters, using contemporary clinical terms, argues that Hölderlin's madness broke out in two distinct phases: a depression triggered by the death of Susette von Gontard in 1802, schizophrenia developed during the second Homburg sojourn 1804–1806.

15. "Hölderlin [. . .], als er längst in den Schutz der Nacht des Wahnsinns hinweggenommen war." Martin Heidegger, *Erläuterungen zu Hölderlins Dichtung* (Frankfurt/M.: Klostermann, 4/1971), 42.

16. Stanley Corngold, *Complex Pleasures: Forms of Feeling in German Literature* (Stanford: Stanford University Press, 1998), 77.

17. Cyrus Hamlin summarizes: "The history of Hölderlin's career as poet and his contribution to literature in the public domain would seem to have ended with the publication of the Sophocles translations and the group of nine *Nightsongs* by Wilmans in 1804, before the poet's return to Homburg. [. . .] The subsequent influence of Hölderlin's work and its critical reception to this day does not include [the] late hymnic fragments, which may be argued to have been drafted later than such completed poems as *Patmos* and *Andenken*." Cf. "'Stimmen des Geschiks': The Hermeneutics of Unreadability (Thoughts on Hölderlin's 'Griechenland')," in *Jenseits des Idealismus*, 253–276: 252.

18. In the past ten years, approximately, there has been a rising interest in Hölderlin's production from 1804 to 1806. For a collection of interesting essays, cf. *Jenseits des Idealismus. Hölderlins letzte Homburger Jahre, 1804–1806*.

19. Cf. Martin Heidegger, *Erläuterungen*.

20. Jakobson and Lübbe-Grothues's assessment of Hölderlin's "strangely intact and enthusiastic wish and capacity for effortless, spontaneous, and purposeful impromptu poetry" serves both desires; it postulates continuity and purpose in madness while acknowledging this continuity's 'strangeness'. Doubly strange in Hölderlin's case, for the idea of effortlessness was alien to his poetic theory; he might have thought, more precisely, that nothing took greater effort to achieve.

21. "Pallaksch" is a nonword that the mad Hölderlin is said to have uttered at times of distress. More on this in the conclusion of this study.

22. "Als ein denkendes und besonnenes Verhalten ist die Reflexion das Gegenteil der Ekstase, der *mania* des Platon." Walter Benjamin, *Der Begriff der Kunstkritik in der deutschen Romantik* (Frankfurt/M.: Suhrkamp, 2/1978), 97.

23. Theodor W. Adorno, "Parataxis: Zur späten Lyrik Hölderlins," *Über Hölderlin*, ed. Jochen Schmidt (Frankfurt/M.: Insel, 1970), 339–378. On the conflict between Heidegger and Adorno concerning Hölderlin, cf. Cyrus Hamlin, "'Stimmen des Geschiks,'" 258–265.

24. Cf. Lange's critique of Benjamin's approach, *Der kalkulierte Wahnsinn*, 200–201.

25. Lacoue-Labarthe, Philippe, "The Caesura of the Speculative," *Glyph* 4 (1978): 57–84, 72. This chapter owes much of its initial conception to this very suggestive essay, as well as other works by the same author (*Typography: Mimesis, Philosophy, Politics*, with an introduction by Jacques Derrida [Cambridge/London: Harvard UP, 1989]; *L'imitation des modernes. Typographies II* [Paris: Editions galilée, 1986]).

26. Most of these fragments or sketches were not readily accessible before Böhm published the second edition of Hölderlin's *Gesammelte Werke* in 1911. The established titles, here quoted after Beißner's Stuttgart edition, have been devised by various editors. The Frankfurt edition lists the untitled fragments under their first lines.

27. Cf. FA 16, 63–64.

28. "Da wo die Nüchternheit dich verläßt, da ist die Grenze deiner Begeisterung. Der große Dichter ist niemals von sich selbst verlassen, er mag sich so weit über sich selbst erheben, als er will. Man kann auch in die Höhe *fallen*, so wie in die Tiefe."—"Reflexion," WBD, 501–504: 501. The modified English translation is based on Friedrich Hölderlin, *Essays and Letters on Theory*, trans. and ed. Thomas Pfau (Albany: SUNY Press, 1988), 45.

29. On the interplay between sobriety and enthusiasm, reason and affect in this and related texts, cf. Rainer Nägele, *Text, Geschichte und Subjektivität in Hölderlins Dichtung—"Uneßbarer Schrift gleich"* (Stuttgart: J.B. Metzler, 1985), 53–4.

30. *Der kalkulierte Wahnsinn*, 221.

31. In Phaedrus, *sophrosune* serves as the counterconcept to mania. *Sophrosune* is untranslatable, combining elements of rationality, self-possession, sobriety.

32. This is, of course, not true for the whole of Hölderlin's oeuvre, where "Asia" as well as the rise of Christianity play an important role. Asia, however, does get subsumed under Greece, and the disappearance of the Christian God marks the beginning of Hesperia, as the late hymn "*Patmos*," among others, shows most clearly.

33. *Essays and Letters*, 149–50, trans. modified: "[. . .] das eigentliche Nationelle wird im Fortschritt der Bildung immer der geringere Vorzug werden. Deswegen sind die Griechen des heiligen Pathos weniger Meister, weil es ihnen angeboren war, hingegen sind sie vorzüglich in Darstellungsgabe, von Homer an, weil dieser außerordentliche Mensch seelenvoll genug war, um die abendländische *Junonische Nüchternheit* für sein Apollonsreich zu erbeuten, und so wahrhaft das Fremde sich anzueignen. //Bei uns ists umgekehrt. Deswegen ists auch so gefährlich, sich die Kunstregeln einzig und allein von griechischer Vortrefflichkeit zu abstrahieren. Ich habe lange daran laboriert und weiß nun, daß außer dem, was bei den Griechen und uns das Höchste sein muß, nämlich dem lebendigen Verhältnis und Geschick, wir nicht wohl etwas *gleich* mit ihnen haben dürfen.//Aber das Eigene muß so gut gelernt sein wie das Fremde. Deswegen sind uns die Griechen unentbehrlich. Nur werden wir ihnen gerade in unserm Eigenen, Nationellen nicht nachkommen, weil, wie gesagt, der *freie* Gebrauch des *Eigenen* das Schwerste ist." WBD, 789.

34. This dialectic between sensibility and form has often been misunderstood in surprising ways; even a reader as careful and knowledgeable as George Steiner asserts that, for Hölderlin, "native to Attic sensibility was a gift of temperance, of 'Junonian Sobriety'," when Hölderlin explicitly states the opposite. Cf. George Steiner,

Antigones: How the Antigone Legend Has Endured In Western Literature, Art, and Thought (New York/Oxford: Oxford UP, 1984), 73.

35. On the issue of Greek failure, cf. Lacoue-Labarthe's essay "Hölderlin and the Greeks," *Typography*, op. cit.

36. Obviously, these terms are not synonymous; by enumerating them as parallel dichotomies, I merely mean to expose their structural complicity.

37. It is interesting to note that Louis Sass's recent extensive study of the relationship between modernity and madness presents a hypothesis that resonates with important elements of Hölderlin's theory. Sass writes about schizophrenia as a disease of modernity with "hyperreflexivity [as] a kind of master theme, able to subsume many specific aspects of schizophrenic consciousness" (*Madness and Modernism*, 11), and he links, as his subtitle suggests, the emergence of this type of madness to modern culture itself.

38. Cf. Blanchot, "Hölderlin's Itinerary," 271.

39. Ernst Cassirer. "Hölderlin und der deutsche Idealismus," *Idee und Gestalt: Goethe, Schiller, Hölderlin, Kleist*, 2nd ed., (Berlin, 1924, Reprint Darmstadt: Wissenschaftl. Buchgesellschaft, 1989); 113–155: 113–4.

40. Cf. Dieter Henrich, *Konstellationen: Probleme und Debatten am Ursprung der idealistischen Philosophie, 1789–1795* (Stuttgart: Klett-Cotta, 1991), and *Der Grund im Bewußtsein: Untersuchungen zu Hölderlins Denken, 1794–1795* (Stuttgart: Klett-Cotta, 1992).

41. For a detailed analysis of Hölderlin's Fichte critique, cf. Henrich, *Der Grund im Bewußtsein*, 40–48 and passim.

42. *Essays and Letters*, 137, trans. modified: ". . . so konnten [die Deutschen] keinen heilsameren Einfluß erfahren als den der neuen Philosophie, die bis zum Extrem auf Allgemeinheit des Interesses dringt, und das unendliche Streben in der Brust des Menschen aufdeckt, und wenn sie schon sich zu einseitig an die große Selbsttätigkeit der Menschennatur hält, so ist sie doch, als Philosophie *der Zeit*, die einzig mögliche. Kant ist der Moses unserer Nation . . . ." WBD, 754.

43. During the time in the *Tübinger Stift*, Hölderlin had come in contact with Fichte, whom he initially much admired. In a letter to Schelling from that time, Hegel asserts that Hölderlin speaks "enthusiastically of Fichte as of a titan." (Quoted after Cassirer, "Hölderlin," 115.) As Henrich points out, "in the years between 1791 and 1794, and in the development of post-Kantian philosophy, Fichte's thought is certainly of primary significance." *Konstellationen*, 10.

44. *Essays and Letters*, 125: "[Fichte] möchte über das Faktum des Bewußtseins in der *Theorie* hinaus, das zeigen sehr viele seiner Äußerungen, und das ist ebenso gewiß, und noch auffallender transcendent, als wenn die bisherigen Metaphysiker über das Dasein der Welt hinaus wollten . . ." WBD, 717.

45. *Essays and Letters*, 125, trans. slightly modified: "[Fichte's] absolutes Ich [. . .] enthaelt alle Realitaet; es ist alles, und ausser ihm ist nichts; es gibt also fuer dieses absolute Ich kein Objekt, denn sonst waere nicht alle Realitaet in ihm; ein Bewusstsein ohne Objekt ist aber nicht denkbar, und wenn ich selbst dieses Objekt bin, so bin ich als solches notwendig beschraenkt, sollte es auch nur in der Zeit sein, also nicht absolut; also ist in dem absoluten Ich kein Bewusstsein denkbar, als absolutes Ich hab ich kein Bewusstsein, und insofern ich kein Bewusstsein habe, insofern bin ich (fuer mich) nichts, also das absolute Ich ist (fuer mich) Nichts." WBD, 717.

46. *Essays and Letters*, 49, trans. slightly modified: "Die Weisen aber, die nur mit dem Geiste, nur allgemein unterscheiden, eilen schnell wieder ins reine Sein zurück, und fallen in eine um so größere Indifferenz, weil sie hinlänglich unterschieden zu haben glauben, und die Nichtentgegensetzung, auf die sie zurückgekommen sind, für eine ewige nehmen. Sie haben ihre Natur mit dem untersten Grade der Wirklichkeit, mit dem Schatten der Wirklichkeit, der idealen Entgegensetzung und Unterscheidung getäuscht, und sie rächt sich dadurch . . ." WBD, 504.

47. It is interesting to note, if only in passing, that Freud will use a similar distinction to clarify the difference between neurosis and psychosis within psychoanalytic theory. Cf. "Neurose und Psychose," *Studienausgabe*, Bd. III (Frankfurt/M.: Fischer, 6/1975), 331–337.

48. Hölderlin's ironic name may be a direct translation of the Greek term for *sophist*, as opposed to the philosopher who does not claim to be wise but to be a "lover of wisdom." In his rejection of empty idealization, he might be referring to the neoplatonist thought Kant abhorred so much (as evidenced in Kant's essay "Über den neuerdings erhobenen apokalyptischen Ton in der Philosophie"). Obviously, one can only speculate as to the specific target of this fragmentary text, but it certainly might also be suggestive as a critique of philosophy in general.

49. *Essays and Letters*, 101: "Es wird gut sein, um den Dichtern, auch bei uns, eine bürgerliche Existenz zu sichern, wenn man die Poesie, auch bei uns, den Unterschied der Zeiten und Verfassungen abgerechnet, zur mechanä der Alten erhebt." WBD, 618.

50. *Essays and Letters*, 101, trans. slightly modified: "Man hat, unter Menschen, bei jedem Dinge, vor allem darauf zu sehen, daß es Etwas ist, d.h. daß es in dem Mittel (*moyen*) seiner Erscheinung erkennbar ist, daß die Art, wie es bedingt ist, bestimmt und gelehret werden kann." WBD, 618.

51. In light of Hölderlin's unsurpassed poetic achievements, this remark may seem inappropriate, and, ultimately, impossible to argue or 'prove'. Hölderlin's own estimation of modern poetry, as expressed in the Böhlendorff letter, however, may serve to legitimize this criticism. Also, it would border on the coy to deny that the extreme difficulty of Hölderlin's work is due in part to a certain indifference to *Darstellungsgabe* when compared, for instance, to the best of Rilke's work.

52. "Many sought in vain to say the most joyful joyfully./Here it speaks, finally, to me, here in mourning speaks out itself." ("Viele versuchten umsonst das Freudigste freudig zu sagen/Hier spricht endlich es mir, hier in der Trauer sich aus.") WBD, 64.

53. "Jetzt hab ich [. . .] dies Geschäft gewählt, weil es zwar in fremden, aber festen und historischen Gesetzen gebunden ist. Sonst will ich, wenn es die Zeit gibt, die Eltern unsrer Fürsten und ihre Sitze und die Engel des heiligen Vaterlands singen." WBD, 564.

54. In a letter to B. R. Abeken, Voß writes in July 1804: "What do you say about Hölderlin's Sophocles? Is the man crazy, or does he only pretend to be and his Sophocles is a secret satire on bad translators? Recently, when I sat with Schiller at Goethe's house, I quite regaled both with it. Read only the IV. Chorus of Antigone—you should have seen Schiller laugh; or Antigone verse 20: 'Was ist's, Du scheinst ein rothes Wort zu färben.' This passage I recommended to Goethe for his optics . . . ." FA 16, 20.

55. For a more detailed account, cf. George Steiner, *Antigones*, 66–106.

56. "Eben darum wohnt in ihnen vor andern die ungeheure und ursprüngliche Gefahr aller Übersetzung: daß die Tore einer so erweiterten und durchwalteten Sprache zufallen und den Übersetzer ins Schweigen schließen." Walter Benjamin, "Die Aufgabe des Übersetzers," *Illuminationen* [Frankfurt: Suhrkamp, 1977], 50–62: 62.

57. "Du scheinst ein rotes Wort zu färben"—Ismene to Antigone, WBD 627.

58. An interesting exception is a fairly recent translation by the poet Steve Berg and the classical scholar Diskin Clay: Sophocles, *Oedipus the King (Greek Tragedy in New Translations)*, trans. Stephen Berg and Diskin Clay, Oxford: Oxford UP, 1990.

59. *Antigones*, 73.

60. *Antigones*, 72.

61. This is a quote from Voß's lengthy and devastating review of Hölderlin's translation in *Jenaische Allgemeine Literatur Zeitung*, FA 16, 24. In all fairness, it must be added that Hölderlin did indeed commit numerous errors, some of them quite entertaining; Voß' review, even though he might have missed the nature and significance of Hölderlin's achievement, is still a hilarious read.

62. Post-Kantian philosophy, Henrich summarizes, "took its departure from the attempt to understand the condition and dynamics of a life that in its recognition (*Erkennen*) always already relates to itself and that is in need of a self-description that would define its place within the whole of that of which we can know." *Konstellationen*, 16.

63. Philippe Lacoue-Labarthe, in an essay on Hölderlin's Sophocles annotations, has called *Antigone* "the most Greek" of tragedies, *Oedipus* the most modern one ("The Caesura of the Speculative," *Glyph* 4 [1978]: 57–84: 68–9). There is some debate about this categorization; Lawrence Ryan has quite persuasively argued for *Antigone*'s greater "modernity." In the course of this chapter, for reasons that will become clear, I side with Lacoue-Labarthe's initial estimation, even though Lacoue-Labarthe himself later suggests that "*Antigone* [is] *itself* at once the most Greek of tragedies *and* the most modern, and that, in order to communicate this same difference, imperceptible in itself, that repetition implies, one had transformed here or there that which it says so as to better say that which it says, *in truth*" (70). Suggestive as Lacoue-Labarthe's arguments are, I think that for Hölderlin, this kind of repetition is, quite simply, impossible; any repetition involved in the Greece-Germany dialectic is a repetition in inversion, and the difference is always irreducibly greater than one "imperceptible in itself."

64. This is not to say, however, that Hölderlin was a "Pre-Socratic." Like Nietzsche, he is a post-Socratic through and through, his reflection and his poetry defined by living in the-time-after-Plato, a historical situation of *Geist* that is unerasable from his work.

65. ". . . in aller Schärfe genommen, ist eine apriorische, von aller Erfahrung durchas unabängige Philosophie . . . so gut ein Unding als eine positive Offenbarung, wo der Offenbarende nur alles dabei tut, und der, dem die Offenbarung gegeben wird, nicht einmal sich regen darf, um sie zu nehmen, denn sonst hätt er schon von dem Seinen etwas dazu gebracht." WBD, 751.

66. Tragedy is "Sprache für eine Welt, wo . . . der Gott und der Mensch, damit der Weltlauf keine Lücke hat und *das Gedächtnis der Himmlischen nicht ausgehet, in der allvergessenden Form der Untreue sich mitteilt*, denn göttliche Untreue ist am besten zu

behalten." WBD, 624. The sentence seems ungrammatical, for if "der Gott und der Mensch" is the subject, the verb should be in the plural, "mitteilen." This might be Hölderlin's mistake or an error in transcription; it might also signify that "Gott und Mensch" become one, or that the divine subsumes the human, for the last clause speaks of divine betrayal alone.

67. "Der kühnste Moment eines Taglaufs oder Kunstwerks ist, wo der Geist der Zeit und Natur, das Himmlische, was den Menschen ergreift, und der Gegenstand, für welchen er sich interessiert, am wildesten gegeneinander stehen . . . ." WBD, 671.

68. "Nur wo Sprache, da ist Welt . . . . Nur wo Welt waltet, da ist Geschichte." Heidegger, *Erläuterungen*, 38.

69. "Eigentliche Sprache des Sophokles, da Aeschylus und Euripides mehr das Leiden und den Zorn, weniger aber des Menschen Verstand, als unter Undenkbarem wandelnd, zu objektivieren wissen." WBD, 671.

70. *Essays and Letters*, 101: "Dann hat man darauf zu sehen, wie der Inhalt sich von diesem [i.e. dem gesetzlichen Kalkul] unterscheidet, durch welche Verfahrensart, und wie im unendlichen, aber durchgängig bestimmten Zusammenhange der besondere Inhalt sich zum allgemeinen Kalkul verhält, und der Gang und das Festzusetzende, der lebendige Sinn, der nicht berechnet werden kann, mit dem kalkulablen Gesetze in Beziehung gebracht wird." WBD, 618.

71. "So wie nämlich immer die Philosophie nur ein Vermögen der Seele behandelt, so daß die Darstellung dieses Einen Vermögens ein Ganzes macht, und das bloße Zusammenhängen *der Glieder* dieses Einen Vermögens Logik genannt wird, so behandelt die Poesie die verschiedenen Vermögen des Menschen, so daß die Darstellung dieser verschiedenen Vermögen ein Ganzes macht, und das Zusammenhängen *der selbständigeren Teile* des verschiedenen Vermögen der Rhythmus, im höhern Sinne, oder das kalkulable Gesetz genannt werden kann." WBD, 670.

72. As I have argued in the first chapter, the *Phaedrus*, a text Hölderlin knew well, suggests a similar self-critique, for there Socrates grounds philosophy in a moment of madness as well.

73. "[Die Regel der Antigonä] ist eine der verschiedenen Sukzessionen, in denen sich Vorstellung und Empfindung und Räsonnement, nach poetischer Logic, entwickelt." WBD, 670. Hölderlin develops a very complex teaching about aesthetic successions in his theory of the "change of tones," according to which idealic, heroic, and naive "tonalities" have to alternate in a specific fashion in order to produce artistic beauty. His allusions to a law of successions in tragedy clearly imply these teachings. Since for the purposes of this investigation, Hölderlin's insistence on the calculability of aesthetic beauty and effect are more important than the specific rules themselves, I will not delve into the extremely difficult tables and texts that work out Hölderlin's schemes.

74. Cf. Nägele's commentary on "Brod und Wein": "Openness ['das Offene'] is emptiness, nothingness, the breach between something, condition that something be seen, in itself, however, it is nothing. The eye that sees openness itself sees nothingness, but not nothingness per se, but a specific nothing, the difference between something and something." *Text, Geschichte und Subjektivität*, 81.

75. The political implications of Hölderlin's tragic thought, or, conversely, his tragic view of history, are too vast a topic to be treated here; nevertheless, it must be kept in mind that Hölderlin writes on the background of the experience of the French

Revolution, at his time the very paradigm of the breakdown and reconstitution of hierarchy. It is not only true that Hölderlin views tragedy through the lens of the Revolution; he also looks at France through the lens of tragedy.

76. The balance resulting from the simultaneity of a double collapse is a familiar metaphor in post-Kantian thought, as Werner Hamacher admirably demonstrates in his essay on Kleist's *Erdbeben in Chili*. Cf. "Das Beben der Darstellung," *Positionen der Literaturwissenschaft: Acht Modellanalysen am Beispiel von Kleists 'Das Erdbeben von Chili,'* ed. D. E. Wellbery (München: Beck, 1985), 149–173.

77. *Essays and Letters*, 111, trans. modified: "Wohl der höchste Zug an der Antigonä. Der erhabene Spott, so fern heiliger Wahnsinn höchste menschliche Erscheinung, und hier mehr Seele als Sprache ist, übertrifft alle ihre übrigen Äußerungen. . . . Es ist ein großer Behelf der geheimarbeitenden Seele, daß sie auf dem höchsten Bewußtsein dem Bewußtsein ausweicht, und ehe sie wirklich der gegenwärtige Gott ergreift, mit kühnem, oft sogar blasphemischem Worte diesem begegnet, und so die heilige lebende Möglichkeit des Geistes erhält." WBD, 672.

78. "Im Zustande zwischen Sein und Nichtsein wird aber überall das Mögliche real, und das Wirkliche ideal, und dies ist in der freien Kunstnachahmung ein furchtbarer aber göttlicher Traum." Cf. "Das Werden im Vergehen," WBD, 540–544: 541.

79. "In der rhythmischen Aufeinaderfolge der Vorstellungen, worin der *Transport* sich darstellt, [wird] *das, was man im Silbenmaße Zäsur heißt*, das reine Wort, die gegenrhythmische Unterbrechung notwendig, um nämlich dem reißenden Wechsel der Vorstellungen, auf seinem Summum, so zu begegnen, daß alsdann nicht mehr der Wechsel der Vorstellung, sondern die Vorstellung selber erscheint." WBD, 619.

80. "In der äußersten Grenze des Leidens besteht nämlich nichts mehr, als die Bedingungen der Zeit oder des Raums." WBD, 624.

81. ". . . die Zeit, weil sie in solchem Momente sich kategorisch wendet und Anfang und Ende sich in ihr schlechterdings nicht reimen läßt." WBD, 624.

82. "Die Darstellung des Tragischen beruht vorzüglich darauf, daß das Ungeheure, wie der Gott und Mensch sich paart, . . . dadurch sich begreift, daß das grenzenlose Eineswerden durch grenzenloses Scheiden sich reiniget." WBD, 623.

83. *Antigones*, 78, 87.

84. "Ich habe gehört, der Wüste gleich sei worde/Die Lebensreiche, Phrygische,/. . ./ Recht der gleich/Bringt mich ein Geist zu Bette." WBD, 652–3.

85. This passage shows once more how far Hölderlin has moved away from the more conventional understanding of inspiration and transcendence that informs his (unfinished) *Empedocles* project. As Blanchot points out in his commentary on this passage, "Empedocles is the desire to go into the other world, and it is this desire which is now called inauthentic. It must be bent back toward the earth." "Hölderlin's Itinerary," 271.

86. "Im Bestimmteren oder Unbestimmteren muß wohl Zeus gesagt werden *Im Ernste* lieber: Vater der Zeit oder: Vater der Erde, weil sein Charakter ist, der ewigen Tendenz entgegen, *das Streben aus dieser Welt in die andre* zu kehren *zu einem Streben aus einer andern Welt in diese.* Wir müssen die Mythe nämlich überall *beweisbarer* darstellen." WBD, 672–673.

87. ". . . der Vater aber liebt,//Der über allen waltet,//Am meisten, daß gepflegt werde//Der feste Buchstab, und Bestehendes gut//Gedeutet. Dem folgt deutscher Gesang." WBD, 182.

88. This is Lacoue-Labarthe's comment on Hegel's omission of the incest in his account of Oedipus. Voß, in fact, criticized Hölderlin's translation for its too carnal imagery.

89. Hölderlin here uses a Virgilian term that signifies a transgression against divine order.

90. *Essays and Letters*, 102–103, trans. modified.—Die *Verständlichkeit* des Ganzen beruht vorzüglich darauf, daß man die Szene ins Auge faßt, wo Oedipus den Orakelspruch *zu unendlich deutet, zum nefas* versucht wird. Nämlich der Orakelspruch . . . konnte heißen: Richtet, allgemein, ein streng und rein Gericht, haltet gute bürgerliche Ordnung. Oedipus aber spricht gleich darauf priesterlich" WBD, 619–620.

91. *Essays and Letters*, 51–52, trans. slightly modified: "Auch im tragisch dramatischen Gedichte spricht sich also das Göttliche aus, das der Dichter in seiner Welt empfindet und erfährt, auch das tragisch dramatische Gedicht ist ihm ein Bild des Lebendigen, das ihm in seinem Leben gegenwärtig ist und war; aber wie dieses Bild der Innigkeit überall seinen letzten Grund in eben dem Grade mehr verleugnet und verleugnen muß, wie es überall mehr dem Symbol sich nähern muß, je unendlicher, je unaussprechlicher, je näher dem *nefas* die Innigkeit ist, je strenger und kälter das Bild den Menschen und sein empfundenes Element unterscheiden muß, um die Empfindung in ihrer Grenze festzuhalten, um so weniger kann das Bild die Emfindung unmittelbar aussprechen, es muß sie sowohl der Form als dem Stoffe nach verleugnen, der Stoff muß ein kühneres fremderes Gleichnis und Beispiel von ihr sein, die Form muß mehr den Charakter der Entgegensetzung und Trennung tragen." WBD, 545–546.

92. Needless to say, numerous critics have taken exception to Heidegger's reading of Hölderlin, among them Theodor W. Adorno, Peter Szondi, Maurice Blanchot, Paul de Man, and Timothy Bahti. I will not refer to their work in detail, since these critiques do not concern Heidegger's speculations about Hölderlin's madness. I am, needless to say, indebted to them nonetheless.

93. "Von *Hölderlin* selbst gilt das Wort, das er in jenem späten Gedicht 'In lieblicher Bläue blühet. . .' von Oedipus gesagt hat: 'Der König Oedipus hat ein Auge zuviel vielleicht.' " *Erläuterungen*, 47.

94. "Das eigenste Schicksal des Dichters sagt alles." *Erläuterungen*, 44. Georg Steiner travels the same path several times in his treatment of Hölderlin's *Antigonä*; cf. *Antigones*, 80, 91, 98.

95. On Heidegger's rejection of "Literaturwissenschaft," and for a critique of Heidegger's method of reading in the specific context of Hölderlin's madness, cf. Dieter Burdorf, *Hölderlins späte Gedichtfragmente: "Unendlicher Deutung voll"* (Stuttgart: J. B. Metzler, 1993), 96–106.

96. "Und ein Jahr päter, nachdem Hölderlin als ein vom Wahnsinn Getroffener in das Haus der Mutter zurückgekehrt ist, schreibt er an denselben Freund [Böhlendorff] aus der Erinnerung an den Aufenthalt in Frankreich: [there follows an excerpt from the Böhlendorff letter]." *Erläuterungen*, 44.

97. "Le dernier philosophe," *L'imitation des modernes*, 203.

98. *Essays and Letters*, 103: "So wird der Orakelspruch und die nicht notwendig darunter gehörige Geschichte von Lajos Tode zusammengebracht." WBD, 620.

99. *Essays and Letters*, 103, trans. modified: "In der gleich darauf folgenden Szene spricht aber, in zorniger Ahnung, der Geist des Oedipus, alles wissend, das *nefas*

eigentlich aus, indem er das allgemeine Gebot argwöhnisch ins Besondere deutet, und auf einen Mörder des Lajos anwendet, und dann auch die Sünde als unendlich nimmt." WBD, 620.

100. *Essays and Letters*, 104, trans. modified: ". . . weil das Wissen, wenn es seine Schranke durchrissen hat, wie trunken in seiner herrlichen harmonischen Form, die doch bleiben kann, vorerst, sich selbst reizt, mehr zu wissen, als es tragen oder fassen kann." WBD, 620.

101. *Essays and Letters*, 105, trans. modified: "Zuletzt herrscht in den Reden vorzüglich das geisteskranke Fragen nach einem Bewußtsein." WBD, 622.

102. Hölderlin's interpretation of the tragedies is undoubtedly his own, but the constellation within which it unfolds—history, subjectivity, metaphysics—is the same one within which Hegel in his *Phenomenology* and Schelling in his *Letters* operate.

103. "Was sagst du? pflanzte Polybos mich nicht"// Beinahe so etwas, wie unser einer. // Wie das? ein Vater, der dem Niemand gleich ist?// Ein Vater eben. Polybos nicht; nicht ich. // Wofür denn aber nennt der mich das Kind?" WBD, 622.

104. "Ich aber will, als Sohn des Glücks mich haltend,//Des wohlbegabten, nicht verunehrt werden.//Denn dies ist meine Mutter. Und klein und groß//Umfingen mich die mitgebornen Monde.//Und so erzeugt, will ich nicht ausgehn, so,//So daß ich nicht ganz, was ich bin, erforsche." WBD, 623.

105. *Essays and Letters*, 107, trans. modified: "Die Darstellung des Tragischen beruht vorzüglich darauf, daß das Ungeheure, wie der Gott und Mensch sich paart, und grenzenlos die Naturmacht und des Menschen Innerstes im Zorn Eins wird, dadurch sich begreift, daß das grenzenlose Eineswerden durch grenzenloses Scheiden sich reiniget." WBD, 623.

106. Cf. the second stanza of *Hälfte des Lebens*, which gives as one of its images the absence of "shadows of the earth."

107. For commentary on Hölderlin's use of "Maß," cf. Nägele, *Text, Geschichte und Subjektivität*, 72.

108. "Ich habe auch hier erfahren, was mir schon manchmal begegnet ist, daß mir nemlich das Vorübergehende und Abwechselnde der menschlichen Gedanken und Systeme fast tragischer aufgefallen ist als die Schicksale, die man gewöhnlich allein die wirklichen nennt, und ich glaube, es ist natürlich, denn wenn der Mensch in seiner eigensten, freiesten Tätigkeit, im unabhängigen Gedanken selbst von fremdem Einfluß abhängt, und wenn er auch da noch immer modifiziert ist von den Umständen und vom Klima, wie es sich unwidersprechlich zeigt, wo hat er dann noch eine Herrschaft? Es ist auch gut, und sogar die erste Bedingung alles Lebens und aller Organisation, daß keine Kraft monarchisch ist im Himmel und auf Erden. Die absolute Monarchie hebt sich überall selbst auf, denn sie ist objektlos; es hat auch im strengen Sinne niemals eine gegeben. . . . Alles greift ineinander und leidet, so wie es tätig ist, so auch der reinste Gedanke des Menschen, und in aller Schärfe genommen, ist eine apriorische, von aller Erfahrung durchaus unabängige Philosophie, . . . so gut ein Unding als eine positive Offenbarung, wo der Offenbarende nur alles dabei tut, und der, dem die Offenbarung gegeben wird, nicht einmal sich regen darf, um sie zu nehmen, denn sonst hätt er schon von dem Seinen etwas dazu gebracht." WBD, 751.

109. It would be a fascinating project to assess whether Hölderlin's reading of Antigone's and Oedipus's respective attitudes towards the sign is informed by, implies,

or amounts to a theory of gender, and whether even, by extension, his theory of history along the lines of the Greece-Germany model might be gendered.

CHAPTER THREE
NIETZSCHE: THE MARKETPLACE OF MADNESS

1. "Protagoras" (314a–b), trans. W.K.C. Guthrie, in *Collected Dialogues*, ed. Edith Hamilton and Huntington Cairns (Princeton: Princeton UP, 1963), 308–352.

2. Christoph Türcke, *Der tolle Mensch: Nietzsche und der Wahnsinn der Vernunft*, (Frankfurt/M.: Fischer, 1989), 163. All translations from the German are mine.

3. "Umgekehrt ist an dem Philosophen ganz und gar nichts Unpersönliches," KSA 3:20.

4. EH, KSA 6: 366–369.

5. Gottfried Benn, "Nietzsche—nach fünfzig Jahren," *Gesammelte Werke in acht Bänden*, ed. Dieter Wellershoff, Bd. IV (Wiesbaden: 1968), 1046–1057: 1051.

6. "Das Genieproblem," *Gesammelte Werke*, Bd. III, 669–684, 684.

7. Wilhelm Lange-Eichbaum, *Nietzsche: Krankheit und Wirkung* (Hamburg: n.p., 1947), 419. For a rather comprehensive bibliography of pathographic texts on Nietzsche, cf. Pia Daniela Volz, op.cit.

8. On Nietzsche's last days and some of the controversies surrounding them, cf. my brief essay "Somatic Archive: Exhibiting Nietzsche," *German Politics and Society* 54:18:1 (Spring 2000), 66–75.

9. Max Nordau, *Entartung*, Bd. I (Carl Duncker, 1893), xx.

10. I am grateful to Charles Bernheimer, who has pointed out to me the pervasive similarities between decadence and the critique of decadence at the turn of the nineteenth century.

11. Georges Bataille, *On Nietzsche*, trans. Bruce Boone, introduction by Sylvère Lotringer, New York: Paragon House, 1992 (trans. of *Sur Nietzsche* [Paris: Éditions Gallimard, 1945]), xix.

12. *Der tolle Mensch*, 7.

13. *Der tolle Mensch*, 169–170.

14. Ibid.

15. Ibid., 7.

16. Ibid., 169–170.

17. *Der tolle Mensch*, 167.

18. Harold Bloom, *The Western Canon: The Books and School of the Ages* (New York: Riverhead, 1995), 351.

19. KSA 6: 373.

20. EH, KSA 6: 367.

21. Ibid.

22. "welchen Sinn hätte *unser* ganzes Dasein, wenn nicht den, dass in uns jener Wille zur Wahrheit sich selbst *als Problem* zum Bewusstsein gekommen wäre? ... An diesem Sich-bewusst-werden des Willens zur Wahrheit geht von nun an—daran ist kein Zweifel—die Moral *zu Grunde*: jenes grosse Schauspiel in hundert Akten, das den

nächsten zwei Jahrhunderten Europa's aufgespart bleibt, das furchtbarste, fragwürdigste und vielleicht auch hoffnungsreichste aller Schauspiele . . . ." GM, KSA 5: 410–411.

23. Ibid.

24. For the history of this fusion, cf. Michel Foucault's analysis in *Madness and Civilization*, op. cit.

25. Letters, quoted after Türcke, 15.

26. Cf. chapter one, section III.

27. Cf., amongst others, the paragraph "Hoch die Physik!," FW, KSA 3: 563.

28. *Reconfigurations*, 175.

29. Terry Eagleton, *The Ideology of the Aesthetic* (Oxford/Cambridge, Mass.: Basil Blackwell, 1990), 234. Nietzsche's physiologism actually differs from Schopenhauer's thoughts on these matters significantly, and "vulgarity" is not necessarily a valid objection; it could even be argued that the very vulgarity of the physiological argument adds to its usefulness as far as it serves as an antidote to what Nietzsche perceives as the "decadence" of dialectical philosophy, a degeneration he often, but not exclusively, accounts for in physiological terms. If, as Plotnitsky notes, Nietzsche's "plural style must always operate both from the inside and from the outside of the deconstructed field" (*Reconfigurations*, 177) of philosophy, the crudeness of some of Nietzsche's thought that coexists along with the most exquisite subtleties may well be seen as part of an overall strategy that combines logic and complexity with something akin to philosophical irresponsibility (which is not the same as intellectual dishonesty).

30. *Reconfigurations*, 177.

31. "Denn eine Gesundheit an sich giebt es nicht, und alle Versuche, ein Ding derart zu definiren, sind kläglich missrathen." FW, KSA 3: 477.

32. "[My] double ancestry, from the highest and the lowest step on the ladder of life, as it were, simultaneously decadent and *beginning*—this, if anything, explains this neutrality, this freedom of any party in relation to the universal problem of life, which perhaps sets me apart."/ "[Meine] doppelte Herkunft, gleichsam aus der obersten und der untersten Sprosse und der Leiter des Lebens, décadent zugleich und *Anfang*—dies, wenn irgend Etwas erklärt jene Neutralität, jene Freiheit von Parthei im Verhältniss zum Gesammtprobleme des Lebens, die mich vielleicht auszeichnet." EH, KSA 6: 264.

33. "Man erräth, dass ich nicht mit Undankbarkeit von jener Zeit schweren Siechthums Abschied nehmen möchte, deren Gewinn auch heute noch nicht für mich ausgeschöpft ist: so wie ich mir gut genug bewusst bin, was ich überhaupt in meiner wechselreichen Gesundheit vor allen Vierschrötigen des Geistes voraus habe. Ein Philosoph, der den Gang durch viele Gesundheiten gemacht hat und immer wieder macht, ist auch durch evensoviele Philosophien hindurchgegangen: er *kann* eben nicht anders als seinen Zustand jedes Mal in die geistigste Form und Ferne umzusetzen,—diese Kunst der Transfiguration ist eben Philosophie. Es steht uns Philosophen nicht frei, zwischen Seele und Leib zu trennen . . . Und was die Krankheit angeht: würden wir nicht fast zu fragen versucht sein, ob sie uns überhaupt entbehrlich ist?" FW, KSA 3: 349–50.

34. Cf. *Ecce Homo*, KSA 6: 265: "All pathological disturbances of the intellect, even that semi-numbness which follows on a fever, have remained utterly foreign to

me." ("Alle krankhaften Störungen des Intellekts, selbst jene Halbbetäubung, die das Fieber im Gefolge hat, sind mir bis heute gänzliche fremde Dinge geblieben.")

35. In those very general terms, the dialectic between illness and health here resembles the dialectic not just between divine fire and poetic control in Hölderlin, but also between the Dionysian and the Apollonian in Nietzsche's *Birth of Tragedy*, a text I am neglecting here because it does not, in its reflection on divine inspiration, decisively depart from romantic theory.

36. On the anti-dialectical nature of Nietzsche's thought, cf. Gilles Deleuze, *Nietzsche and Philosophy*.

37. "Ich erwarte immer noch, dass ein philosophischer *Arzt* im ausnahmsweisen Sinne des Wortes—ein Solcher, der dem Problem der Gesammt-Gesundheit von Volk, Zeit, Rasse, Menschheit nachzugehn hat—einmal den Muth haben wird, meinen Verdacht auf die Spitze zu bringen und den Satz zu wagen: bei allem Philosophiren handelte es sich bisher gar nicht um 'Wahrheit', sondern um etwas Anderes, sagen wir um Gesundheit, Zukunft, Wachsthum, Macht, Leben...." FW, KSA 3: 349.

38. "... die Schwachen werden immer wieder über die Starken Herr—das macht, sie sind die grosse Zahl, sie sind auch klüger." GD, KSA 6: 120.

39. "Ich weiss nicht mehr, ob du, mein lieber Mitmensch und Nächster, überhaupt zu Ungunsten der Art, also 'unvernünftig' und 'schlecht' leben *kannst*; das, was der Art hätte schaden können, ist vielleicht seit vielen Jahrtausenden schon ausgestorben und gehört jetzt zu den Dingen, die selbst bei Gott nicht mehr möglich sind." FW, KSA 3: 470.

40. "Auch der schädlichste Mensch ist vielleicht immer noch der allernützlichste, in Hinsicht auf die Erhaltung der Art." FW, KSA 3: 369.

41. In a passage that I will analyze later, he speaks less optimistically about the future of mankind; interestingly enough, he asserts that this future is threatened by madness.

42. "Wie die Vernunft in die Welt gkommen ist? Wie billig, auf eine unvernünftige Weise, durch einen Zufall." M, KSA 3: 116.

43. "*Das vernünftige Denken ist ein Interpretiren nach einem Schema, welches wir nicht abwerfen können.*" KSA 12: 194.

44. WL, KSA 1: 875–890. All further quotations from this essay will be marked by page number only.

45. Prominent examples would be both Socrates' ideas and Descartes' *Meditations on First Philosophy*, the seminal text of modern philosophy, where Descartes sets out to create a mode of recognition totally independent of perception.

46. Paul de Man, "Rhetoric of Tropes," *Allegories of Reading: Figural Language in Rousseau, Nietzsche, Rilke, and Proust* (New Haven: Yale UP, 1979), 103–118.

47. "Mit schöpferischem Behagen wirft er die Metaphern durcheinander und verrückt die Gränzsteine der Abstraktion.... [der intuitive Mensch begehrt, über das Leben zu herrschen], indem er als ein 'überfroher Held' jene [hauptsächlichsten] Nöthe nicht sieht und nur das zum Schein und zur Schönheit verstellte Leben als real nimmt." 888–890.

48. "[H]ätten wir noch, jeder für sich eine verschiedenartige Sinnesempfindung, könnten wir selbst nur bald als Vogel, bald als Wurm, bald als Pflanze percipiren,

oder sähe der eine von uns denselben Reiz als roth, der andere als blau, hörte ein Dritter ihn sogar als Ton, so würde niemand von einer solchen Gesetzmässigkeit der Natur reden, sondern sie nur als ein höchst subjectives Gebilde begreifen." 885.

49. It is interesting to note that one of the classical essays in the contemporary philosophy of consciousness, Thomas Nagel's "What Is It Like to Be a Bat?", elaborates on the implications of Nietzsche's remark. Nagel argues, in brief, that the "problem of consciousness" poses an insurmountable problem for scientific reductions of the mind/body problem (in *The Nature of Consciousness: Philosophical Debates*, ed. Ned Block et al. [Cambridge: MIT Press, 1997], 519–528).

50. Schöffler-Weiss, *Taschenwörterbuch der englischen und deutschen Sprache*, Bd. II (Stuttgart: Ernst Klett, 1965), 360.

51. Cf. "Über den Nachtheil und Nutzen der Historie für das Leben," UB II, KSA 1: 245–334, section I.

52. In "Structure, Sign, and Play," Jacques Derrida distinguishes between radical play in "a world of signs without fault, without truth, and without origin," and "*sure* play: that which is limited to the *substitution* of *given* and *existing, present,* pieces." ("Structure, Sign, and Play in the Discourse of the Human Sciences," *Writing and Difference*, 292.) Nietzsche's artist would play the latter game.

53. Cf. especially the last paragraph of "The Rhetoric of Tropes."

54. *Allegories of Reading*, 112.

55. "[W]eil aber der Mensch zugleich aus Noth und Langeweile gesellschaftlich und heerdenweise existiren will, braucht er einen Friedensschluss und trachtet darnach dass wenigstens das allergröbste bellum omnium contra omnes aus seiner Welt verschwinde." 877.

56. It is important to note that Nietzsche does indeed formulate this thesis as early as this—even before he writes *Daybreak* and *Gay Science*. Ignoring "Truth and Lie," Maudemarie Clark argues that the *Genealogy* and *Beyond Good and Evil* reject Nietzsche's earlier theory of morality because he then postulates a "*pre-moral* period of mankind," which she reads to coincide with the period Nietzsche calls *Sittlichkeit der Sitte* in *Daybreak* (Cf. *Nietzsche's Attack on Morality*, diss., University of Wisconsin-Madison [Ann Arbor, Michigan, 1976], 96.). "Truth and Lie," however, shows that Nietzsche was theorizing about this pre-moral period as early as 1873. This suggests that Nietzsche's history of morality encompasses not two, but three periods: pre-moral state, *Sittlichkeit,* and *Moral.*

57. "Was ist ein Wort? Die Abbildung eines Nervenreizes in Lauten. . . . [Der Sprachbildner] bezeichnet nur die Relationen der Dinge zu den Menschen und nimmt zu deren Ausdrucke die Kühnsten Metaphern zu Hülfe. Ein Nervenreiz zuerst übertragen in ein Bild! erste Metapher. Das Bild wieder nachgeformt in einem Laut! Zweite Metapher. Und jedesmal vollständiges Uebersprungen der Sphäre, mitten hinein in eine ganz andre und neue." 878–879.

58. Metaphors of enclosed space abound in Nietzsche's text: chamber (87), "Wolkenkukuksheim" (879), pyramid (881), dome (882), edifice (882), jail (883).

59. "Wenn Jemand ein Ding hinter einem Busche versteckt, es eben dort wieder sucht und auch findet, so ist an diesem Suchen und Finden nicht viel zu rühmen: so aber steht es mit dem Suchen und Finden der 'Wahrheit' innerhalb des Vernunft-Bezirks." 883.

60. "Rhetoric of Tropes," 118.

61. Ibid.

62. "Wenn eine rechte Wetterwolke sich über ihn [den Stoiker] ausgiesst, so hüllt er sich in seinen Mantel und geht langsamen Schrittes unter ihr davon." 890.

63. "Verschweigt die Natur ihm nicht das Allermeiste, selbst über seinen Körper, um ihn, abseits von den Windungen der Gedärme, dem raschen Fluss der Blutströme, den verwickelten Fasererzitterungen, in ein stolzes gauklerisches Bewusstsein zu bannen und einzuschließen! Sie warf den Schlüssel weg: und wehe der verhängnissvollen Neubegier, die durch eine Spalte einmal aus dem Bewusstseinszimmer heraus und hinab zu sehen vermöchte und die jetzt ahnte, dass auf dem Erbarmungslosen, dem Gierigen, dem Unersättlichen, dem Mörderischen der Mensch ruht, in der Gleichgültigkeit seines Nichtwissens, und gleichsam auf dem Rücken eines Tigers in Träumen hängend." 877.

64. Wilhelm Reich, *The Function of the Orgasm*, trans. Vincent R. Carfagno (New York: Simon & Schuster, 1973), 60.

65. "[E]s könnte selbst zur Grundbeschaffenheit des Daseins gehören, dass man an seiner völligen Erkenntnis zugrunde gienge." JGB, KSA 5: 65–7.

66. Cf. *Madness and Civilization*, op. cit., especially Chapters II and III.

67. Cf. *Daybreak* I, sections 1 and 9.

68. "Wenn trotz jenem furchtbaren Druck der 'Sittlichkeit der Sitte', unter dem alle Gemeinwesen der Menschheit lebten, viele Jahrtausende lang vor unserer Zeitrechnung und in derselben im Ganzen und Grossen fort bis auf den heutigen Tag (wir selber wohnen in der kleinen Welt der Ausnahmen und gleichsam in der bösen Zone): wenn, sage ich trotzdem neue und abweichende Gedanken, Werthschätzungen, Triebe immer wieder herausbrachen, so geschah diess unter einer schauderhaften Geleitschaft: fast überall ist es der Wahnsinn, welcher dem neuen Gedanken den Weg bahnt." M, KSA 3: 26.

69. Samuel Weber, *Institution and Interpretation* (Minneapolis: University of Minnesota Press, 1987), 159.

70. "Es schien, dass man mit [der Wahrheit] nicht zu leben vermöge, unser Organismus war auf ihren Gegensatz eingerichet; alle seine höheren Functionen, die Wahrnehmungen der Sinne und jede Art von Empfindung überhaupt, arbeiteten mit jenen uralt einverleibten Grundirrthümern. Mehr noch: jene Sätze wurden selbst innerhalb der Erkenntniss zu den Normen, nach denen man 'wahr' und 'unwahr' bemass—bis hinein in die entlegensten Gegenden der reinen Logik. Also: die *Kraft* der Erkenntnisse liegt nicht in ihrem Grade von Wahrheit, sondern in ihrem Alter, ihrer Einverleibtheit, ihrem Charakter als Lebensbedingung. Wo Leben und Erkennen in Widerspruch zu komen schienen, ist nie ernstlich gekämpft worden; da galt Leugnung und Zweifel als Tollheit." FW, KSA 3: 469.

71. On the many transitions that were necessary before *Erkenntnis* could become a "continuously growing power" and "the drive to truth could *prove* itself as a life-preserving force," cf. the long paragraph from which the citation above is taken, FW, KSA 3: 469–471.

72. As I have argued in the first chapter, Plato's *Phaedrus* illustrates a similar concept of madness that both validates and subverts the philosophy that grants it its privilege.

73. "Ursprünglich gehörte die ganze Erziehung und Pflege der Gesundheit, die Ehe, die Heilkunst, der Feldbau, der Krieg, das Reden und Schweigen, der Verkehr unter einander und mit den Göttern in den Bereich der Sittlichkeit: sie verlangte, dass man Vorschriften beobachtete, *ohne an sich* als Individuum zu denken. Ursprünglich also war Alles Sitte." M, KSA 3: 22.

74. "[E]s ist gar nicht auszurechnen, was gerade die seltneren, ausgesuchteren, ursprünglicheren Geister im ganzen Verlauf der Geschichte dadurch gelitten haben müssen, dass sie immer als die bösen und gefährlichen empfunden wurden." M, KSA 3: 24.

75. " 'Ach, so gebt doch Wahnsinn, ihr Himmlischen! Wahnsinn, dass ich endlich an mich selber glaube! . . . Der Zweifel frisst mich auf, ich habe das Gesetz getödtet, das Gesetz ängstigt mich wie ein Leichnam einen Lebendigen: wenn ich nicht *mehr* bin als das Gesetz, so bin ich der Verworfenste von Allen. Der neue Geist, der in mir ist, woher ist er, wenn er nicht von euch ist? Beweist es mir doch, dass ich euer bin; der Wahnsinn allein beweist es mir.' " M, KSA 3: 28.

76. "eine geheime Lehre von Kunstgriffen und diätetischen Winken . . . : unsinniges Fasten, fortgesetzte geschlechtliche Enthaltung, in die Wüste gehen oder auf einen Berg oder eine Säule steigen. . . ." M, KSA 3: 27.

77. "in jener Zeit, in welcher as Christenthum am reichsten seine Fruchtbarkeit an Heiligen und Wüsten-Einsiedlern bewies und sich dadurch selber zu beweisen vermeinte, gab es in Jerusalem grosse Irrenhäuser für verunglückte Heilige, für jene, welche ihr letztes Korn Salz daran gegeben hatten." M, KSA 3: 28.

78. Nietzsche develops a somewhat similar train of thought in *Daybreak*, in a section on "the moral insanity of the genius": "As long as the genius lives in us, we are courageous, even as mad, and pay no regard to life, health, and honor. . . . But suddenly, it leaves us, and as suddenly deep anguish descends on us" ("So lange der Genius in uns wohnt, sind wir beherzt, ja wie toll, und achten nicht des Lebens, der Gesundheit und der Ehre. . . . Aber auf einmal verlässt er uns, und ebenso plötzlich fällt tiefe Furchtsamkeit auf uns") M, KSA 3: 307.

79. "Vergessen wir auch jene Gehörs-Hallucinationen nicht, die, als 'Dämonion des Sokrates", in's Religiöse interpretiert worden sind." GD, KSA 6: 69.

80. "Jene Moralisten dagegen, welche wie die Nachfolger der *sokratischen* Fußstapfen die Moral der Selbstbeherrschung und Enthaltsamkeit dem *Individuum* als seinen eigensten *Vortheil*, als seinen persönlichsten Schlüssel zum Glück an's Herz legen, *machen die Ausnahme*—und wenn es uns anders erscheint, so ist es, weil wir unter ihrer Nachwirkung erzogen sind: sie alle gehen eine neue Strasse unter höchlichster Missbilligung aller Vertreter der Sittlichkeit der Sitte,—sie lösen sich aus der Gemeinde aus, als Unsittliche, und sind, im tiefsten Verstande, böse. Ebenso erschien einem tugendhaften Römer alten Schrotes jeder *Christ*, welcher 'am ersten nach seiner *eigenen* Seligkeit trachtete',—als böse." M, KSA 3: 23.

81. "Alle Dinge, die lange leben, werden allmählich so mit Vernunft durchtränkt, dass ihre Abkunft aus der Unvernunft dadurch unwahrscheinlich wird. Klingt nicht fast jede genaue Geschichte einer Entstehung für das Gefühl paradox und frevelhaft? *Widerspricht* der gute Historiker nicht fortwährend?" M, KSA 3: 19.

82. "Während es uns heute noch immer wieder nah gelegt wird, dass dem Genie, anstatt eines Kornes Salz, ein Korn Wahnwurz beigegeben ist, lag allen früheren

Menschen der Gedanke viel näher, dass überall, wo es Wahnsinn giebt, es auch ein Korn Genie und Weisheit gäbe,—etwas 'Göttliches', wie man sich zuflüsterte." M, KSA 3: 27.

83. Cf. the brief discussion of Foucault in the introduction.

84. "das Ausbrechen des Beliebens im Empfinden, Sehen und Hören, der Genuss in der Zuchtlosigkeit des Kopfes, die Freude am Menschen-Unverstande." FW, KSA 3: 431.

85. *"Die grösste Gefahr.*—Hätte es nicht allezeit eine Überzahl von Menschen gegeben, welche die Zucht ihres Kopfes—ihre 'Vernünftigkeit'—als ihren Stolz, ihre Verpflichtung, ihre Tugend fühlten, welche durch alles Phantasiren und Ausschweifen des Denkens beleidigt oder beschämt wurden, als die Freunde 'des gesunden Menschenverstandes': so wäre die Menschheit längst zu Grunde gegangen! Ueber ihr schwebte und schwebt fortwährend als ihre grösste Gefahr der ausbrechende *Irrsinn*— das heisst eben Genuss in der Zuchtlosigkeit des Kopfes, die Freude am Menschen-Unverstande. Nicht die Wahrheit und Gewissheit ist der Gegensatz der Welt des Irrsinnigen, sondern die Allgemeinheit und Allverbindlichkeit eines Glaubens, kurz das Nicht-Beliebige im Urtheilen." FW, KSA 3: 431.

86. This understanding has been vigorously attacked by Maudemarie Clark, in *Nietzsche's Attack on Morality*. While Clark marshals a great number of Nietzsche passages that criticize morality in its entirety, she neglects to follow Nietzsche's argument that something that is a lie or a deception is therefore not yet useless or dispensable.

87. Cf. this chapter, section II.

88. Nietzsche and Philosophy, 95–96.

89. Ibid., 97.

90. "Und die grösste Arbeit der Menschen bisher war die, über sehr viele Dinge mit einander übereinzustimmen und sich ein *Gesetz der Uebereinstimmung* aufzulegen—gleichgültig, ob diese Dinge wahr oder falsch sind." FW, KSA 3: 431.

91. In *Beyond Good and Evil*, Nietzsche concentrates much of his efforts on a critique of truth as value; while pertinent and desirable, any extended discussion of this critique would far exceed the limits of this enterprise.

92. "Wir fragten nach dem *Werthe* dieses Willens. Gesetzt, wir wollen Wahrheit: *warum nicht lieber* Unwahrheit? Und Ungewissheit? Selbst Unwissenheit? . . . Und sollte man's glauben, dass es uns schliesslich bedünken will, als sei das Problem noch nie bisher gestellt, als sei es von uns zum ersten Male gesehn, in's Auge gefasst, *gewagt*? Denn es ist ein Wagnis dabei, und vielleicht giebt es kein grösseres." JGB, KSA 5: 15.

93. " 'Ich komme zu früh, sagte er dann, ich bin noch nicht an der Zeit. Diess ungeheure Ereigniss ist noch unterwegs und wandert,—es ist noch nicht bis zu den Ohren der Menschen gedrungen. Blitz und Donner brauchen Zeit, das Licht der Gestirne braucht Zeit, Thaten brauchen Zeit, auch nachdem sie gethan sind, um gesehen und gehört zu werden. Diese That ist ihnen immer noch ferner, als die fernsten Gestirne,—*und doch haben sie dieselbe gethan!*' " FW, KSA 3: 481–2.

94. " 'Wohin ist Gott? rief er, ich will es euch sagen! *Wir haben ihn getödtet,*—ihr und ich! Wir Alle sind seine Mörder!" FW, KSA 3: 480–1.

95. Earlier in the *Gay Science*, Nietzsche suggests that to be born too late, as an "atavism," can also lead to madness: "I prefer to understand the rare human beings of an age as suddenly emerging late ghosts of past cultures and their powers—as atavisms

of a people and its *mores*. . . . Now they seem strange, rare, extraordinary; and whoever feels these powers in himself must nurse, defend, honor and cultivate them against another world that resists them, until he becomes either a great human being or a mad and eccentric one—or perishes early." ("Die seltenen Menschen einer Zeit verstehe ich am liebsten als plötzlich auftauchende Nachschösslinge vergangener Culturen und deren Kräften: gleichsam als den Atavismus eines Volkes und seiner Gesittung. . . . Jetzt erscheinen sie fremd, selten, ausserordentlich: und wer diese Kräfte in sich fühlt, hat sie gegen eine widerstrebende andere Welt zu pflegen, zu vertheidigen, zu ehren, gross zu ziehen: und so wird er damit entweder ein grosser Mensch oder ein verrückter und absonderlicher, sofern er überhaupt nicht bei Zeiten zu Grunde geht.") FW, KSA 3: 381–2. Note, however, that Nietzsche does not empower these "rare" beings with legislative or prophetic power.

96. *Der tolle Mensch*, 124.

97. "Nietzsches Wort 'Gott ist tot'," *Holzwege* (Frankfurt/M.: Klostermann, 6/1980), 205–263: 215.

98. "Das innere Glück und Elend der Menschen ist ihnen nämlich je nach ihrem Glauben an diese oder jene Motive zu Theil geworden,—*nicht* aber durch Das, was wirklich Motiv war! Alles diess Letztere hat ein Interesse zweiten Ranges." FW, KSA 3: 410–1.

99. "Nietzsches Wort," 221.

100. "Was thaten wir, als wir diese Erde von ihrer Sonne losketteten? Wohin bewegt sie sich nun? Wohin bewegen wir uns? Fort von allen Sonnen? Stürzen wir nicht fortwährend? Und rückwärts, seitwärts, vorwärts, nach allen Seiten? Giebt es noch ein Oben und ein Unten?" FW, KSA 3: 481.

101. "Es gab nie eine grössere That,—und wer nur immer nach uns geboren wird, gehört um dieser That willen in eine höhere Geschichte, als alle Geschichte bisher war!" FW, KSA 3: 481.

102. *Der tolle Mensch*, 26.

103. "Nietzsches Wort," 217.

104. Max Weber, *The Protestant Ethic and the Spirit of Capitalism*, quoted after Philip Rieff, *The Triumph of the Therapeutic: Uses of Faith after Freud* (Chicago/London: U of Chicago P, 1966), xvii.

105. "Nietzsches Wort," 262–263.

106. Ibid., 262.

107. "Nietzsches Wort," 262.

108. "Alle Erlebnisse leuchteten anders, denn ein Gott glänzte aus ihnen; alle Entschlüsse und Aussichten auf die ferne Zukunft ebenfalls: denn man hatte Orakel und geheime Winke und glaubte an die Vorhersagung. 'Wahrheit wurde anders empfunden, denn der Wahnsinige konnte ehemals als ihr Mundstück gelten,—was *uns* schaudern oder lachen macht." FW, KSA 3: 495.

109. "*Wir Hyperboreer*. Weder zu Wasser, noch zu Lande kannst du den Weg zu den Hyperboreern finden. Pindar. Jenseits des Nordens, des Eises, der Härte, des Todes—*unser* Leben! *Unser* Glück!" KSA 12: 201.

110. "Nicht die Wahrheit und Gewissheit ist der Gegensatz der Welt des Irrsinnigen, sondern die Allgemeinheit und Allverbindlichkeit eines Glaubens, kurz das Nicht-Beliebige im Urtheilen." FW, KSA 3: 431.

111. "Wie dürfte man den Mittelmäßigen ihre Mittelmäßigkeit verleiden! Ich thue, wie man sieht, das Gegentheil: denn jeder Schritt weg von ihr—so lehre ich—führt *ins Unmoralische.*" KSA 12: 528.

112. "der Haß gegen die Mittelmäßigkeit ist eines Philosophen unwürdig; es ist fast ein Fragezeichen an seinem *Recht* auf 'Philosophie'. Gerade deshalb, weil er die Ausnahme ist, hat er die Regel in Schutz zu nehmen, hat er allem Mittleren den guten Muth zu sich selber zu erhalten." KSA 12: 560.

113. "aber die Gegentriebe sind immer noch so mächtig, dass man im Grunde von der Zukunft der Menschheit mit wenig Vertrauen reden darf." FW, KSA 3: 431–2.

114. "Fortwährend verschiebt sich noch das Bild der Dinge, und vielleicht von jetzt ab mehr und schneller als je; fortwährend sträuben sich gerade die ausgesuchtesten Geister gegen jene Allverbindlichkeit—die Erforscher der *Wahrheit* voran!" FW, KSA 3, 432.

115. M, KSA 3: 17.

116. ". . . und schon das langsame Tempo, welches [der Allerweltsglaube] für alle geistige Processe verlangt, jene Nachahmung der Schildkröte, welche hier als die Norm anerkannt wird, macht Künstler und Dichter zu Ueberläufern. . . ." FW, KSA 3: 432.

117. "Die Helden, Märtyrer, Genies und Begeisterten sind uns nicht still, geduldig, fein, kalt, langsam genug." KSA 12, 322.

118. "Der Irrsinn ist bei Einzelnen etwas Seltenes,—aber bei Gruppen, Parteien, Völkern, Zeiten die Regel." JGB, KSA 5: 100.

119. "Nicht nur die Vernunft von Jahrtausenden—auch ihr Wahnsinn bricht an uns aus. Gefährlich ist es, Erbe zu sein." Z, KSA 4: 100.

120. "Die wahre Welt haben wir abgeschafft: welche Welt blieb übrig? die scheinbare vielleicht? . . . Aber nein! *mit der wahren Welt haben wir auch die scheinbare abgeschafft!*" GD, KSA 6, 81.

121. Jacques Derrida, "The Ends of Man," *Margins of Philosophy* (Chicago: U of Chicago P, 1972), 135.

122. "Inmitten des Oceans des Werdens wachen wir auf einem Inselchen, das nicht grösser als ein Nachen ist, auf, wir Abenteurer und Wandervögel, und sehen uns hier eine kleine Weile um: so eilig und so neugierig wie möglich, denn wie schnell kann uns ein Wind verwehen oder eine Welle über das Inselchen hinwegspülen, sodass Nichts mehr von uns da ist! Aber hier, auf diesem kleinen Raume, finden wir andere Wandervögel und hören von früheren,—und so leben wir eine köstliche Minute der Erkenntnis und des Errathens, unter fröhlichem Flügelschlagen und Gezwitscher mit einander und abenteuern im Geiste hinaus auf den Ozean, nicht weniger stolz als er selber!" M, KSA 3: 227.

CONCLUSION
LOGOS AND PALLAKSCH: PAUL CELAN'S "TÜBINGEN JÄNNER"

1. We may, for instance, read Aristotle's *Poetics* as the answer of *techne* to the tradition of *mania*.

2. In the mid-1970s, there were nearly 10,000 articles and books that qualified for the *Index of Scientific Writings on Creativity*. Albert Rothenberg and Bette Greenberg,

The Index of Scientific Writings on Creativity: Creative Men and Women and *The Index of Scientific Writings on Creativity: General (1566–1974)*, (Hamden, Conn.: Archon Books, 1974), cf. Albert Rothenberg, *Creativity and Madness: New Findings and Old Stereotypes*, 7fn1.

3. Cf., among others, Jamison, *Touched By Fire*, or Ludwig, *The Price of Greatness*.

4. E. R. Dodds, *The Greeks and the Irrational* (Berkeley: University of California Press, 1951), 74.

5. Leon E. A. Berman, "An Artist Destroys His Work: Comments on Creativity and Destructiveness," *Creativity and Madness: Psychological Studies of Art and Artists*, 59–78: 61.

6. These and the following remarks should *not* be construed as a generalized attack on the behavioral or social sciences, nor even as an attack on the sometimes subtle work that has been done on the present correlations between mental illness and creativity; I am strictly arguing against retrospective arrogations.

7. As Dodds points out, the distinction between divine madness and "the ordinary kind which is caused by disease" has been important to ancient accounts of privileged madness long before Plato. (*The Greeks and the Irrational*, 65)

8. Catherine Brown, "In the Middle," *Journal of Medieval and Early Modern Studies* 30:3, Fall 2000, 547–73:562–3.

9. In his essay "Of Divine Places," the contemporary French philosopher Jean-Luc Nancy writes that "wherever thought comes up against the furthest extreme, the limit, against truth, or ordeal, in short wherever it thinks, it encounters something that once bore or seems to have borne, at one time or another, a divine name." Such encounters, according to Nancy, do not mean that the divine returns—on the contrary, "God disappears even more surely and definitively through bearing all the names of a generalized and multiplied difference." In the end, we can say "*nothing about the god* that cannot immediately be said about 'the event,' about 'love,' about 'poetry.' " "Of Divine Places," trans. Michael Holland, in: Jean-Luc Nancy, *The Inoperative Community*, ed. Peter Connor (Minneapolis: University of Minnesota Press, 1991), 110–150: 3–4; quoted in modified translation after Hent de Vries' excellent essay "Winke," *The Solid Letter: Readings of Friedrich Hölderlin*, ed. Aris Fioretos (Stanford: Stanford University Press, 1999), 94–120: 96.

10. It is worth mentioning that the concept of *furor poeticus* proper, so important to the debates of the pre- or early Enlightenment, had already lost much of its currency by Hölderlin's time. On the question of the divine in Hölderlin's work, cf. a number of recent excellent readings in *The Solid Letter*, op. cit., esp. Jean-Luc Nancy, "The Calculation of the Poet" (44–73); Philippe Lacoue-Labarthe, "Poetry's Courage" (74–93), and Hent de Vries, "Winke" (94–120).

11. I am writing these words during the late summer of the year 2000, i.e., during the U.S. presidential campaign; the outgoing president has asked God to forgive him his sexual escapades, one candidate claims Jesus as his most important influence, and one vice-presidential candidate has just suggested that there can be no morality without religion. In this light, it seems hasty to take recourse to the death of God, or, from the perspective of a secular humanist, optimistic to the point of naivete. I will maintain, however, that the faith in God to which so many profess in every poll lacks all *intellectual* relevance. After Nietzsche, there has not been a single nonsecular theoretical

or aesthetic development of international importance, no matter how often religion has been and no doubt will be evoked in political contexts. Perhaps this is a controversial statement; so be it.

12. Accident here includes the possibility that the etiologies of mental illness and creativity overlap, that there may be, for instance, a somatic constellation of factors that favors both illness and *poiêsis*, but even if that is the case, madness and creation will still coexist, not co-incide.

13. Roberto Calasso, *Literature and the Gods*, trans. Tim Parks (New York: Alfred A. Knopf, 2001), 192.

14. The reader will recognize the two examples Hegel stresses in the relevant section of G. W. F. Hegel, *Die Phänomenologie des Geistes* (Frankfurt/M.: Suhrkamp, 1986), 82–91.

15. Cf. Chapter Three, section two.

16. V. S. Ramachandran and Sandra Blakeslee, *Phantoms in the Brain: Probing the Mysteries of the Human Mind* (New York: William Morrow, 1998), 131. The (very rare) condition described in this anecdote is "somatoparaphrenia, the denial of ownership of one's own body parts," speculatively related to anosognosia (denial of illness) and the experience of phantom limbs.

17. Aeschylus, *Agamemnon* (1210–12), Crane, Gregory R. (ed), *The Perseus Project*, http://www.perseus.tufts.edu, August 2000, my translation.

18. To Blindness per-/suaded eyes./Their—"a riddle is what purely/springs forth"—, their/remembrance of/swimming Hölderlin towers, seagull-/circumwhirred.// Visits of drowned carpenters to/these/diving words://If there came,/if there came a man,/if there came a man to the world, today, with/the lightbeard of the/patriarchs: he might,/if he spoke of this/time, he/might/only babble and babble,/ever-, ever-/ moremore. //("Pallaksch. Pallaksch.") This translation is mine, and since it is not meant to "translate" in any deeper sense, but only to give an approximation, I will not repeat here everything that has been said about the impossibility of translating poetry, or Celan's poetry.

19. Christoph Theodor Schwab, a friend and one of Hölderlin's frequent visitors, calls "pallaksch" Hölderlin's "favorite expression" ("Lieblingsausdruck"). *Hölderlin. Sämtliche Werke*, Historisch-Kritische Ausgabe, ed. Norbert v. Hellingrath and Friedrich Seebass and Ludwig v. Pigenot (München/Leipzig: 1913–23, Bd. VI), 444. Cf. the end of this chapter.

20. "Soll ich? Muß ich? Hör ich's da auch, sagt's der Wind auch? Hör ich's immer, immer zu, stich tot, tot" ("Should I? Must I? Do I hear it there, too, does the wind say it, too? Hear it always, always, on, on, stick dead, dead."). Georg Büchner, *Gesammelte Werke*, ed. Gerhard P. Knapp (Goldman: n.p., 1970), 175.

21. For more detailed references and further speculations on the role of "January," cf. Rainer Zbikowski, " 'schwimmende Hölderlintürme': Paul Celans Gedicht 'Tübingen, Jänner'—diaphan," in *'Der glühende Leertext': Annäherungen an Paul Celans Dichtung*, ed. Otto Pöggeler and Christoph Jamme (München: Fink, 1993), 185–211.

22. The correlating verses from the King James or the Oxford Annotated Bible fail to reproduce important elements of this passage. Literally translated, it is: "Yea, God will once speak to this people in an unintelligible language and in a foreign

tongue, he, who said to them: 'This is rest; create rest for the weary, and that is refreshment!' But they wouldn't listen. Hence, the word of the lord will go out to them thus: 'Zawlazaw zawlazaw, kawlakaw kawlakaw.' "

23. Jacques Derrida, "Cogito and the History of Madness," *Writing and Difference*, trans. Alan Bass (Chicago: U of Chicago P, 1978), 31–63.

24. Cf. especially the *Phaedrus* and the *Ion*.

25. "... das geisteskranke Fragen nach einem Bewußtsein ..."; Friedrich Hölderlin, *Anmerkungen zum Ödipus, Sämtliche Werke ('Frankfurter Ausgabe')*, historisch-kritische Ausgabe, ed. Friedrich Sattler, Bd. XVI (Frankfurt/M.: Stroemfeld/Roter Stern, 1988), 247–258: 255.

26. Thanks to Arkady Plotnitsky for his gift of a definition of madness as "that which cannot be deconstructed."

27. Derrida, "Cogito," 61.

28. Peter Szondi has very cogently and sensitively written on the need to *also* attempt to recognize and retrieve these conventional, as it were pre-poetic images from Celan's poetry. Cf. *Celan-Studien* (Frankfurt/M.: Suhrkamp, 1967).

29. Friedrich Hölderlin, *Werke, Briefe, Dokumente*, Nach der Kleinen Stuttgarter Hölderlin-Ausgabe, ed. Friedrich Beißner, Ausgewählt und mit Nachwort von Pierre Bertaux (München: Winkler, 1963), 150–154: 153.

30. For other readings about or touching on "Tübingen, Jänner," cf. Bernhard Böschenstein, "Hölderlin and Celan," *Hölderlin-Jahrbuch* 1982–83, 147–155; B. Böschenstein, "'Tübingen, Jänner,'" in: *Über Paul Celan*, ed. Dietling Meinecke (Frankfurt/M.: Suhrkamp, 1973, 101–112; Sigrid Bogumil, *Celan's Wende, Entwicklungslinien in der Lyrik Paul Celan's I. Neue Rundschau* H. 4 (1982): 81–110; S. Bogumil, "Celan's Hölderlinlektüre im Gegenlicht des schlichten Wortes," *Celan-Jahrbuch* 1, ed. Hans-Michael Speier (Heidelberg: Carl Winter, 1987), 81–125; Philippe Lacoue-Labarthe, *La poésie comme expérience* (Paris: Christian Bourgois, 1986); Rainer Zbikowski, "'schwimmende Hölderlintürme': Paul Celan's Gedicht 'Tübingen, Jänner'—diaphan," in *'Der glühende Leertext': Annäherungen an Paul Celan's Dichtung*, ed. Otto Pöggeler and Christoph Jamme, 185–211.

31. In "Hölderlin and Celan" (op.cit.), Bernhard Böschenstein suggests, without further explanation, that the blind eyes parallel the poet's diving words. In "'Tübingen, Jänner'" (op.cit., 101), Böschenstein suggests that the "eyes have let themselves be convinced (*überzeugen*) that blindness is proper to them"—ignoring the strong distinction between "überreden" (persuade) and "überzeugen" (convince), where only the latter connotes conviction. Other readings offer only slight modifications of this view, and none explain sufficiently whose *Rede* has caused the blindness.

32. "With yellow pears, and ample with wild roses, the land hangs into the lake, you comely Swans, and drunken with kisses you dunk your heads into sacredly sober water."

33. In light of the multiple allusions set free by "Der Rhein," we might have to count Rousseau, too, among the possible patriarchs with the beards of light. Hölderlin, at least, seems to attribute to him the mad language of "the purest ones," a line echoing with the enigma of pure origin. The potentially blinding language of the purest philosopher poet, we might spin this reading further, must turn into babble as well; enlightenment, the rhetoric of freedom and progress, must turn (or has turned)

into babble in "this time." The mad language of purity, prophecy, divinity, the most ancient mode of elevated speech, is dead.

34. "into death/however, a man, too, can/remember what is best," a reference to Plato's *Symposium*.

35. Cf. *Republic* 597b: "We get, then, these three beds: one that has its being in nature . . . that God produces . . . And then there was one which the carpenter made. . . . And one which the painter made."

36. It is always possible to read "pallaksch," in this poem, not only as modern patriarchs' mournful babble, borrowed from a not-anymore-poet, but also as a laconic, ironic play on "platsch," the onomatopoetic German term used to imitate the sound of something hitting the water, destroying reflection.

37. One dictionary actually lists "(*ausbrechen*) escape (*aus* from); (*Gefängnis*) to break out (of prison)" as the primary meaning of *entspringen*. Cf. Schöffler-Weis, *Taschenwörterbuch*, Deutsch-Englisch (Stuttgart: Klett, 1965), 266, col. 1.

38. Gilles Deleuze, "To Have Done with Judgment," *Essays Clinical and Critical*, trans. Daniel W. Smith and Michael A. Greco (Minneapolis: University of Minnesota Press, 1997), 126–135.

39. Quoted after Sigrid Bogumil, "Celan's Hölderlinlektüre im Gegenlicht des schlichten Wortes," op.cit., 93.

40. Hölderlin, *Sämtliche Werke*, op. cit., Bd. VI, 444.

BIBLIOGRAPHY

Ackermann, Robert John. *Nietzsche, a Frenzied Look*. Amherst: University of Massachusetts Press, 1990.

Adorno, Theodor W. "Parataxis: Zur späten Lyrik Hölderlins." In *Über Hölderlin*, ed. Jochen Schmidt. Frankfurt/Main: Insel, 1970. 339–378.

Ansell-Pearson, Keith. *Nietzsche contra Rousseau: A Study of Nietzsche's Moral and Political Thought*. Cambridge: Cambridge University Press, 1991.

Aristotle. *Poetics*. In *Classical Literary Criticism: Translations and Interpretations*, ed. A. Preminger et al. New York: Unger, 1974. 108–139.

Bataille, Georges. *On Nietzsche*. Trans. Bruce Boone. Introduction by Sylvère Lotringer. New York: Paragon House, 1992.

———, *L'expérience intérieure*. Paris: Gallimard, 1954.

Benardete, Seth. *The Rhetoric of Morality and Philosophy: Plato's 'Gorgias' and 'Phaedrus'*. Chicago/London: Chicago University Press, 1991.

Benjamin, Walter. *Der Begriff der Kunstkritik in der deutschen Romantik*. Frankfurt/Main: Suhrkamp, 1978.

Benn, Gottfried. *Gesammelte Werke in acht Bänden*. Ed. Dieter Wellerschoff. Wiesbaden: Limes 1968.

Bergmann, Frithjof. "Nietzsche's Critique of Morality." In *Reading Nietzsche*, ed. Robert Solomon and Kathleen Higgins. New York: Oxford University Press, 1988.

———, "Tübingen, Jänner." In *Über Paul Celan*, ed. Dietling Meinecke. Frankfurt/Main: Suhrkamp, 1973. 101–112.

Bernhard Böschenstein. "Hölderlin and Celan." *Hölderlin-Jahrbuch* (1982–83): 147–155.

Bertaux, Pierre. *Friedrich Hölderlin*. Frankfurt/Main: Suhrkamp, 1978.

Blanchot, Maurice. *The Space of Literature*. Trans. Ann Smock. Lincoln: University of Nebraska Press, 1982.

Blondel, Eric. *Nietzsche, The Body and Culture: Philosophy as a Philological Genealogy*. Stanford: Stanford University Press, 1991.

Bloom, Allan. "An Interpretation of Plato's *Ion*." In *The Roots of Political Philosophy: Ten Forgotten Socratic Dialogues*, ed. Thomas L. Pangle. Ithaca: Cornell University Press, 1987. 371–395.

Bloom, Harold. *The Western Canon: The Books and School of the Ages.* New York: Riverhead, 1995.

Bogumil, Sigrid. "Celans Wende, Entwicklungslinien in der Lyrik Paul Celans I". *Neue Rundschau* H. 4 (1982): 81–110.

———. "Celans Hölderlinlektüre im Gegenlicht des schlichten Wrotes." In *Celan-Jahrbuch* 1, ed. Hans-Michael Speier. Heidelberg: Carl Winter, 1987. 81–125.

Brown, Catherine. "In the Middle." *Journal of Medieval and Early Modern Studies* 30:3. Fall 2000. 547–573.

Büchner, Georg. "Gesammelte Werke". Ed. Gerhard P. Knapp. Goldman: n.p., 1970.

Burdor, Dieter. *Hölderlins späte Gedichtfragmente: "Unendlicher Deutung voll".* Stuttgart: J. B. Metzler, 1993.

Burger, Ronna. *Plato's Phaedrus: A Defense of a Philosophic Art of Writing.* Tuscaloosa: University of Alabama Press, 1980.

Calasso, Roberto. *Literature and the Gods.* Trans. Tim Parks. New York: Knopf, 2001.

Carter, R. E. "Plato and Inspiration." *Journal of the History of Philosophy* 5 (1967): 111–121.

Cassirer, Ernst. "Hölderlin und der deutsche Idealismus." In *Idee und Gestalt: Goethe, Schiller, Hölderlin, Kleist.* 2nd ed. Berlin, 1924. Reprint, Darmstadt: Wissenschaftl. Buchgesellschaft, 1989. 113–155.

Celan, Paul. *Die Niemandsrose.* Frankfurt/Main: Suhrkamp, 1963.

Clark, Maudemarie. "Nietzsche's Attack on Morality". Ph.D. diss. University of Wisconsin-Madison, 1976.

———. *Nietzsche on Truth and Philosophy.* Cambridge: Cambridge University Press, 1990.

Classical Literary Criticism: Translations and Interpretations. Ed. A. Preminger et al. New York: Unger, 1974.

Corngold, Stanley. *Complex Pleasures: Forms of Feeling in German Literature.* Stanford: Stanford University Press, 1998.

Creativity and Madness: Psychological Studies of Art and Artists. Ed. Barry M. Panther et al. Burbank: American Institute of Medical Education, 1995.

Del Caro, Adrian. *Nietzsche Contra Nietzsche.* Baton Rouge: Louisiana State University Press, 1989.

Deleuze, Gilles. *Nietzsche and Philosophy.* Trans. Hugh Tomlinson. New York: Columbia University Press, 1983.

———. *Essays Clinical and Critical.* Trans. Daniel W. Smith and Michael A. Greco. Minneapolis: University of Minnesota Press, 1997.

de Man, Paul. "Rhetoric of Tropes." In *Allegories of Reading: Figural Language in Rousseau, Nietzsche, Rilke, and Proust.* New Haven: Yale University Press, 1979. 103–118.

———. "The Image of Rousseau in the Poetry of Hölderlin." Trans. Andrzej Warminski. In *The Rhetoric of Romanticism.* New York: Columbia University Press, 1984. 19–45.

Derrida, Jacques. "Cogito and the History of Madness." *Writing and Difference.* Chicago: University of Chicago Press, 31–63.

———. "La parole souflée." *Writing and Difference*. Trans. with additional notes by Alan Bass. Chicago: University of Chicago Press, 1978. 169–195.

———. "Plato's Pharmacy." *Dissemination*. Trans. Barbara Johnson. Chicago: University of Chicago Press, 1981. 61–171.

———. *Margins of Philosophy*. Trans. with additional notes by Alan Bass. Chicago: University of Chicago Press, 1982. 207–272.

Diamond, Stephen A. *Anger, Madness, and the Daimonic: The Psychological Genesis of Violence, Evil, and Creativity*. Albany: State University of New York Press, 1996.

Dodds, E. R. *The Greeks and the Irrational*. Berkeley: University of California Press, 1951.

Eagleton, Terry. *The Ideology of the Aesthetic*. Oxford/Cambridge, Mass.: Basil Blackwell, 1990.

Felman, Shoshana. *Writing and Madness (Literature/Philosophy/Psychoanalysis)*. Trans. Martha N. Evans and S. Felman. Ithaca: Cornell University Press, 1985.

Ferrari, G. R. F. *Listening to the Cicadas: A Study of Plato's Phaedrus*. Cambridge: Cambridge University Press, 1987.

Fioretos, Aris, ed. *The Solid Letter: Readings of Friedrich Hölderlin*. Stanford: Stanford University Press, 1999.

Foucault, Michel. "Nietzsche, Freud, Marx." *Cahiers de Royaument: Philosophie 6* (1967): 183–192.

———. *Folie et déraison. Histoire de la Folie à l'age classique*. Paris: Plon, 1961.

———. "Nietzsche, Genealogy, Morals." In *Language, Countermemory, Practice*. Ed. Donald F. Bouchard. Ithaca: Cornell University Press, 1977.

Freud, Sigmund. *Studienausgabe*. Frankfurt/Main: Fischer, 1975.

Gadamer, Hans-Georg. "Plato und die Dichter." *Platos dialektische Ethik und andere Studien zur platonischen Philosophie*. Hamburg: Felix Meiner, 1968.

Gasché, Rodolphe. "*Ecce Homo* or the Written Body." *The Oxford Literary Review* 7 (1985): 3–24.

Geertz, Clifford. *After the Fact: Two Countries, Four Decades, One Anthropologist*. Cambridge University Press, 1995.

Gillespie, Michael Allen, and Tracy B. Strong, eds. *Nietzsche's New Seas: Explorations in Philosophy, Aesthetics, and Politics*. Chicago: University of Chicago Press, 1988.

Goethe, Johann Wolfgang. "Plato als Mitgenosse einer christlichen Offenbarung (1796)." In *Ion*. Cambridge: Cambridge University Press, 42–46.

Griswold, Charles L. Jr. *Self-Knowledge in Plato's Phaedrus*. New Haven/London: Yale University Press, 1986.

Hallman, Max O. "Nietzsche's Environmental Ethics." *Environmental Ethics* 13 (1991): 99–125.

Hamacher, Werner. "Das Beben der Darstellung." In *Positionen der Literaturwissenschaft: Acht Modellanalysen am Beispiel von Kleists 'Das Erdbeben von Chili,'* ed. D. E. Wellbery. München: Beck, 1985. 149–173.

Hamlin, Cyrus. "'Stimmen des Geschiks': The Hermeneutics of Unreadability (Thoughts on Hölderlin's 'Griechenland')." In *Jenseits des Idealismus: Hölderlins letzte Homburger Jahre, 1804–1806*. Bonn: Bouvier, 253–276.

Hegel, G. W. F. *Die Phänomenologie des Geistes. Werke* 3. Frankfurt/Main: Suhrkamp, 1986.

Heidegger, Martin. *Erläuterungen zu Hölderlins Dichtung.* Frankfurt/Main: Klostermann, 1971.

―――. "Nietzsches Wort 'Gott ist tot'." *Holzwege.* Frankfurt/Main: Klostermann, 1980. 205–263.

Henrich, Dieter. *Konstellationen: Probleme und Debatten am Ursprung der idealistischen Philosophie, 1789–1795.* Stuttgart: Klett-Cotta, 1991.

―――. *Der Grund im Bewußtsein: Untersuchungen zu Hölderlins Denken, 1794–1795.* Stuttgart: Klett-Cotta, 1992.

Hölderlin, Friedrich. *Werke, Briefe, Dokumente.* Nach dem Text der von Friedrich Beißner besorgten Kleinen Stuttgarter Hölderlin-Ausgabe. Ausgewählt von Pierre Bertaux. München: Winkler, 1963.

―――. *Sämtliche Werke.* Historisch-Kritische Ausgabe. Ed. D. E. Sattler. Frankfurt: Roter Stern, 1983.

―――. *Essays and Letters on Theory.* Trans. and ed. Thomás Pfau. Albany: State University of New York Press, 1988.

―――. *Die Briefe: Briefe an Hölderlin, Dokumente.* Bd. 2, *Sämtliche Werke und Briefe in drei Bänden.* Herausgegeben von Jochen Schmidt in Zusammenarbeit mit Wolfgang Behschnitt. Frankfurt/Main: Deutscher Klassiker-Verlag, 1992.

Jakobson, Roman, and Grete Lübbe-Grothues. "Two Types of Discourse in Hölderlin's Madness." In *Cognitive Constraints on Communication.* Synthese language library, 18. Ed. Lucia Vania and Jaakko Hintikka. Dordrecht: D. Reidel, 1984. 115–136.

Jamison, Kay Redfield. *Touched By Fire: Manic-Depressive Illness and the Artistic Temperament.* New York: Free Press, 1993.

Jamme, Christoph. " 'Ein kranker oder gesunder Geist?' Berichte über Hölderlins Krankheit in den Jahren 1804–1806." In *Jenseits des Idealismus: Hölderlins letzte Homburger Jahre, 1804–1806, 279–289.*

Jenseits des Idealismus: Hölderlins letzte Homburger Jahre, 1804–1806. Neuzeit und Gegenwart. Philosophische Studien, 5. Bonn: Bouvier, 1988.

Jung, C. G. "Commentary on 'The Secret of the Golden Flower.' " *Alchemical Studies.* Ed. R. F. C. Hull. *Collected Works.* Vol XIII. Routledge and Kegan Paul: London, 1978.

Kant, Immanuel, "Von einem neuerdings erhobenen vornehmen Ton in der Philosophie." *Werke* III. Ed. Wilhelm Weischedel. Frankfurt/Main: Insel, 1958. 377–397.

Kofman, Sarah. *Nietzsche et la scène philosophique.* Paris: Union Générale d'Éditions, 1979.

Lacoue-Labarthe, Philippe. "The Caesura of the Speculative." *Glyph* 4 (1978):57–84.

―――. *L'imitation des modernes.* Typographies II. Paris: Editions galilée, 1986.

―――. *La poésie comme expérience.* Paris: Christian Bourgois, 1986.

―――. *Typography: Mimesis, Philosophy, Politics.* With an introduction by Jacques Derrida. Cambridge/London: Harvard University Press, 1989.

Lampert, Laurence. *Nietzsche and Modern Times: A Study of Bacon, Descartes, and Nietzsche.* New Haven: Yale University Press, 1993.

Lange, Wolfgang. *Der kalkulierte Wahnsinn: Innenansichten ästhetischer Moderne.* Frankfurt/Main: Fischer, 1992.

Lange-Eichbaum, Wilhelm. *Nietzsche: Krankheit und Wirkung.* Hamburg: n.p., 1947.

Ludwig, Arnold M. *The Price of Greatness: Resolving the Creativity and Madness Controversy.* New York: Guilford, 1995.

Megill, Alan. *Prophets of Extremity: Nietzsche, Heidegger, Foucault, Derrida.* Berkeley/ Los Angeles: University of California Press, 1985.

Monroe, Russell R. *Creative Brainstorms: The Relationship Between Madness and Genius.* New York: Irvington, 1992.

Murdoch, Iris. *The Fire and the Sun: Why Plato Banished the Artists.* Oxford: Oxford University Press, 1977.

Nagel, Thomas. "What Is It Like to Be a Bat?" In *The Nature of Consciousness: Philosophical Debates,* ed. Ned Block et al. Cambridge: MIT Press, 1997. 519–528.

Nägele, Rainer. *Text, Geschichte und Subjektivität in Hölderlins Dichtung—"Uneßbarer Schrift gleich."* Stuttgart: J. B. Metzler, 1985.

Nägele, Rainer. *Reading After Freud.* New York: Columbia University Press, 1987.

Nancy, Jean-Luc. *The Inoperative Community,* ed. Peter Connor. Foreword Christopher Fynsk. Minneapolis: University of Minnesota Press, 1991.

Nehamas, Alexander. *Nietzsche: Life as Literature.* Cambridge, Mass.: Harvard University Press, 1985.

Nietzsche, Friedrich. *Sämtliche Werke. Kritische Studienausgabe in 15 Bänden.* Hg. Giorgio Colli und Mazzino Montinari. Deutscher Taschenbuch-Verlag: München, 1988.

Nordau, Max. *Entartung.* Carl Duncker, 1893.

Nussbaum, Martha. *The Fragility of Goodness: Luck and Ethics in Greek Tragedy and Philosophy.* Cambridge: Cambridge University Press, 1986.

Peters, Uwe Henrik. *Hölderlin: Wider die These vom edlen Simulanten.* Reinbek: Rowohlt, 1982.

Picht, Georg. *Nietzsche.* Stuttgart: Klett-Cotta, 1988.

Pieper, Josef. *Enthusiasm and Divine Madness.* Trans. Richard and Clara Winston. New York: Harcourt, Brace & World, 1964.

Plato on Beauty, Wisdom, and the Arts. Ed. J. Moravcsik and P. Temko. Totowa: Rowman & Littlefield, 1982.

Plato. *Plato's Phaedrus.* Trans. with introduction and commentary by R. Hackforth. Cambridge: Cambridge University Press, 1952.

———. *Collected Dialogues.* Ed. Edith Hamilton and Huntington Cairns. Princeton: Princeton University Press, 1963. 308–352.

———. *Ion.* Griechisch-deutsch. Ed. Hellmut Flashar. München: Ernst Heimeran, 1963.

———. *Phaidros.* Ed. and trans. Wolfgang Buchwald. München: Ernst Heimeran, 1964.

———. *The Republic of Plato.* Trans. Allan Bloom. New York: Basic Books, 1968.

———. *The Being of the Beautiful: Plato's Theaetetus, Sophist, and Statesman.* Trans. with commentary by Seth Benardete. Chicago/London: Chicago University Press, 1984.

————. *Sämtliche Werke in zehn Bänden.* Griechisch und Deutsch. Nach der Übersetzung Friedrich Schleiermachers. Ergänzt durch Übersetzungen von Franz Susemihl und anderen. Ed. Karlheinz Hülser. Frankfurt/Main: Insel, 1991.

Plotnitsky, Arkady. *Reconfigurations. Critical Theory and General Economy.* Gainesville: University of Florida Press, 1993.

————. *In the Shadow of Hegel: Complementarity, History, and the Unconscious.* Gainesville: University of Florida Press, 1993.

Pöggeler, Otto, and Christoph Jamme, eds. *'Der glühende Leertext': Annäherungen an Paul Celans Dichtung.* München: Fink, 1993.

Price, A. W. *Love and Friendship in Plato and Aristotle.* Oxford: Oxford University Press, 1989.

Price, A. W. "Plato and Freud." In *The Person and the Human Mind,* ed. Christopher Gill. Oxford: Clarendon Press, 1990. 247–270.

Ramachandran, V. S. and Sandra Blakeslee. *Phantoms in the Brain: Probing the Mysteries of the Human Mind.* New York: William Morrow, 1998.

Reich, Wilhelm. *The Function of the Orgasm.* Trans. Vincent R. Carfagno. New York: Simon & Schuster, 1973.

Rieff, Philip. *The Triumph of the Therapeutic: Uses of Faith after Freud.* Chicago/London: University of Chicago Press, 1966.

Rothenberg, Albert. *Creativity and Madness: New Findings and Old Stereotypes.* Baltimore: Johns Hopkins University Press, 1990.

Rothenberg, Albert and Bette Greenberg. *The Index of Scientific Writings on Creativity: Creative Men and Women* and *The Index of Scientific Writings on Creativity: General (1566–1974).* Hamden, Conn.: Archon Books, 1974.

Rowe, C. J. *Plato: Phaedrus.* London, 1986.

————. "Philosophy, Love, and Madness." In *The Person and the Human Mind,* ed. Christopher Gill. Oxford: Clarendon Press, 1990. 227–246.

Sass, Louis. *Madness and Modernism: Insanity in the Light of Modern Art, Literature, and Thought.* New York: Basic Books, 1992.

Sinaiko, Henry L. *Love, Knowledge, and Discourse in Plato: Dialogue and Dialectic in Phaedrus, Republic, Parmenides.* Chicago: University of Chicago Press, 1965.

Staten, Henry. *Nietzsche's Voice.* Ithaca: Cornell University Press, 1990.

Steiner, George. *Antigones: How the Antigone Legend Has Endured In Western Literature, Art, and Thought.* New York/Oxford: Oxford University Press, 1984.

Szondi, Peter. *Celan-Studien.* Frankfurt/Main: Suhrkamp, 1967.

————. *On Textual Understanding and Other Essays.* Trans. Harvey Mendelsohn. Foreword Michael Hayes. Minneapolis: University of Minnesota Press, 1986.

Thiele, Leslie Paul. *Friedrich Nietzsche and the Politics of the Soul.* Princeton: Princeton University Press, 1990.

Tigerstedt, E. N. "Plato's Idea of Poetical Inspiration." *Commentationes Humanarum Litterarum* 44 (1970): 18–20.

Türcke, Christoph. *Der tolle Mensch: Nietzsche und der Wahnsinn der Vernunft.* Frankfurt/Main: Fischer, 1989.

Understanding the Phaedrus: Proceedings of the II Symposium Platonicum. Ed. Livio Rossetti. Sankt Augustin: Academia Verlag, 1992.

Verdenius, W. J. "Der Begriff der Mania in Platons *Phaidros*." *Archiv für Geschichte der Philosophie* 44 (1962): 132–150.

Vogel, Klaus. *Der Wilde unter den Künstlern: Zur Strategie des Anderen seit Friedrich Hölderlin.* Historische Anthropologie, 15. Berlin: Dietrich Reimer, 1991.

Volz, Pia Daniela. *Nietzsche im Labyrinth seiner Krankheit: Eine medizinisch-biographische Untersuchung.* Tübingen: Königshausen & Neumann, 1990.

Vries, Hent de. "Winke." *The Solid Letter: Readings of Friedrich Hölderlin.* Cultural Memory in the Present, ed. Aris Fioretos. Stanford: Stanford University Press, 1999. 94–120.

Weber, Samuel. *Institution and Interpretation.* Minneapolis: University of Minnesota Press, 1987. Theory and History of Literature 31.

Weinholz, Gerhard. *Zur Genese des 'Wahnsinns' bei Friedrich Hölderlin: Ein Erklärungsmodell aus dem Kontext seines Lebens und seiner Zeit.* Literaturwissenschaft in der Blauen Eule, 2. Essen: Blaue Eule, 1990.

Weissberg, Liliane. *Geistersprache: Philosophischer und literarischer Diskurs im späten achtzehnten Jahrhundert.* Würzburg: Königshausen & Neumann, 1990.

White, Alan. *Within Nietzsche's Labyrinth.* New York: Routledge, 1990.

White, David A. *Rhetoric and Reality in Plato's* Phaedrus. Albany: State University of New York Press, 1993.

Wilcox, Joel F. "Cross-Metamorphosis in Plato's Ion." In *Literature as Philosophy: Philosophy as Literature,* ed. Donald G. Marschall. Iowa City: University of Iowa Press, 1987. 155–174.

Yack, Bernard. *The Longing for Total Revolution: Philosophical Sources of Social Discontent from Rousseau to Marx and Nietzsche.* Princeton: Princeton University Press, 1986.

Zaslavsky, Robert. *Platonic Myth and Platonic Writing.* Washington, D.C.: University Press of America, 1981.

Zbikowski, Rainer. " 'schwimmende Hölderlintürme': Paul Celans Gedicht 'Tübingen, Jänner' – diaphan," In *'Der glühende Leertext': Annäherungen an Paul Celans Dichtung,* ed. Pöggler and Jammer. 185–211.